TEACH YOUR OWN

BOOKS BY JOHN HOLT

How Children Fail

How Children Learn

The Underachieving School

What Do I Do Monday?

Freedom and Beyond

Escape from Childhood

Instead of Education

Never Too Late

Teach Your Own

Learning All the Time

A Life Worth Living: Selected Letters

TEACH YOUR OWN

*The Indispensable Guide to Living and
Learning with Children at Home*

JOHN HOLT AND
PATRICK FARENGA

hachette
BOOKS

NEW YORK

This book is dedicated to all those who have supported *Growing Without Schooling* and John Holt's work and ideas. This book could not have been written without your courage and determination to teach your own children and share your stories.

CONTENTS

HOMESCHOOLING RESOURCES

ACKNOWLEDGMENTS

THIS THIRD EDITION could not have been written without the ongoing support and encouragement from my family, friends, and colleagues in the unschooling/homeschooling, alternative school, and learning center communities.

In particular, I want to thank everyone at the Alliance for Self-Directed Education for their unwavering support for unschooling and their friendship over the years, and especially to September James for helping me update the appendices of this book with ASDE's resources.

I also want to thank Peter Bergson, Aaron Falbel, Peter Gray, Steve Hargadon, Milva McDonald, Carlo Ricci, Sophia Sayigh, Susannah Sheffer, and Cevin Soling for our conversations related to self-directed education that made me rethink and refine my ideas.

Dan Ambrosio suggested creating this new edition to me and through his skillful editing made it happen. I especially want to thank Merloyd Lawrence, who edited John Holt's last four books. For many years she has helped preserve and expand John's literary legacy, and her kind advice has proven invaluable to me many times.

—Patrick Farenga

NOTE: *Growing Without Schooling* (GWS) magazine is mentioned throughout this book. GWS was the first magazine about homeschooling, founded by John Holt in 1977. When John died in 1985, I became the magazine's publisher. My colleagues Donna Richoux, Susannah Sheffer, and Meredith Collins were subsequent editors of GWS after John's death. GWS ceased publication in December 2001. All 141 issues of GWS can be found at www.johnholtgws.com. ∎

FOREWORD

LEARNING: LOST AND FOUND

AS A VETERAN HOMESCHOOLER AND AUTHOR, I field many questions about the lost educational and social opportunities homeschoolers face by not attending school, especially "How will my children get into college or find work without a proper school transcript?" and "How will my children socialize if they're not in school?" The COVID-19 pandemic made these questions pertinent to every parent, not just to those considering homeschooling. Further, headlines such as "Research Shows Students Falling Months Behind During Virus Disruptions"[1] and "'A Lost Generation': Surge of Research Reveals Students Sliding Backward, Most Vulnerable Worst Affected" exacerbated our fears about children falling behind in school and therefore in life, causing further anxiety in families.

Don't let the hype upset you; your children will continue to learn and grow whether or not they are in school. Homeschoolers matriculate in and out of school, get into college, and find work they want to do without running through school's curricular gauntlet. Our lives and careers often do not run in the same patterns as educational institutions, or as we, ourselves, wish. Missing months or years of standard school learning does not take an equivalent amount of time to regain, if one needs to learn it at all.

Education is an important element of civil society, but it has become a sedentary institution, serving much more as a gatekeeper for employment opportunities instead of enabling active learning for students. Both in-person and online education continue to operate on the assumption that by exposing all children to the same information at the same time they will learn it. This core belief is hard to shake; generations of school reforms to make schooling more personalized have tried it and failed. Ivan Illich summarized this situation in *The Futility of Schooling* (1968): "And yet it is politically inexpedient and intellectually disreputable to question the elusive goal of providing equal educational opportunities for all citizens by giving them access to an equal number of years in school."

To even question the order in which school subjects are taught is to invite being labeled naïve or an enemy of education. For instance, in school the main reason for making sure children can read by the end of third grade is school management issues, not a child's biological development. In puberty, hair growth is spontaneous and happens to all healthy children over a range of time; there is no equivalent biological process in our bodies that triggers "You will learn to read now." Reading is a learned behavior, and forcing someone to learn something they don't want to do can actually delay or impede learning.

However, the curriculum after third grade requires competent reading skills to succeed in school. Homeschoolers have long noted, and research shows, that when children are not forced to learn to read at home, boys tend to learn to read later than girls do. Once a child decides to learn to read, they learn quickly, catching up to their age-mates' reading abilities in weeks or months, not years. Further, the studies show that children who haven't been compelled to read due to their age, read more for personal pleasure and information as they get older than do those who were forced to learn to read at a particular age. There are many different paths and texts that turn people into readers, not just school's path.[2]

This is why John preferred to refer to his work as unschooling; to describe learning that doesn't have to take place in school or at home and does not resemble school learning. Homeschooling has become the default word that captures many forms of learning without attending school. John often used unschooling and homeschooling interchangeably in his talks and writing, but it is clear that duplicating school at home is not what John meant when he used the word homeschooling.

John started out as a typical school reformer, inventing clever ways of presenting curricular material to his classes, using alternative assessments, and giving his students as much choice and freedom as he could in school. With each book he wrote he moved further away from reforming school and towards reforming society to be more welcoming of children. He eventually described his work as reintegrating children into daily life and adult society, as they were until the rise of compulsory schooling placed them in an educational silo. In the first (1981) edition of *Teach Your Own*, he wrote: "We who believe that children want to learn about the world, are good at it, and can be trusted to do it with very little adult coercion or interference, are probably no more than one percent of the population, if that. And we are not likely to become the majority in my lifetime. This doesn't trouble me much anymore, as long as this minority keeps on growing. My work is to help it grow."

Published forty years ago and never out of print, *Teach Your Own* encourages us to rethink how children learn and grow in our society and, in doing so, to reframe education as a communal, social endeavor that supports families and individuals through school and community resources. Taking a more cooperative stance with families who want to be with their children during school hours, educators and parents can see how different learning schedules can be leveraged instead of viewed as outliers to be banished from the enterprise of education. Not everyone can or wants to homeschool, but the new combinations of learning—at home, in school, and in one's community—open new opportunities for everyone's learning. The variety of educational paths homeschoolers have forged—in terms of finding work worth doing, gaining college admissions, and becoming responsible citizens—are noteworthy. So what learning is lost by not attending school?

So far, the research on learning loss during the pandemic confirms what we already know from other studies of test scores: the poorest school districts and families are the most negatively affected and the wealthier ones are stable or thriving. The solutions proposed are more intensive tutoring and schooling during vacation breaks to make up for the lost learning time. But learning is not internalized simply by attending more classes and taking more tests.

The basis for the claim that school learning can be lost and must be replaced as soon as possible is based on research about summer learning loss, which is used as the basis for determining pandemic learning loss. Education writer Alfie Kohn notes that the evidence for summer learning loss is "much less persuasive than people realize" and "none of the research on this topic actually shows a diminution in learning—just a drop in standardized test scores (in some subjects, in some situations, for some kids)."[3]

Dr. Peter Gray examined the studies about summer learning loss and discovered some interesting data regarding reading and math. Dr. Gray writes, "Although the results are somewhat inconsistent from study to study, most studies show either no significant change or an average increase in reading ability." Some studies of students' "summer slide" broke out two types of math abilities: math calculation and math reasoning. Gray points out that math calculations are typically learned by rote and "hardly anyone does such calculations outside of school; we all have calculators of computers." Math reasoning is about children's "understanding of math concepts and their ability to use those concepts to solve problems. Indeed, the scores for calculation went down over the summer, but the scores for reasoning went up!…Maybe instead of expanding the school year to reduce a summer slide in calculation we should expand summer vacation to reduce the school-year slide in reasoning."[4]

Learning loss can be recovered more quickly than we think. Many parents learn this lesson when they start homeschooling, usually when they must relearn something they could do in school, such as how to multiply and divide improper fractions, but haven't done since. Later in this book you will see how this is a common technique in homeschooling: learning alongside children, rather than always directly instructing. This models for children how we actively learn rather than how we passively receive instruction. Since learning is typically iterative and cumulative over time—it is rarely a one-and-done event—your effort and dedication to the task or project is also communicated to the children.

Learning loss also reveals how doing poorly in one subject doesn't mean you can't do well in other subjects in school, so it begs the question: Why must teachers always double-down on a student's weaknesses? Why not focus on strengths? Such weaknesses can be addressed later if they are, indeed, holding the student back from accomplishing what they want to do. Learning loss doesn't happen only by not being in school; it is often the result of attending school!

In fact, most universities and community colleges offer remedial classes to students who are deficient in math or other core subjects. Isn't summer school a recovery program for learning lost during school hours? Isn't after-school tutoring a form of recovering learning that got lost in the classroom?

Our oldest daughter, Lauren, developed a strong interest in criminal justice issues when she was fifteen and we enrolled her in a course on the subject at our local community college that was taught by a working detective. Lauren got a lot out of the two-semester course, especially the realization that she did not want to work in the criminal justice system. Instead, she developed an interest and concern about why so many people, teenagers in particular, get themselves into trouble with the law and how to help them. This led her to take the Introduction to Psychology course the next year, which totally engaged her. At sixteen, she went to the department head to ask if she could work toward a degree in psychology and was told she needed to show proficiency with statistics before she could proceed to the next level of classes. Since Lauren hated math and, as a result, we'd downplayed it in our unschooling, this was a big blow to her. However, the professor told her she could take Fundamentals of Mathematics, a six-month course offered by the college, and if she passed, she could enter the psychology program. Lauren was the youngest student in the class, which was filled with recent high school graduates and older people. She passed and went on to earn her associate's degree, which enabled her to transfer to a four-year college as a junior. She earned her bachelor's in psychology there and then went to work as a social worker in Texas and Massachusetts. During that time, she completed her master's degree in social work and moved into administrative roles, which she found to be even more draining than fieldwork. Lauren took up yoga to relieve her job stress and over time discovered she was happier being a yoga instructor than a social work administrator; she now runs her own yoga studio. Even if you make up for lost learning, as Lauren did with math, there is always more to learn—as long as we remain open to the possibilities of learning new things and can find support to try them.

And what about all those courses and tests we've successfully passed but which we don't remember or use in or out of school once the test is over? That's a lot of lost learning—and lost personal time.

About 25 percent of American high school students learn a foreign language, often for one or two years, mainly because most colleges and universities require one or two years of a foreign language for admission, rather than the students' personal interest in learning one. Students graduate from high school and get into American colleges all the time, yet the United States has low rates of dual-language speakers despite our expertly created foreign language programs: "According to the U.S. Census Bureau, only 20 percent of Americans can converse in two or more languages, compared with 56 percent of Europeans. Experts estimate about half of the human race is bilingual, at least."[5]

Ireland made Irish its national language and compels students to study Irish in its public schools. All public government signs are in Irish, and there is an active cultural movement to preserve Irish language and culture. Nonetheless, after fourteen years of compulsory schooling in Gaelic, only three out of ten Irish feel confident speaking the language.[6]

In New Zealand there is a debate about whether its native language, Maori, should be taught to all students as a way to preserve national identity and culture. David Seymour, leader of the New Zealand political party ACT, compared learning the Maori language in schools to Ireland's experience. "Look at the Irish. They've had compulsory Gaelic for ninety years, it's turned Gaelic into sort of the Brussels sprout of languages in Ireland. People eat it only because they're forced to do so and it makes them resent it."[7]

Michael D. Higgins, the current president of Ireland, visited New Zealand and offered his experience and thoughts about learning a language as a compulsory subject in schools. Higgins said, "I am in favor of encouraging people, bringing people to the language rather than forcing it.... You must lure them to the language, make the language attractive."[8]

Most adults resist such thoughts and believe, if given a choice, children will always choose to learn nothing, especially difficult things like math and foreign languages. Further, the thinking goes, "We must make children learn math or Spanish now because their brains are pliable and open to new things. It will be much harder to learn when they are older, if they even have the time or ability to learn such things as parents or workers."

Young children *can* learn languages more easily than adults, but plenty of adults successfully learn languages long after they've graduated from school. Indeed, some learn to speak conversationally simply by living in a foreign land or local enclave and engaging with the native speakers. A large study from MIT shows that the grammar-learning ability of children doesn't start to decline until they are seventeen years old, much later than previously thought. Also, this ability declines much more slowly than thought, which is why adults can learn a language nearly as well as children.[9]

Ironically, the reason US educators tell us we don't remember our foreign language studies is because we don't have opportunities to use the language outside of class, which makes me wonder: Why make people learn things they aren't likely to use, especially since the grade can affect their school record? An economist considered the lost opportunity costs for students studying a foreign language and concluded: "Any honest scale will tell you that the costs of foreign language instruction dwarf the benefits. Think about it: Even ignoring teacher's salaries, we're currently burning two years of class time per graduate. The payoff? Making less than one student in a hundred fluent."[10]

Besides the myth that learning a second language is easier done by young people, schooling fetishizes another claim about youthful learning and scientific discoveries. There is a perception that young people make better scientists because most major scientific discoveries are made by scientists in their thirties, followed by diminishing achievements as they age. Though this was true for a short time in the twentieth century, research shows that "inventors peak in their late 40s and tend to be highly productive in the last half of their careers.... [but] the highest-value patents often come from the oldest inventors—those over the age of 55.... A study of Nobel physics laureates found that, since the 1980s, they have made their discoveries, on average, at age 50. The study also found that the peak of creativity for Nobel winners is getting higher every year."[11]

John Holt described himself as a not very musical child and a late bloomer as a writer. In his book *Never Too Late*, John writes about learning to play the cello as a middle-aged man. John wrote the book as his musical biography but also "to question the widely held idea that what happens to us in the first few years of our lives determines everything that will happen later, what we can be, what we can do." [12] John writes in this book that teaching *is* like medicine and therefore should be given in the right dose at the right time. If given the wrong dose or at the wrong time, such teaching can poison a child's curiosity.

The number of students who give up on math, reading, or any subject because they think they are "not good at it" could be reduced if there wasn't this institutional prejudice that failing is due to some personal flaw or issue, not because the teacher or subject matter was not appropriate for them at that time. Having a more agile curriculum, one that prioritizes students' interests and strengths, is a big reason homeschooling succeeds.

The number of places and things for students to use at any time are limited to school and its calendar. This is the unappreciated value of homeschooling and alternative schools: both have lots of experience and success working with children outside of the classroom setting, calendar, and curriculum. Their examples show how a variety of people, play, and other activities can fill a child's day instead of a steady stream of instruction. Schools could benefit, especially during pandemic times, by loosening up on direct instruction and consulting with their colleagues about how to leverage outdoors and online resources for local interactions that engender social and emotional learning.

There's more on how schools are responding to homeschooling later in this book, but since schools are wedded to their regimens and the public doesn't question this much, it is unlikely they will change. Some educators claim homeschoolers are harming their children because only formal schools know what works to make children learn. Carol Black, a filmmaker (*Schooling the World*) and author, gives this concise reply:

What "works?" Direct instruction. How do we know? Tests. Who designs the tests? The same people who have always designed the tests. What do the tests correlate with? Success in school. What does success in school correlate with? (Hint: it's not creativity, compassion, critical thinking, scientific curiosity, artistic vision, sustainability, justice, spiritual insight, sense of humor, interpersonal skill, practical competence, or entrepreneurial success.)

Success in school correlates with more school success through a narrow band of verbal and analytical skills that are valued and measured in schools. More school success correlates with access to the elite institutions and sites of economic and political power that require school success as a gatekeeper for entry. (Oh, yeah. And it correlates with family income.)[13]

INSTRUMENTAL VERSUS SELF-DIRECTED EDUCATION

ADAM DICKERSON EXPLORES John Holt's philosophy of learning in a scholarly book and notes the similarities between Aristotle and Holt regarding active learning and how it molds the learner.[14] Aristotle wrote, "For the things we have to learn before we can do, we learn by doing, e.g., men become builders by building and lyre-players by playing the lyre; so too we become just by doing just acts, temperate by doing temperate acts, brave by doing brave acts." This is similar to Holt's ideas about children's learning: children learn best by doing things, and by gaining competence and more access to the world, their learning and growth increase. In school, we must be taught before we can do.

Dickerson describes human activities that require attention from the doer as *practices*, and practices have external and internal goods. The external goods are "related to the practice only contingently, rather than (as internal goods are) playing a constitutive role in making it the practice it is." The example of learning to play chess is used: "The only way to embody those internal goods is in stretches of chess-playing that demonstrate particular virtues (e.g., strategic brilliance, elegance, etc.). Hence, to strive to play excellent chess requires that the player choose to play chess for its own sake." But if chess becomes a means to an end—solely to win fame and fortune—its practice becomes instrumental rather than autotelic (for its own sake).[15] The primary pursuit of high grades in school is an instrumental practice that is embraced by teachers and parents, but it has significant downsides.

In school, families are often put in an unfair competitive position due to how much income they have. On a rudimentary level, those who can afford private tutoring for passing tests pay for it, and those who can't afford tutoring must do what they can. On a higher level, the social capital that a middle- or upper-class child has—a secure home life, safe neighborhood, and easy access to books, technology, and knowledgeable people—provides many more educational, social, and employment opportunities for the cultural transmission of knowledge outside the classroom. This makes the school grading system inherently unfair toward poor families. Though not considered cheating by education officials, this dynamic is felt as deeply unfair by those affected by it. By pretending the school meritocracy is fair, when it is increasingly clear to all who participate that it designed to favor those who are already advantaged in life, we undermine credibility in the school system. The instrumental use of school grades to justify outcomes, to sort the haves and have nots in society, corrupts education.

High-stakes testing in India can make or break a student's social mobility, and the test-coaching industry is deeply entrenched among the country's middle and upper classes. This helps to explain the do-or-die attitude some Indian parents display as they help their children cheat on exams. News reports and video from 2015 show a large number of Indian parents scaling the outer walls of a school to pass their children cheat sheets during the high-stakes exams.[16]

It's clear to these parents that school perpetrates an educational caste system, and they will do everything in their power to help their children escape the caste of dropouts and failed students, and its accompanying economic despair. It doesn't matter to these parents that their children don't know the content that school is testing because, unlike the wealthy, they can't purchase or use other ways to escape their education caste. The crazy scene of parents passing test answers through a window to their children in school makes sense if you buy into the notion of school as the be-all and end-all of one's destiny, a notion our all-too-serious educationists like to encourage through advertising, law, and custom. Powerless to change those factors, a sane response is to game the system yourself, to change what you can.

In the United States, studies consistently show that students from wealthy school districts do better on standardized tests, and even if their test scores aren't good, wealth can still get a not-so-bright child into a university through some well-planned gifts or flat-out bribery. This clear, systemic unfairness is what emboldens parents to help their children cheat in order to get ahead in life. As in the chess example earlier, instrumental motivations drive schools to create and use tests that, intentionally or not, are biased against certain groups of students (poor, minority, non-native speakers, etc.), and this gives permission to the instrumental motivations of adults and students to cheat. The adage, "The corruption of the best is the worst" is an appropriate motto for the times we live in. In academia, all sorts of scholarly work are now in question due to issues of falsification of data and plagiarism. RetractionWatch.com writes that academic journals in 2020 alone retracted 1,800 papers.

In the United States our deadly earnestness about the need for even more school tests has led some teachers and parents to band together to opt out of the standardized testing regime, but it is far from a done deal. Alternative schools, other countries, and homeschoolers have used other types of assessments to determine how to help people do things better for decades, yet the testing and grading industry remains in control of education, citing the impartial nature of their scientifically produced test scores. Education has become a modern idol worshipped with test scores, instead of a human activity that enhances our lives.

An Indian journalist writes, "Other nations have managed to diminish the role of standardized testing or discard it altogether. Students in Finland, long the model of a successful national education system, take just one national test and only if they are moving on to university. Instead, the country relies on formative assessment—measuring students as they learn, not after, and providing constant feedback and coaching."[17] Nonetheless, the power of the state, combined with the power of standardized testing and bureaucracy, continues to trump individual needs and goals in education.

Forty years ago, John wrote at the end of this book, "Our chief educational mission is not to find a way to make homes more like schools. If anything, it is to make schools *less* like schools." Let's hope this change will happen someday. For now, though, you can make the change yourself and try homeschooling. ■

INTRODUCTION

JOHN HOLT

THIS BOOK IS ABOUT WAYS we can teach children, or rather allow them to learn, outside of schools—at home or in whatever other places and situations (and the more the better) we can make available to them. It is in part an argument in favor of doing it, in part a report of the people who are doing it, and in part a manual of action for people who want to do it.

Many events, some public, some personal, some in my own mind, led me to write this book. It began in the late 1950s. I was then teaching ten-year-olds in a prestige school. I was also spending a lot of time with the babies and very young children of my sisters, and of other friends. I was struck by the difference between the tens (whom I liked very much) and the ones and twos. The children in the classroom, despite their rich backgrounds and high IQs, were with few exceptions frightened, timid, evasive, and self-protecting. The infants at home were bold adventurers.

It soon became clear to me that children are by nature and from birth very curious about the world around them, and energetic, resourceful, and competent in exploring it, finding out about it, and mastering it. In short, much more eager to learn, and much better at learning, than most of us adults. Babies are not blobs, but true scientists. Why not then make schools into places in which children would be allowed, encouraged, and (if and when they asked) helped to explore and make sense of the world around them (in time and space) in the ways that most interested them?

I said this in my first two books, *How Children Fail* (1964) and *How Children Learn* (1966). They were soon widely read and translated in many other countries. Along with others saying much the same thing, I found myself busy as a lecturer, TV talk show guest, and so on. Many people, among educators, parents, and the general public, seemed to be interested in and even enthusiastic about the idea of making schools into places in which children would be independent and self-directing learners. I was even asked to give a course on Student-Directed Learning at the Harvard Graduate School of Education. For a while it seemed to me and my allies that within a few years such changes might take place in many schools and, in time, even a majority.

When parents told me, as many did, that they were dissatisfied with their children's schools, I urged them to form committees, hold meetings, and organize public support for school reform, pressuring school boards and if need be electing new ones. In a few places, parents actually did this.

At first I did not question the compulsory nature of schooling. But by 1968 or so I had come to feel strongly that the kinds of changes I wanted to see in schools, above all in the ways teachers related to students, could not happen as long as schools were compulsory. I wrote about this in an article, "Not So Golden Rule Days," which appeared first in the *Center Magazine* of the Center for the Study of Democratic Institutions and later in my third book, *The Underachieving School.*

Since compulsory school attendance laws force teachers to do police work and so prevent them from doing real teaching, it would be in *their* best interests, as well as those of parents and children, to have those laws repealed, or at least greatly modified. In the article, I suggested some political steps or stages in which this might be done.

In such ways many of us worked, with great energy, enthusiasm, and confidence, for this kind of school reform. As people do who are working for change, we saw every sign of change, however small, as further proof that the change was coming. We had not yet learned that in today's world of mass media ideas go in and out of fashion as quickly as clothes. For a while, school reform was in fashion. There is no way we could have known that it was only fashion. One only finds out later what is fashion and what has lasting effect.

There were signs, even then. I had been one of a number of speakers invited to Minneapolis, a liberal city in a liberal state, to talk to a large conference of Minnesota teachers. At my meeting there were perhaps seven hundred. After my talk, during the questions, which had seemed friendly, a stout woman, thin pressed-together lips turned way down at the corners, said in a harsh angry voice, "What do you do with the children who are just plain lazy?" The entire audience burst into loud applause. I was startled and shocked. When the applause died down, I replied as best I could, and the meeting resumed its normal polite course. Later, I pushed aside the awkward memory of that little incident. I did not want to hear what it was plainly saying, that for a second the silent majority had spoken and said, "Children are no damned good."

In my travels I was often invited to visit schools and classes by people who said, "We've read your books, we think they're wonderful, and we're doing all the things you talked about." Well, they usually were, but not in the way they meant—they were doing all the mistaken and harmful things that I described in the books and had once done myself. People also talked to me with great enthusiasm about innovative programs. But these were always paid for with federal money, and as time went on, it always turned out that when the federal money stopped, so did the program. People might feel badly about losing these wonderful programs. But pay for them with local money, their own money? It was never considered.

When I went to places to talk, I was always met at the airport by two or three people. Usually, we were friends from the start. They had read my books, saw things much as I did. We always had a good time together, talking about the things we agreed on, sharing success stories, horror stories, hard-luck stories. They always made me feel so at home that, by lecture time, I assumed that with a few exceptions the people there must all be like my friends. Only slowly did I realize that the people who brought me in to speak were almost always a tiny minority in their own school or community, and that my task was to say out loud in public what people were sick of hearing *them* say, or even what they had been afraid to say at all. They hoped that if people heard me—famous author, guest on the *Today* show, and so on—they might pay attention.

From many such experiences I began to see, in the early 1970s, slowly and reluctantly, but ever more surely, that the movement for school reform was mostly a fad and an illusion. Very few people, inside the schools or out, were willing to support or even tolerate giving more freedom, choice, and self-direction to children. Of the very few who were, most were doing so not because they believed that children really wanted and could be trusted to find out about the world, but because they thought that giving children some of the appearances of freedom (allowing them to wear old clothes, run around, shout, write on the wall, etc.) was a clever way of getting them to do what the school had wanted all along—to learn those school subjects, get into a good college, and so on. Freedom was not a serious way of living and working, but only a trick, a "motivational device." When it did not quickly bring the wanted results, the educators gave it up without a thought and without regret.

At the same time, I was seeing more and more evidence that most adults actively distrust and dislike most children, even their own, and quite often especially their own. Why this should be so, I talked about in my books *Escape From Childhood* and *Instead of Education*. In a nutshell, people whose lives are hard, boring, painful, meaningless—people who suffer—tend to resent those who seem to suffer less than they do, and they will make them suffer if they can. People who feel themselves in chains, with no hope of ever getting them off, want to put chains on everyone else.

In short, it was becoming clear to me that the great majority of boring, regimented schools were doing exactly what they had always done and what most people wanted them to do. Teach children about Reality. Teach them that Life Is No Picnic. Teach them to Shut Up and Do What You're Told. Please don't misunderstand me on this. People don't think this way out of pure meanness. A man writing, sympathetically, to a radical paper, about life in small towns in Iowa, where in order to pay their debts, many full-time farmers have to do extra work in meatpacking plants—as he says, "shoveling lungs"—said, "The work ethic has been ground into these folks so thoroughly that they think anyone who doesn't hold down, continually, a full-time *painful* job is a bum." They don't want their kids to be bums. Back to the Basics, for most of them, is code for No More Fun and Games in School. Most of them don't care particularly about reading, as such. They read little themselves—like most Americans, they watch TV. What they want their children to learn is how to *work*. By that they don't mean to do good and skillful work they can be proud of. They don't have that kind of work themselves, and they never expect to. They don't even *call* that "work." They want their children, when their time comes, to be able, and *willing*, to hold down full-time painful jobs of their own. The best way to get them ready to do this is to make school as much like a full-time painful job as possible.

Of course, they would be glad to see their children go to a "good" college, become lawyers, doctors, corporation executives, part of that world of wealth and power they see every day on TV. But this is like winning the lottery. You may hope for it—about the only hope you've got—but you don't plan on it. Anyway, most people know by the time their children finish second or third grade that they are not going to win the big prize. What's left is that full-time painful job. To get them ready for that is what most schools are for, always were for.

Just the other day, this truth was once again thrust in my face. Taking a cab to the airport, I fell into conversation with the driver, a cheerful, friendly man. He asked me where I was going and what I did. I said I wrote books about children, schools, and education, and also published a little magazine about people teaching their children at home. He said he didn't think that was a very good idea, and he went on to talk about schools and what was wrong with them. As soon as I reached the airport, I wrote down all I could remember of his words. The fragments I quote here give a fair picture of the whole.

Early in our talk he said,

Seems to me the students are directing the teachers these days, instead of the other way round....When I was a kid, if I'd ever talked back to a teacher, I would have got a face full of knuckles. (Laughed.) Then I would have had to hope to God he didn't tell my father about it.

Print can't convey the approval, even the *pleasure*, with which he said this. I rarely meet people who have this faith in violence to solve problems. When I do, they scare me. I thought in the cab, "What have I got myself into now?" During the ride, I said little, tried once or twice without success to change the subject, and at the end said nothing at all. He did all the talking, getting angrier and angrier. Yet when we reached the airport, he said good-bye and wished me a good trip, in the most friendly way. I looked at him as we parted. In the city I see many faces that look angry, brutal, and cruel. He did not look that way at all.

After saying the words quoted above, he said, "God help any of my children if they had ever talked back to a teacher," with such ferocity that it froze the tongue in my mouth. Yet I wonder now what he would have done if they had, and whether in fact he had actually ever done it. Suppose one of his children had claimed to be the victim of a teacher's injustice. My guess is that he would have told them to forget about justice, that the teacher was the boss, and that their job was to do whatever the teacher said.

This thought recalled a scene in Frederick Wiseman's film *High School*, in which a student and a disciplinary vice-principal were arguing. The student, wearing glasses, good at using words, obviously not a poor kid, was stubbornly insisting that he hadn't done something he was accused of doing, and therefore, that he shouldn't be punished for it. The vice-principal, a big man, a former athlete and probably once a poor kid, was just as stubbornly trying to explain to the student that it didn't make any difference whether he had done what he was accused of or not; the people in charge had *decided* that he had done it, and there was nothing for him to do but take his punishment—"like a man," he said, implying that only crybabies and troublemakers whine about justice. Theories about what was true, or fair, were beside the point. In the real world, Authority had declared him guilty and he was going to be punished, and he might as well accept it.

Later in our conversation the driver spoke admiringly of Catholic schools, saying,

> I know a guy who had a couple of high school kids who were kind of wild. He sent them to Saint [Name] School. There, if a kid talked back to one of the priests, he'd deck him, right then and there, no questions asked. (He laughed approvingly.)

I know well and on the whole believe all the conventional arguments about the futility and destructiveness of violence. None of them would have made the slightest dent on this driver. For in our conversation, he told me that all six of his children had gone to college, earned the money for it themselves, and made it through. One had finished at the top of her class of 170 at a school for dental technicians. Another was trying to get into medical school, but (so the driver said) had not yet been able to, because he was not black or Puerto Rican or Mexican. (He talked a long time, and very bitterly, about this.) But in any case, here he was, driving a cab, and here were his six children, all college graduates, on their way to higher levels of society. Here was all the proof he needed that his threats and toughness worked. Not for a moment would he ever have considered the possibility that his children might have done what he wanted not so much because they feared his fist as because they valued his good opinion.

We must be clear about this. It is not because he is cruel himself that this father, like many others, insists that the schools be harsh and cruel to his children. It is because he believes that this is how the world really works, that only by being tough on kids can we help them to live better than we do, working at good jobs instead of waiting on tables and driving crummy cabs. Nor is it only working-class people who take this harsh view of life. Let me tell again a story I told in an earlier book. A boy in one of my fifth-grade classes was the son of a mid-level executive in a large corporation, perhaps not extremely wealthy but certainly in the top 5 percent in income. In the two or three years before the boy came to my class he had done poorly in his studies and had been a behavior problem both at school and at home. Expert "help" had been called on, and it had not helped. In my less rigid class, the boy found many things to do that interested him, became the class chess champion, did much better in his studies, particularly math, which he had always hated, and became much better behaved, both at school and at home. His mother, a gentle and soft-spoken woman, came to see me one day after school. She said how pleased she and her husband were that their son was doing so much better in his schoolwork and was so much more pleasant and easy to live with. She told me how much he enjoyed my class, and how much he talked about all the interesting things that went on in it. Then she paused a while, frowning a little, and finally said, "But you know, his father and I worry a little about how much fun he is having in school. After all, he is going to have to spend the rest of his life doing things he doesn't like, and he may as well get used to it now."

As long as such parents are in the majority, *and in every social class they are*, the schools, even if they wanted to, and however much they might want to, will not be able to move very far in the directions I and many others have for years been urging them to go. These parents do not want their children in or anywhere near classes in which children learn what interests them most, for the satisfaction and joy of doing it. They want their children to believe what countless teachers and parents have told me: "If I wasn't *made* to do things, I wouldn't do anything." They don't want them to think that the best reason for working might be that the work itself was interesting, demanding, and worth doing. For the real world, as they see it, doesn't run that way and can't be made to run that way.

While the question "Can the schools be reformed?" kept turning up no for an answer, I found myself asking a much deeper question. Were schools, however organized, however run, necessary at all? Were they the best place for learning? Were they even a good place? Except for people learning a few specialized skills, I began to doubt that they were. Most of what I knew, I had not learned in school, or in any other such school-like "learning environments" or "learning experiences" as meetings, workshops, and seminars. I suspected this was true of most people.

As time went on, I even began to have more and more doubts about the word *learning* itself. One morning in Boston, as I walked to work across the Public Garden, I found myself imagining a huge conference, in a hotel full of signs and posters and people wearing badges. But at this conference everyone seemed to be talking about *breathing*. "How are you breathing these days?" "Much better than I used to, but I still need to improve." "Have you seen Joe Smith yet—he certainly breathes beautifully." And so on. All the meetings, books, discussions were about Better Breathing. And I thought, if we found ourselves at such a conference, would we not assume that everyone there was sick or had just been sick? Why so much talk and worry about something that healthy people do naturally?

The same might be said of our endless concern with "learning." Was there ever a society so obsessed with it, so full of talk about how to learn more, or better, or sooner, or longer, or easier? Was not all this talk and worry one more sign that there was something seriously the matter with us? Do vigorous, healthy, active, creative, inventive societies—Periclean Greece, Elizabethan England, the United States after the Revolution—spend so much time *talking* about learning? No; people are too busy *doing* things and learning from what they do.

These ideas led into my book *Instead of Education* where I tried to make clear the distinction between *doing*, "self-directed, purposeful, meaningful life and work" and *education*, "learning cut off from life and done under pressure of bribe or threat, greed and fear." Even as I wrote it I planned a sequel, to be called *Growing Up Smart—Without School*, about competent and useful adults who during their own childhood spent many years out of school, or about families who right now were keeping their children out.

During the late 1960s and early 1970s I knew a number of groups of people who were starting their own small, private, alternative schools. Most of them did not try to start their own school until they'd spent years trying to get their local public schools to give them some kind of alternative. When they finally decided to make a school of their own, they had to persuade other parents to join them, reach some agreement on what the school would be like, find a place for it that the law would accept and that they could afford, get the okays of local fire, health, safety, officials, get enough state approval so that their students would not be called truants, and find a teacher or teachers. Above all, they had to raise money.

One day I was talking to a young mother who was just starting down this long road. She and a friend had decided that they couldn't stand what the local schools were doing to children, and that the only thing to do was start their own. For many months they had been looking for parents, for space, for money, and had made almost no progress at all. Perhaps if I came up there and talked to a public meeting....

As we talked about this, I suddenly thought, Is all this really necessary? I said to her, "Look, do you really want to run a school? Or do you just want a decent situation for your own kids?" She answered without hesitation, "I want a decent situation for my own kids." "In that case," I said, "why go through all this work and trouble—meetings, buildings, inspectors, money? Why not just take your kids out of school and teach them at home? It can't be any *harder* than what you are doing, and it might turn out to be a lot easier." And so it soon proved to be—a lot easier, a lot more fun.

In talking with young families like these, I found that what they most needed was support and ideas from other families who felt the same way. For this reason, I began publishing a small, bimonthly magazine called *Growing Without Schooling*, in which parents could write about their experiences teaching their children at home. Some of the material in this book first appeared in that magazine. Of this material, some is quoted from books, magazines, news stories, court decisions, and so on. Some was written by me. Much of it comes from letters from parents. The letters quoted here are only a small part of the letters we have printed in the magazine, which in turn are only a very small part of those that people have sent us.

The ones quoted here are of course some of the best, but many others that we might have printed are just as good. I have had to break up many of these letters so as to fit the parts under different chapter headings. This may have caused a loss of some of the impact and flavor of the originals, which were often very long and covered many topics. Still, what we have quoted will give some idea how affectionate, perceptive, and eloquent most of these letters are. Reading the mail sent to *Growing Without Schooling* has been one of the great rewards of doing this work. I hope readers of this book will enjoy these letters as much as I have.

1

CHILDREN ARE NOT THE FUTURE— THEY ARE THE PRESENT

WHEN THE COVID-19 PANDEMIC LOCKDOWNS CAME, many parents started pulling their hair out trying to teach their children at home and cursing homeschooling as a result. However, participating in daily classroom lessons using a computer at home is *remote learning*, not homeschooling. For most of the public though, homeschooling *is* simply doing school at home, and now that perception is further primed by schools' need to supply conventional schoolwork through the internet. This is why John Holt used the word *unschooling* to describe learning at home: it doesn't have to occur only at home nor resemble learning in school. You are in control of your time with unschooling; the school is in control of your time during remote learning.

First-time homeschoolers often start by purchasing and following a packaged curriculum to ensure their children are learning the same things at the same ages as conventionally schooled students. The conventional school curriculum is easily adaptable to homeschooling, since most parents spent their early lives learning in a classroom and know the routine. But if you decide to recreate conventional public or private schooling in your home, you're pretty much locked into a school schedule of learning, teaching the way you were taught, and evaluating your efforts the way school does. This is not something every child or parent wants to do at home five days a week, especially if school wasn't working for them in the first place.

Certainly, some families succeed at doing school at home, and there are plenty of curricula companies, consultants, and books to help you do so. Further, daily lessons designed for a class of ten or more children can be finished more quickly by a family at home. This leaves everyone with more time to study a topic, or to put it away and move on to something else. Some families find they can complete a daily, prepackaged elementary school curriculum in one to three hours, leaving lots of time for play, socializing, and thinking. Other families just want to have the curriculum on hand to see what children in school are learning at a particular age, treating it as guidelines rather than directives. In any case, you don't need to turn your home into a miniature school to help your children learn and grow.

The well-known and often described boredom of students during school can become a familiar complaint from children when school is transplanted into the home: "If I have to do school then I'd rather go back and at least be miserable with my friends." As you will read, there are many ways to help children grow without resorting to conventional school schedules, techniques, and discipline.

Experienced homeschoolers and those who study education alternatives know you don't need to use grades, standardized test regimens, and school's seat-time metrics to judge how well a child is learning. You know because the child can demonstrate knowledge and mastery of topics by performing and documenting their ability to do science, history, math, and so on.

Homeschoolers see how reading, writing, science, and math are integrated and learned outside of school settings because they often occur when children participate in the tasks of daily life—fixing things, cleaning, cooking, using a computer, and so on. Children want to join us in our efforts to make things, do things, learn things, and we can invite them to do so. Many homeschoolers find their children not only enjoy helping around the house, but it gives them a sense of self-efficacy and accomplishment. If there are things children want to learn that parents can't help with, they find classes, outside help from friends or relatives, online courses, books, videos, or tutors to help them.

As the pandemic resulted in parents spending more time at home with their children, some parents began to see how reading, writing, math, and more are learned through their children's questions and cultural transmission. Further, supervising schools' remote learning is making parents see how much time their children spend being bored or confused in class while the teacher instructs or manages technical and student-behavior issues. Yet we tell children they need to endure the bad parts of school now so they can reap its benefits in the future as adults.

It's hard to change the culture of schooling when the entire enterprise is judged by how well people move to its next levels: the more graduates who go on to higher levels of schooling, the better the system is judged to be doing. In 1971 Ivan Illich explained in *Deschooling Society* how the need for schooling feeds upon itself, and this gets more evident the longer I live and see how much younger we put our children into school and how much older we keep them in.

Certainly, school does help *some* poor children obtain better lives, but it is not able to address the needs of the great number of children who become poor adults after graduation. The problem isn't just how schools operate, but the public perception that more school is the best way to make people get ahead in our society, and schools' willingness to feed that perception. We put money into educational programs like teaching social justice, civics, and ecology and think we are solving the problem because—Children are the future! We are teaching children to be better than we adults and we have record numbers of graduates! The future will necessarily be better because so many more people have been educated!

President Obama took this rhetoric to new heights when he claimed we are in a worldwide education competition that is "a race to the top, that we are going to out-educate the world and win the future."[18] As much as I like President Obama, his vague goal begs the question: How will we even know if we won the future since the future is always the future. Does time stop?

Such cheerleading and hubris about education cause us to be blind to other solutions before our eyes. Education has become the illusory fix for all of society's ills, including poverty. Why are we hoping that children will just graduate from school and move up in the world without directly addressing the issue of poverty? Generations of college graduates have yet to fix the poverty issue.

Increasing wages, providing public healthcare, job and skill training, better unions, and so on deal head-on with the issue of poverty. Politicians and educators need to support direct action to ameliorate poverty, instead of more educational posturing about the next generation. Doing so will not only relieve many parents of worry about living on the razor's edge, but also increase overall family security, which the children feel. Secure children learn better than insecure ones and secure adults sleep more soundly than insecure ones. Children can help us with these problems, according to their abilities, too. Helping to care, feed, and deliver things for those in need are all possible ways children can participate. Such efforts are usually a weekend or after-school project for children, or a year of service when they are much older, but why couldn't it be something they do as part of their schooling in their local communities?

The virus is scary, but it is also a learning moment. Some children will naturally want to study the science and nature of the virus, but others will want to pitch in with the adults and help do something about it. Being off of school's curriculum schedule enables children to do both in their own ways, often with the support of their parents and other adults. Here are two stories of schoolchildren who chose to help others instead of focus on the goals of school during this pandemic. After reading these, can you say what they did outside of school was less important than what they would be doing in school?

Seven-year-old Zohaib Begg spent three years in the hospital when he was younger and when he learned about the strain the virus is putting on his local hospital, he decided he wanted to do something to help them. ABC News reported that when Begg learned that some hospitals were running short of headgear, he thought they could use shower caps—and he knew that they were at hotels.

> First he collected shower caps from the hotels, but it turned out the hotels also had gloves and face masks to donate.
> Zohaib was able to collect more than 6,000 caps, masks, and gloves.[19]

The *New Yorker* noted the achievements of seventeen-year-old Avi Schiffmann,

> who launched a homemade Web site to track the movement of the Corona virus. Since then, the site, ncov2019.live, has had more than hundred million visitors....In a politicized pandemic, where rumor and panic run amok, the site has become a reputable, if unlikely, watchdog.[20]

Avi's mom describes him as a C-student in school, but this project shows how competent and motivated he actually is. It's always good to see parents who appreciate the value of supporting their children's self-directed learning, especially when it involves subjects outside the school curriculum. These stories also show how adults can support young people who want to help us deal with our current problems now, instead of in the future.

A documentary film, *Unschooled* (2020), featured the Natural Creativity Center (NCC) in the Germantown section of Philadelphia. In several scenes you see Peter Bergson, the center's founder, describe how low-income, inner-city children could benefit from the same freedom and nurturing his middle-class enrollees enjoyed in a similar center he founded with his wife more than forty years ago in the suburbs. A psychologist and a lawyer in the film criticize Peter's efforts seeing him as just another white guy who wants to help but doesn't understand the real problem: these kids need credentials and discipline to succeed in the *future*, not free choice, including time to play, and a sense of being accepted for who they are.

The three teens who are featured had trauma in their lives that public school was contributing to or ignoring, and they came from families in struggling neighborhoods on top of that. Patience, kindness, and respect for each teen is shown to pay off educationally in this film—but it takes time and doesn't match either the public school schedule or methods.

As we watch the time and effort NCC puts into building trustful relationships with its students, we also see how it causes discomfort for both their families and the officials overseeing the project for the city and state. Many parents openly express their doubts that letting their young teenagers play and talk freely, and pursue their own interests, is somehow educational. NCC has a long-term view of how people learn, and when the young people return for a second year we see them using the center's materials and mentors much more actively now that they have developed a baseline of trust in the NCC staff and the established processes. At the end of the second year, all three teens flourish in different ways and their parents recognize and appreciate the changes.

I think the movie title, *Unschooled*, refers to the adults in it far more than the young people. The adults are having their ideas about schooling challenged and, like most people, they resist change and push back. I know from my own experiences that supporting a child's self-directed learning is a tough idea for most parents and educators to grasp, often because they don't understand what their role should be if not instructor or director of education: "If children learn on their own, then what do I do?" This attitude is clearly shown in the film as various professionals criticize the lack of direct instruction and how such permissive ideas about children and learning are not educationally worthy, especially for inner-city youth. The adults don't teach in the standard way at the Natural Creativity Center (or in most alternative schools and homeschooling learning centers). They act primarily as facilitators and mentors, allowing the children to explore on their own and ask for help or companionship as needed. New concepts and opportunities may be offered but they are not imposed. NCC focuses on the power of self-motivation, based on personal interests and passions, as opposed to a compulsory curriculum. This is not a modern way of teaching, but an ancient and proven one that has fallen into disuse.

When you are homeschooling and your children resist doing schoolwork, they will probably ask why they have to learn something that you don't remember from school and that you're struggling to teach them. If you say, "Because it will teach you self-discipline" or "Because the school said so," or some other excuse that doesn't truly answer their question, you are sending the strong message that the only reason for doing it now is just because "I said so." Children eventually get the message that though we adults don't really believe this particular thing is important, we're forcing them to do it "just because." Children can revolt from such treatment in many ways—silently through self-harm, openly with their parents and society, or through passive-aggressive tactics.

For example, Chinese students in quarantine and learning the state curriculum at home had to download and use an app called Dingtalk for all their schoolwork. The students organized a large-scale effort to post one-star reviews of Dingtalk to get it removed from the Apple App Store. This effort was copied by American students who targeted Zoom and Classroom apps.[21]

The students made the news but lost the fights, but their fights are worth noting for their creativity and effort. What students present to us externally as compliance is not necessarily what's happening inside them: resentment, anger, humiliation, revenge for being made to do busywork during a worldwide crisis—those are likely the thoughts and emotions percolating inside in them.

We don't have to structure schooling so it feels constraining to so many students, which is another reason why I see homeschooling as a hopeful path for education. Homeschooling shows us the many possibilities that exist for learning when children are reintegrated into the real world. In the words of George Bernard Shaw, "What we want to see is the child in pursuit of knowledge, and not knowledge in pursuit of the child."

Since schooling seems stuck in the economic and social models of the nineteenth and twentieth centuries—school as a factory that manufactures children into educated adults—shouldn't we be updating our model?

NEW INSIGHTS INTO CHILDREN'S LEARNING

The metaphors we use to describe children and how they learn are telling. We describe children's minds as being blank slates that need to be written upon, empty vessels to be filled, or lamps that need to be lit. All indicate an adult doing something to a child to make them learn. Upon hearing the motto of the Lamplighter School, "A student is not a vessel to be filled but a lamp to be lighted," John Holt replied: "I've heard of that place, but they've got it all wrong. Their lamps are *already* lit. They just need to stop doing the types of things that blow them out."[22]

Research and psychology support this position in many ways, as you'll see throughout this book. A group of researchers sum up their findings quite clearly in the title of their paper: "The Double-Edged Sword of Pedagogy: Instruction Limits Spontaneous Exploration and Discovery." Direct instruction advocates claim self-directed learning is inefficient and ineffective, but what these researchers found from their experiments was that after direct instruction from teachers, "children are less likely to perform potentially irrelevant actions but also less likely to discover novel information." In other words, directly instructed students are compliant but less adventurous in their thinking. The less we instruct, the more children can explore and make sense of the world in their own minds.

The researchers note how young children will turn their attention to where there is more to be learned, demonstrating their innate strengths as independent learners.

> Although the negative effects of instruction on exploration may seem disheartening, the results suggest a striking competence in young children: they are able to negotiate the trade-off between exploration and instruction such that they explore more when they can rationally infer that there is more information to be learned. Moreover, children demonstrate this competence remarkably early. By preschool, children seem actively to evaluate their teachers both for the knowledge they have and their ability to demonstrate it. Thus, well before children are immersed in formal education, they are sensitive to some conditions that promote effective instruction.[23]

Young children are much more capable at learning from the world than we give them credit for; let's celebrate that and encourage their explorations as much as we can. This knowledge can help you get more relaxed about homeschooling young children, too.

Alison Gopnik's book *The Gardener and the Carpenter: What the New Science of Child Development Tells Us About the Relationship Between Parents and Children* is full of current research and stories about how "parenting" has become something parents should do to children. It is a verb, a task or technique, rather than simply being a parent, a noun, to their children. The book is full of interesting insights that can give you confidence to let your children explore the world much as possible:

> All this scientific research points in the same direction: Child-hood is designed to be a period of variability and possibility, exploration and innovation, learning and imagination.[24]
>
> …children learn more from the unconscious details of what caregivers do than from any of the conscious manipulations of parenting.[25]

LEARNING IS A BY-PRODUCT OF DOING

School is often described as preparation for life, but what are children doing if not living right now alongside us? At the time of this writing, they are enduring, in their own ways, the anxieties and disappointments caused by the pandemic and, like the adults around them, they are improvising solutions to a unique situation. It's important that we tell our children when we don't know what's going to happen and to discuss it with them, even if it is upsetting to them and to us. It isn't easy to do, but being open with our children about how we display and cope with our emotions and difficulties is important too. Having time to build your relationship with your child is one of the best benefits of homeschooling—if you stop worrying about the future and take advantage of the present.

This is a point homeschooling makes plain to those willing to see it: all learning is interrelated. In school we divide science from literature, history from math, philosophy from physical education, and so on. But in life there are no such divisions. A child might want to learn chess and be shown how to play at first, but in order to get better at it they also need to become a better reader, internalize intricate strategies, and play and observe lots of chess. In the course of doing this, the history, culture, and social world of chess are also discovered.

In the Foreword, I wrote about an economist who questioned the value of learning foreign languages in high school compared to learning or doing something else. In the comments to the article, several people state that even if you don't learn a foreign language, being compelled to learn it is still worthwhile because of its learning by-products: It is an introduction to a language. It expands the mind. The experience teaches you discipline. Even if you don't end up using it, having it will increase your value as an employee in the future. It makes you a well-rounded individual.

This is exactly the same thing that happens when you learn things you want to do, like how to bake cookies. But the by-products of baking cookies for a child (discipline to complete the task, measuring, tasting, reading, etc.) are not considered as educationally valuable as the by-products learned by forcing oneself to complete a language course you saw no need to take. The older I get the more I wonder what I would be doing had I been allowed to play and study piano in school instead of doing a forced march through French, Spanish, algebra, and Latin. We don't know how much time we have on earth, and to think of the amount of time we spend in school being bored, confused, or doing things we don't want to do makes me mourn for what is truly lost—my personal time. Many adults say they make children do things "for their own good," because the young don't appreciate how what they do now affects the future. Perhaps. But the young sure know what they want to do now.

Many misinterpret this reasoning and call for patience to mean children should be allowed to do whatever they want, whenever they want. John Holt did not argue, as some claim, that children should do whatever they want. In *Freedom and Beyond* he wrote, "As there is no life without structure, so there is no life without constraints." John further notes that adults "often and rightly intervene in the lives of children" because adults know the social agreements and rules better than they do. Adam Dickerson writes that John does not "speak of the individual-independent-of-society (there is no such thing), but only of the individual-in-her-social-context."[26] This is seen in John's description of the three types of discipline.

The Discipline of Reality—you play the wrong note in a song and that tells you if it was the right or wrong thing to get the result you wanted.

The Discipline of Culture, of Society, of What People Really Do— "Children sense around them this culture, this network of agreements, customs, habits, and rules binding the adults together. They want to understand it and be part of it."[27]

The Discipline of Superior Force—coercing people into doing one thing rather than another. John writes, "There is bound to be some of this in a child's life. Living as we do surrounded by things that can hurt children, or that children can hurt, we cannot avoid it....But we ought to use this discipline when it is necessary to protect the life, health, safety, or well-being of people or other living creatures, or to prevent destruction of things that people care about. But we ought not to assume too long, as we usually do, that a child cannot understand the real nature of the danger from which we want to protect him."[28]

Throughout *Teach Your Own* and in the many issues of the magazine he founded, *Growing Without Schooling* (*GWS*), John discusses how children choose to learn simple and difficult things in their own ways. *GWS* has thousands of examples of children who display their love for acrobatics, martial arts, music, dance, sports, science, math, social action, caregiving, and so on. This love drives them to seek higher levels of excellence and to learn more and meet more people, which can lead to all sorts of explorations and personal development.

But the amount of sustained attention, *love*, one gives to a practice depends on the amount of control the practitioner has in the process. Studies continue to show that having control over one's learning makes it easier to retain and use what was learned. Alfie Kohn has written at length about the studies and research on learning, particularly how intrinsic motivations enhance learning better than extrinsic motivations in his book *Punished by Rewards*. Clinical psychologist Naomi Fisher writes that as she researched and explored cognitive evaluation theory (how to facilitate motivation in others), she learned intrinsic motivation cannot be manipulated in others: "You can't force it; you can only facilitate it."[29] Despite this evidence, and folk wisdom like "You can lead a horse to water, but you can't make it drink," we remain obsessed with having children delay gratification for what they want to learn now so they can learn something adults think may be important for them in the future.

This disconnect between the goals of schools and homeschoolers is stark. A few researchers have noticed this. A school may ask a homeschooler to show how they will remediate their child's reading because the child is five months behind the reading level of fifth-graders in school, or they scored poorly on their last two math tests. The homeschool parents find this worry to be unfounded because they know their child enjoys reading and uses numbers correctly and will increase their proficiency with time. In *Homeschooling in America*, Professor Joseph Murray writes:

> In short, what counts as evidence of success in public schools has de facto become the measure of progress in homeschools, at least for researchers....

Most of the outcomes pursued by homeschooling families, such as learning for understanding, developing habits of inquiry, and learning across content areas, never appear in research studies on the effects of homeschooling.[30]

Another desired outcome not mentioned in Murray's list but mentioned often in books and materials created by homeschoolers (and unschoolers in particular) is *joy*. Joy in learning, joy in living. There is scant education research about joy in learning in the classroom, but a study by Finnish educators

> identified the circumstances that were most likely to produce joy in the classroom. No doubt many pupils would agree with this example of their findings: "The joy of learning does not include listening to prolonged speeches."
>
> Such teacher-centric lessons are much less likely to generate joy than are lessons focused on the student, the authors report.[31]

Education has been conflated with schooling so much in our culture that the terms are interchangeable, making it nearly impossible to separate the large-scale enterprise of institutional schooling from the small-scale project of personal growth. In his first book, *How Children Fail*, based on his experiences teaching fifth grade in private schools, John wrote that the only difference between good students and bad ones is the good students are careful not to forget what they studied until after the test. This charade of learning infects all compulsory school systems as instrumentalist learning is valued more than learning for its own sake. ∎

2

HOMESCHOOLING, PARENTING, AND HIGHER EDUCATION

MANY FAMILIES' ATTEMPTS TO COPE WITH LEARNING at home during the COVID-19 pandemic caused concepts like remote learning, learning pods, and hybrid homeschooling to come into our discussions.

The failure of remote learning is apparent—not only were the schools and students ill-prepared for the move, they also failed to factor in the amount of screen time students had to use (if they had a computer and internet access), as well as parents' worries about the amount time their children already spent sitting in front of a computer.

Pandemic learning pods depend on the amount of risk you are willing to share with another person or family. This usually involves another family that you trust and one that has similar health and learning profiles as yours. In addition, some of these families hire a private tutor to work with their children at home during the day so both sets of parents are free.

Hybrid homeschooling is a mix of conventional schooling and learning at home. It can be with a public or private school that allows children to attend part-time, say two days a week and the rest at home. This can also involve homeschooling learning centers, if any exist in your area.

When homeschooling was in its early stages, school officials tried to stop it by claiming people's homes weren't properly set up to be schools. They took families to court for not having the same types of safety protocols as schools, such as clearly labeled emergency exits, and for parents not being certified teachers. Over time, homeschooling families won those cases and, since schools receive per-pupil funding each year based on the number of students enrolled in them, schools made it clear that there is no middle ground: you're either in school or out.

We might see court cases by the schools to shut these options down if they affect school funding. After all, isn't hiring a full-time teacher for your pod the creation of an unlicensed private school? Should hybrids receive public funding?

For decades, homeschooling grew at such a slow rate that school funding mechanisms were not seriously threatened, but the pandemic has changed that. *Education Week* writes that 58 percent of school districts surveyed cite homeschooling "as being a major contributor to enrollment declines caused by COVID-19—more than any other single reason, such as losing students to charter schools, private schools, or 'pandemic pods.'"[32] Typically, about 3 percent of school-age children are homeschooled each year, but according to an EdWeek Research Center survey of parents, "9 percent of parents who weren't home schooling their children last school year said they planned to home school their children at least some of the time this school year."[33]

There is doubt among researchers about the actual size of the increase due to issues with self-reporting and the phrasing of the survey questions, but in any case this is a remarkable boost for homeschooling. I hope schools will welcome rather than fight the varieties of education that homeschooling engenders instead of attempting to standardize homeschooling into conventional school at home or eliminate it all together. In the United States, homeschoolers do not receive any federal government support or funding, though some states offer tax relief for homeschool educational expenses and Education Savings Accounts can be used by all families. Once the pandemic is over, it will be interesting to see how many of the newcomers continue homeschooling.

Germany and Sweden officially banned homeschooling several years ago, and France is on track to severely limit it, on the grounds that homeschooling creates a parallel society that undermines democracy. This is an unproven assumption, particularly since homeschooling has a strong record of its children actively participating in society as government employees, teachers, scientists, entrepreneurs, artists, and so on. It's ironic that allowing family choice is considered a danger to democracy; perhaps the idea that freedom is an inherent part of the definition of democracy is more an American idea than a European one? Compulsory attendance in government schools does not automatically create a unified society, as illustrated by the ongoing strife these countries have over immigrants and the variety of private schools they allow to operate, so these actions are much more about political agendas than education.

LEARNING IN THE REAL WORLD

John was deeply impressed by the work of the self-taught anthropologist Jean Liedloff, the author of *The Continuum Concept*. He was moved with her descriptions not only of how the Yequana Indians cared for their children but also with how children were allowed to play undisturbed while the adults did their things throughout the day. If they wished, the children could observe the adult activities, often on the periphery, and participate if possible. Liedloff notes the absence of any formal teaching and how conversation, observation, and mimicking adult behavior leads to tribal children's intellectual development. Hunting and gathering expeditions, sharp knives and tools, tribal councils and rituals were all accessible to the young.

Carol Black's essay "On the Wildness of Children" presents research that supports Liedloff's observations.

> In many rural land-based societies, learning is not coerced; children are expected to voluntarily observe, absorb, practice, and master the knowledge and skills they will need as adults—and they do. In these societies—which exist on every inhabited continent—even very young children are free to choose their own actions, to play, to explore, to participate, to take on meaningful responsibility. "Learning" is not conceived as a special activity at all, but as a natural by-product of being alive in the world.
>
> Researchers are finding that children in these settings spend most of their time in a completely different attentional state from children in modern schools, a state psychology researcher Suzanne Gaskins calls "open attention." Open attention is widely focused, relaxed, alert; Gaskins suggests it may have much in common with the Buddhist concept of "mindfulness." If something moves in the broad field of perception, the child will notice it. If something interesting happens, he can watch for hours. A child in this state seems to absorb her culture by osmosis, by imperceptible degrees picking up what the adults talk about, what they do, how they think, what they know.[34]

We don't live in a primitive society, goes the counterargument, so our children must learn in modern-day society. This objection doesn't address the issue though. The problem is that we don't allow our children to live and learn in modern-day society much at all. They must live and learn under the assumptions of school, in segmented areas with texts, songs, teachers, and information made just for children, and for longer periods of their lives. Children must learn to focus on what the school wants them to focus on, so open attention becomes a deficit in a school environment.

What would happen if we allowed children to learn and share the world with adults more than we do now? Can a person's open attention develop into useful skills and employment? The strong growth of the homeschooling movement around the world shows an incredible array of living and learning situations created by families, including taking children to work, reclaiming the home as a center of productivity as well as leisure, and creating clubs and associations based on the interests and activities of members regardless of their age. School has a role in this new production, but it is not the lead player. In this scenario, it is a communal resource to be used as wanted or needed, like a public library.

WORKING WITH, NOT ON, CHILDREN

Many parents rely on the childcare that school provides while they work or care for others, so this system is pretty firmly in place going forward. But cracks are showing all over schooling today and, rather than redesign or offer alternatives, those in charge double-down on giving children more of what they've gotten: longer school days, more homework, and more rigorous curriculum.

Once you challenge schools' concepts of learning, discipline, and merit you can see there are other ways to handle those things besides the usual displays of force: time-outs, detentions, lower grades, threats, and so on. After starting homeschooling, some discover—and especially if they move on to unschooling—that they no longer have to think and behave as if they are performing for school's approval, and they start to figure out what it is they really want to do with each day. Unschoolers call this the deschooling process. For children, it can follow the general formula that for each year a child spent in school you need to give them a month of rest from school to help them reset and get comfortable learning at home.

For adults, deschooling is about changing their schooled habits of mind. In their research on unschooling, Peter Gray and Gina Riley collected responses from parents about what they felt were the biggest challenges they faced as unschoolers. The most common challenge is responding to people's incredulous questions about teaching children at home.[35] If you say you homeschool, people assume you have a classroom instead of a living room in your home; if you say you unschool they imagine your home being overrun by feral children who will never fit in the real world. The interesting thing about homeschooling and unschooling is that people change not only how they view education but also how they act as parents.

John wrote about how parents can turn their children into "praise junkies." "Babies do not learn in order to please us, but because it's their instinct and nature to want to find out about the world. If we praise them for everything they do, after a while they are going to start learning, doing things, just to please us, and the next step is that they are going to become worried about not pleasing us. They're going to become just as afraid of doing the wrong thing as they might have been if they had been faced with the threat of punishment."[36]

This is a big one to let go of: controlling your children's time and thoughts. By giving your children freedom to learn in their own ways, you are also giving yourself a chance to see new possibilities for your children, and to unlearn the old ways of learning we've internalized from our years of schooling. You are not a teacher trying to keep a large number of children attentive to your instruction, you are working one-on-one with your own child and you can enjoy the time and space you have with your child in your own way, not the school's way. You don't need to worry that one child saying no to the lesson will incite a showdown with you in front of the class. In homeschooling, you can accept your child's response respectfully and move on to the next thing, just as you would if a friend said no to you.

Delia Tetelman, who operates the Unschooling Every Family: Embracing Neurodivergent and Disabled Learners Facebook page, describes unschooling as freedom, especially the freedom to say no. Tetelman says that unschooling parents learn to respect the process more than the outcome, and they learn to focus on strengths-based and interest-based learning and how to accommodate for weaknesses. Paying such close attention to a child takes time and effort. How can a teacher with many students in their class do so, especially when the teacher needs to complete assignments and move to the next subject to keep the students on school's schedule?

School teaches us to believe we need more school to advance in our lives and that's how the need for education feeds upon itself, devouring our current income in the promise of increased income to come from our latest education credentials. I was raised to think that higher education was about improving one's knowledge and character, not primarily as a ticket for a job. The line I was fed whenever I challenged something in school was, "Even if you don't enjoy it, attending school makes you a well-rounded individual able to function in a democracy."

It wasn't until I started work with John Holt that I realized how strange this logic is, especially for an institution that claims to be necessary for democracy to work. How can democracy be learned in a place where it isn't practiced?

Most people start homeschooling by replicating school at home and loosen up as they see their children are learning and growing in many ways outside the school curriculum. Homeschooling parents, over time, also realize they don't have to be their children's sole teacher and that other children, private tutors, homeschool parents, and some public schools offer classes and support to homeschoolers. If you decide to unschool, you have access to all those resources, but you are not limited to them. Your entire community, and all its people, places, and things, are yours to explore and enjoy.

There is another thing you can let go of once you start homeschooling your children: conventional parenting techniques. Homeschooling parents can work *with* their children, not *on* their children, and that means letting go of many of our assumptions about how children and adults are supposed to relate. The standardized school regimen is perfectly suited for corporate-style management, but you don't have to use that style to manage your home. Instead, you can be much more personal, warm, and accommodating of new ideas that your children offer, which means building a meaningful relationship with your children, not one based on mere obedience to authority. There are many examples of how this is done in *Teach Your Own*.

In 1983, when John revised his book *How Children Learn*, he wrote: "All I am saying in this book can be summed up in two words—Trust Children. Nothing could be more simple—or more difficult. Difficult, because to trust children we must trust ourselves—and most of us were taught as children that we could not be trusted."[37]

I think education is primarily about relationships, not education administration. People can use democratic meetings, nonviolent communication techniques, parent effectiveness training, the latest reading method, and so on as they see fit. But, ultimately, education is about trusting oneself and others to learn and grow without requiring an outside system or authority to force it. John Holt fretted that he was making parents too self-conscious about their interactions with their children; feeling pressure to do unschooling "the right way" can be just as fear-and-shame producing as feeling pressure to do school the right way, and fear and shame inhibit learning.

THE CIVIL LIBERTIES OF CHILDREN

John is famous for his child advocacy and in his book *Escape From Childhood: The Needs and Rights of Children*, he explores how we can gradually grant children the same rights as adults. He wrote a long letter to the American Civil Liberties Union seeking help for children's rights; here's a portion of it:

> [Compulsory school attendance laws are] a very serious infringement of the civil liberties of children and their parents, and would be so no matter what schools were like, how they were organized, or how they treated children, in other words, even if they were far more humane and effective than in fact they are.
>
> … [Y]ou will surely agree that if the government told you that one hundred and eighty days of the year, for six or more hours a day, you had to be at a particular place, and there do whatever people told you, you would feel that this was a gross violation of your civil liberties. The State, of course, justifies doing this to children as a matter of public policy, saying that only thus can it keep them from being ignorant and a burden to the state. But even if it were true that children were learning important things in schools and that they could not learn them anywhere else, neither of which I admit, I would still remind the ACLU that since in other and often more difficult cases, i.e., the Nazi rally in Skokie, Ill., it does not allow the needs of public policy to become an excuse for violating the basic liberties of citizens, it ought not to in this case.[38]

John later wrote that the ACLU sees "as a civil liberty matter the right of children to go to school, but not their right not to go." John decided to give up trying to abolish compulsory laws because he saw that "what makes schools compulsory, far more than these laws, is the fact that they have a virtual monopoly on the various kinds of grades, credits, transcripts, diplomas, and credentials which people must have to do almost all kinds of work in society, above all the most interesting, respected, and well-paid work."[39] Forty years later, and the civil liberties of children are being not only ignored but openly violated. Children are being forced into labor, warfare, and sexual abuse around the world, while poverty ravages their lives even in developed countries. In the United States, children are the poorest age group in the country,[40] yet we insist the best way to deal with that is to make sure they are educated—and being educated usually means being a college graduate.

IF EVERYONE GOES TO COLLEGE . . .

Some colleges are having record-breaking online enrollments during the pandemic. This isn't a surprise; during most economic downturns people turn to education credentials to boost their chances of employment. But what happens if everyone goes to college?

The rungs on school's meritocratic ladder have long been weak and narrow for the poor, especially in higher education. But now that the middle class is being negatively affected by higher education costs for degrees they may not use or complete, there is more skepticism that the best way to pursue future happiness is to complete a four-year college program. Citing increased income and status, many have chased advanced education degrees, such as law and MBAs, but have found the market overpopulated with similar graduates seeking the same jobs. MBA programs have seen steady enrollment declines for several years, but the pandemic seems to have changed that with enrollments soaring in 2020.

I hope their time and money is well spent, because many current holders of four-year college degrees are not happy with their investments of time and money. Not only are many college graduates underemployed, there is also a trend of people who have a traditional bachelor's degree who later enter community college to study what they really want to learn or get supplementary skills.[41]

A platitude that drives parents and school counselors to insist teenagers go to college is the instrumentalist idea that owning a college degree automatically gives you more money in the world of work. Anthony Carnevale, director of the Georgetown University Center on Education and the Workforce, champions this notion: "But the value of a college degree in the workplace is without question.... The road to success starts with one step. That step is still going to college."[42]

Tell that to a social worker who is still paying off their MSW degree, or to a schoolteacher (or anyone) still paying off their college loans! Not all college degrees give you a financial boost upon graduation or later in life. Research done by the Georgetown University Center also showed large differences in the earnings of college majors. Engineering and pharmaceutical majors "earn an average of $3.4 million more over their lifetimes than college graduates with some of the lowest-paying degrees, some of which include human services and education roles."[43]

As of September 2020, 43.2 percent of recent college graduates and 33.8 percent of all college graduates are underemployed—defined by the Federal Reserve Bank of New York as "the share of graduates working in jobs that typically do not require a college degree."[44] These numbers have been more or less in the same range since 1990, which is remarkable considering the big push educational institutions have been making to encourage everyone to graduate from college.

In the 1970s, my parents said I had to go to college because so many people had college degrees, they were the equivalent of high school degrees, so I needed a college degree to stand out from the crowd. It was quite common then to hear educators claim the liberal arts were valuable because they taught transferable skills; English majors could move into communication fields, philosophers could use logic skills to move into computer coding, and so on. Indeed, counselors and teachers urged students to follow their passions in college and throughout life in order to find their work–life balance. By the 1980s so many liberal arts degrees had glutted the market that specialized degrees, such as MBAs and law degrees, were viewed as better investments for those seeking to make lots of money with their degrees. By the early twenty-first century, both fields were saturated.

Colleges seem to have given up their mission of conserving, developing, and sharing knowledge for its own sake and have instead become handmaidens to industry, serving as their human resource department. Higher education institutions are also reluctant to give up their four-year tuition streams and support short-term, specialized certificates for skills or life-experience credits. Colleges have touted that their degrees confer benefits far beyond better job prospects because of all the networking connections you make there, the honors you get for good grades, and how a degree can increase your value as an employee later in life, and so on. It's such oft-repeated truisms that are leading students and their families to go into debt for college degrees.

Millions of former and current college students are now protesting to get the government to forgive their unreasonable college loan debts, because the job doors the degrees were supposed to open are not there. Learning throughout our lives can be supported by higher education in ways other than a four-year marathon of classes, but the education establishment is quite set in its ways. However, agile businesses are forging new paths toward employment.

James Marcus Bach is an expert in software testing and the author of *Secrets of A Buccaneer-Scholar: How Self-Education and the Pursuit of Passion Can Lead to a Lifetime of Success*. We met at an unschooling conference several years ago and I asked James about his self-education experiences. How was he able to work for companies like

Google and Apple without conventional degrees or certificates? James replied that he could never work at Google since they were so degree oriented in their hiring process; however, Apple gave him a chance. I mention James because of how quickly things are changing for people without college degrees. Google is now not only hiring people like James—they recruit them.

A *Forbes* magazine article about 2020 recruiting trends reported that some of the largest tech giants, including Google and Apple, are moving away from requiring candidates to have college degrees.[45] Companies are no longer limiting themselves to candidates who can afford a college education because the internet has created an abundance of opportunities for individuals to learn skills on their own, without the need for an expensive university education.

There is still a long way to go before we can say people will be considered for employment based on their personal skills, character, and merits instead of the school they graduated from, but I think these developments are encouraging signs that self-directed education is gaining public acceptance. Homeschooling is growing more rapidly than ever at this moment, and its ideas about children, families, communities, and social learning are receiving serious attention from parents around the world. But this is a small piece of the changes we need to make to create, in John's words, "a life worth living and work worth doing—that is what I want for children (and all people), not just, or not even, something called 'a better education.' "[46] ■

3

LIVING WITH CHILDREN

CHILDREN, THEIR NATURE AND NEEDS

MANY PEOPLE WHO QUITE LIKE and enjoy children still seem to be in the grip of the old idea that in civilizing them we have to give up or destroy some important part of them. To me that idea seems mistaken and harmful. It simply is not true that every virtue is some kind of suppressed vice, or that civilized human beings are nothing but cowed savages. As Abraham Maslow used to say, this explains human virtues only by "explaining them away." Such explanations do not fit everyday experience. A famous child psychiatrist has long been quoted as saying that the infant is a psychopath. I take the side of a mother I know well, who after raising seven babies said, "Babies are nice people."

Paul Goodman once wrote of the "wild babytribe," an affectionate and accurate expression. Children do often seem to me like talented barbarians, who would really like to become civilized. Many free schools, and some kindly and well-meaning parents, have suffered from the notion that there was something wild and precious in children that had to be preserved against the attacks of the world for as long as possible. Once we get free of this idea, we will find our lives with children much easier and the children themselves much happier. As I write this, I have spent much time recently with young babies, and my overwhelming impression is that basically they want to fit in, take part, and do right—that is, do as we do. If they can't always do it, it is because they lack experience, and because their emotions sweep them away.

Oddly enough, the reactionary view and the romantic liberal view of children are like opposite sides of the same coin. The hard-nosed types say that to fit children for the world we have to beat the badness out of them. The romantic child worshippers say that in fitting children for the world we destroy most of the goodness in them. One group claims that children are undersized and defective adults; the other, that adults are oversized and defective children. Neither is true. There really are ways to help children, as they grow, to keep and build on all their best qualities. How we may do this is the subject of this chapter.

We can learn much from *The Continuum Concept*, by Jean Liedloff, as important a book as any I have ever read. Liedloff (along with a number of others—Frederick Leboyer, Ashley Montagu, John Bowlby, etc.) says and *shows* that babies grow best in health, happiness, intelligence, independence, self-reliance, courage, and cooperativeness when they are born and reared in the "continuum" of the human biological experience, that is, as "primitive" mothers bear and rear their babies, and probably always have through all the millions of years of human existence. What babies have always enjoyed, needed, and thrived on, for the first year or so of their lives, until they reach the crawling and exploring stage, is constant *physical* contact with their mothers (or someone equally well known and trusted).

Babies have always had this, at least up until the last thousand years or so, and all newborn babies, knowing nothing of history but everything of their own animal nature, expect it, want it, need it, and suffer terribly if they do not get it.

Here, in only one of many passages of extraordinary vividness and sensitivity, is Liedloff's description of the early life of a baby among the Yequana Indians of the Amazon basin, with whom she lived for some time:

> From birth, continuum infants are taken everywhere. Before the umbilicus comes off, the infant's life is already full of action. He is asleep most of the time, but even as he sleeps he is becoming accustomed to the voices of his people, to the sounds of their activities, to the bumpings, jostlings, and moves without warning, to stops without warning, to lifts and pressures on various parts of his body as his caretaker shifts him about to accommodate her work or her comfort, and to the rhythms of day and night, the changes of texture and temperature on his skin, and the safe, right feel of being held next to a living body.[47]

The result of this kind of treatment is not, as most modern people might expect, a timid, clinging, whiny, dependent infant, but the exact opposite. Liedloff writes:

> When all the shelter and stimulus of his experience in arms have been given in full measure, the baby can look forward, outward, to the world beyond his mother.... The need for constant contact tapers off quickly when its experience quota has been filled, and a baby, tot, or child will require reinforcement of the strength it gave him only in moments of stress with which his current powers cannot cope. These moments become increasingly rare and self-reliance grows with a speed, depth, and breadth that would seem prodigious to anyone who has known only civilized children deprived of the complete in-arms experience.[48]

As Liedloff shows, children so reared very quickly notice what people are doing around them and want to join in and take part as soon and as far as their powers permit. No one has to *do* anything in order to "socialize" the children or *make* them take part in the life of the group. They are born social; it is their nature. One of the most peculiar destructive ideas that "civilized" people have ever invented is that children are born bad and must be threatened and punished into doing what everyone around them does. No continuum culture expects children to be bad as a matter of course, to misbehave, to make trouble, to refuse to help, to destroy things, and cause pain to others, and in cultures with long traditions of child-rearing these common (to us) forms of child behavior are virtually unknown.

Some years ago, a group of American child experts went to China to study Chinese children, child-rearing, and schools. To their Chinese counterparts they eagerly asked what *they* did when their children had tantrums, fought, teased, whined, broke things, hurt people, and so on. The Chinese looked at them with baffled faces. The Americans might as well have asked, "What do you do when your children jump three hundred feet straight up in the air?" The Chinese could only say over and over, "Children don't do those things." The American visitors went away equally baffled. It never occurred to them to suppose that one reason Chinese children are not bad in the way so many of ours seem to be is that nobody expects them to be. Being small, ignorant, inexperienced, and passionate, they may now and then stray off the path of good behavior. But correcting them is only a matter of patiently pointing out that they *have* strayed, that here we don't do things like that. No one assumes that their deep intent is to do wrong, and that only a long hard struggle will break them of that intent and force them to do right.

In short, the problem children of the affluent Western world are as much a product of our culture as our automobiles. What we call psychology, our supposed knowledge of "human nature," is and can only be the study of the peculiar ways of severely deprived people, so far from the norms of long-term human biological experience that it would not be stretching matters to call them (us) freaks. Liedloff's description of "modern," "medical," "scientific" childbirth, and the ensuing days and months as a baby must experience them, is enough to make one weep, or have nightmares, or both. It's a wonder we're no worse off than we are.

But I wish that Ms. Liedloff had said early in the book what she finally says at the end, that some or many of the most harmful effects of severe early deprivation (of closeness and contact) can be largely made up for or cured if a human being is richly supplied with these necessities, in ways she suggests, later in life. This is important. Many sensitive and loving mothers and fathers who bore and raised children in the modern "civilized" way, upon reading this book and realizing what they had unknowingly denied their children, might be almost overwhelmed by guilt and grief. With enough kindness, tenderness, patience, and courtesy, one can make up for much of this early loss.

It is impossible for me to say how important I think this book is. For most of the past twenty-five years it has become clearer to me all the time that our worldwide scientific and industrial civilization, for all its apparent wealth and power, was in fact moving every day closer to its total destruction. What is wrong? What can we do? Many people have pointed toward some useful answers. But only in the last year or two has it become clear to me that one of the most deep-rooted of the causes of our problems is the way we treat children, and above all babies. I am equally convinced that no program of social and political change that does not include and begin with changes in the ways in which we bear and rear children has any chance of making things better.

I hope that many people will read *The Continuum Concept*, the more the better, and above all mothers and fathers of young children and babies, parents-to-be, people who have no children but think someday they might, young marrieds or marrieds-to-be, teenagers, babysitters, older brothers and sisters of babies, and also doctors, nurses, psychologists, and so forth. In short, anyone who may have any contact with, or anything to do with, babies or little children. The human race, after all, changes with every new generation, and only a generation or two of healthy and happy babies might be enough to turn us around.

BORN KIND

From a letter to an old friend of mine, an elementary school teacher:

> Loved being with your kindergarten class. I don't remember when I have ever struck up so strong a friendship with a child so quickly as I did with Molly. Our conversation was very serious, the kind of talk you might expect to have with someone much older. Above all, I was so touched with her concern about me. At one point—I didn't tell you this—I was squatting down beside a table at which some of the children were working. After a long time I stood up, and as is always the case, I was a little stiff, and took a few seconds to get the kinks in my knees and back straightened out. Molly and a couple of the others asked me what I was doing, and I explained that when people my age squat down for a long time they tend to get a little stiff. It must have been at least an hour later, when I was again squatting down beside some children, that Molly said to me, "Don't squat down too long." Surprised, I said, "Why not?" She said, "You'll get stiff." I had forgotten all about the earlier time. Then, as I said to you, when she saw where I had bumped and scratched the top of my head a week or so earlier in Maine, she was very concerned, wanted to know how I had done it, and did it hurt. This is much more empathy than I would have expected from such a little person, much as I like them.

ALL OF JOHN HOLT'S BOOKS CONTAIN IDEAS and advice for adults to live and learn with children, but often in subtle and unconventional ways. For instance, the observation that children are "born kind" is not the same as they're being born without need of any moral upbringing as they are innately good. In our office I heard John talk angrily about people who he felt belonged in jail, who were just "bad cats" (John's phrase for such people), and children who were willfully bad in some pretty awful ways. He didn't view all people as innately good; he didn't view all people as innately bad, either. He simply wanted us to recognize that there is a tendency toward kindness present in children to which they respond, and that working with that tendency, rather than ignoring it, quashing it, or distorting it, can make living and learning with children easier for us all. The chances that good behavior, character, and morals will take root in an atmosphere of kindness are much better than if we assume the worst in children and use kindness only as a reward for good behavior, rather than the norm for our relationships. ∎

ON SAYING NO

SINCE FEW OF US raise children in continuum ways, most of us still have the task of teaching them to live by our rules. We tend to make this task much more difficult than it needs to be, not least of all by the way in which we use the word *no*.

Not long ago I visited a friend who had a beautiful, lively, affectionate year-old Husky pup. He had only one fault. He loved to be petted, and if you had been petting him, and stopped, or if he had just come up to you, he would put his paw up on your leg, let it fall, put it up again, and so over and over until you did *something*. This dirtied clothes, scratched skin, and hurt. His owner had tried now and then to break him of this habit, by scolding him, pushing him away, or whatever, but it hadn't done much good. He was too busy with his work to spend much time on it. One day I thought that as long as I was visiting, had some time, and loved the pup, I would see if I could break him of this habit.

So every time he came up to me I would pat him for a while and then stop and wait, my hand poised to block his paw when it came up. When he raised it, I would catch it a few inches off the floor and lower it gently to the ground, saying at the same time just as gently, "No, no, keep the paw on the floor." Then I would pat him, say what a nice dog he was, and after a while stop again. Soon the paw would come up once more, and I would catch it and go over the whole thing once again. Sometimes I would do this with him sitting, sometimes with him standing. After a few repeats I would back away from him; then, as he came toward me, I would say in a gentle but warning voice, "Now, keep those paws down," or "Now remember, four on the floor." I would have my hand ready to catch the paw when it rose, which at first it always did. But before long he began to get the idea, and quite often the tone of my voice, the sound of my words, and perhaps the position of my body and hand, would be enough to remind him, and he would keep the paw down. I was only there for a few days and can't claim that I broke him of the habit altogether. But he was certainly much better about it, and usually only one warning and paw catch would be enough to remind him.

The point is that even a young dog is smart enough to know that *no* does not have to be just a *signal*, an explosion of angry noise. It can be a word, conveying an idea. It does not have to say, "You're a bad dog, but we're going to beat the badness out of you." It can say instead, "You're a good dog, but this thing that you're doing isn't what we do around here, so please don't do it anymore." Even a young dog can understand that, and act on it.

And if a dog, why not a child? Except in rare times of great stress or danger, there is no reason why we cannot say no to children in just as kind and gentle a tone as we say yes. Both are *words*. Both convey ideas which even tiny children are smart enough to grasp. One says, "We don't do it that way," the other says, "That's the way we do it." Most of the time, that is what children want to find out. Except when overcome by fatigue, or curiosity, or excitement, or passion, they want to do right, do as we do, fit in, take part.

Soon after my visit with friend and dog, I visited two other friends, and their delightful fifteen-month-old boy. Around dinner time, in the little kitchen-dining room, I took out my cello and began to play. The baby was fascinated, as I hoped he would be. He stopped what he was doing and came crawling across the floor toward the cello at top speed. His parents looked a bit nervous, but I said, "Don't worry, I'll defend the cello, I won't let him hurt it." He came to the cello, pulled himself up to a standing position, and began to touch and pluck at the strings, below the bridge. At the same time, keeping the bow (which he might have been able to damage) out of his reach, I plucked the cello strings above the bridge, which made nice sounds. Now and then I could see that he was being overcome with a wave of excitement, and that he wanted to bang on the cello, as little babies like to bang on things. But when his hands began to make these impulsive gestures, I would catch them, like the paw of the pup, and slow them down, saying softly, "Gently, gently, easy, easy, be nice to the cello." When his motions grew smaller and calmer I would take my hands away. For a while he would caress the wood and pluck at the strings. Then he would begin to get excited again. But as soon as he did, I would catch and slow down his hands again, saying as before, "Gently, gently, nice and easy." After a while he would crawl away, while I talked with his parents. Then I would play some more, and he would come crawling over for more looking and touching. I might have to say, "Gently, gently," once or twice, but hardly more than that. Most of the time this tiny boy, still just a baby, was as gentle and careful with the cello as I was. And all this in only one evening, the first time he had ever seen such a strange and fascinating object.

Louise Andrieshyn, a parent in Manitoba, says about this:

You've made an excellent point about the difference between "No" the angry signal and "No" the meaningful word.... There is a third kind of "No," perhaps the most common of all, neither an angry explosion nor a meaningful word—the no, no, no that goes on all day with some parents. This constant hassling is simply a running, ineffective banter.

The parents don't even *mean* it; there's no anger or even much reprimand in their voices…our cultural expectation is that kids are bad, always getting into trouble, and parents must be dictators controlling their kids (in the name of "protection").

How to cope with these 3 kinds of "No" is much more difficult, though, than you make it sound.

You're saying, if we can become aware of how we use "No" we can change our use of it.…

As parents, we can simply SHUT UP! If we can sit back and listen to ourselves, we can hear how much negative harassment we throw at our kids. If a parent would seriously and objectively listen to what he says (through his child's ears), he would be appalled and could probably with some effort change that kind of no.

I think here of Lisey (then three) who was pouring herself a glass of milk yesterday. She had gotten it from the fridge, opened it, poured from a fat two-quart carton a very small juice glass of milk, had drunk it, then had gotten a paper towel and was wiping up the milk spilled on the table. There was more milk spilled than the towel could absorb so as she wiped now, the milk was being pushed off the table onto the floor.

I walked in at this point and started with the running "no, no" commentary in a whiny voice: "Ooooh no, Lisey, you should have asked someone to pour you a glass of milk—no, don't wipe it up, it's going on the floor, now stop, don't do it, I'll do it, it's bad enough on the table—look, now you've got it on the floor—you're making more work for me."

Happily at this point, I was struck by a rare beam of sanity and it said to me, "Oh, quit being such a bitch, Lisey has just poured her first glass of milk all by herself and you're ruining the whole thing for her."

And suddenly I looked and saw a very little girl trying very hard to grow up—trying to wipe up herself the mess she had made getting herself a drink of milk. And I said, "Lisey, I think Sparkle (dog) would like this extra milk."

Lisey stopped and looked at me. I had finally said something of meaning. All the negative harassment up till then she had been trying to ignore.

I said, "If you get Sparkle's dish we can put the milk in it."

She got it and we did.

And immediately she began an animated chatter about how Sparkle would like this milk and how she had poured them both a drink of milk, and so on. Until then, she had barely said one word. In fact, if I had pushed her far enough—"Okay, Lisey, get out of the kitchen while I clean up your mess"—she would have probably ended up crying (over spilled milk!).

But the happy ending here did not require too much effort on my part because I wasn't very emotionally involved. My mind could still be objective about the situation to the extent of being able to control and change it.

TESTING ADULTS

In his very good book *Growing With Your Children*, Herbert Kohl—like just about everyone who writes about children—says that they have to keep testing adults in order to find limits. I absolutely disagree. They do it all the time, no question about that. But I don't think they *have* to do it, or do it primarily for that reason, and I don't think we ought to let them do it. If they want to find out, as they do, the rules of family life and human society, there are other and better ways to do it.

One year, when I was teaching fifth grade, I had a boy in my class who had been kicked out of his local public schools—no small feat. He was a perfectly ordinary-looking, middle-sized, middle-class white kid, didn't pull knives or throw furniture, no *Blackboard Jungle* stuff. It took me a while to understand *why* the public schools had shown him the door. In a word, he was an agitator, always stirring things up. One day, when everyone was trying to do something, I forget what, and he was trying to prevent them, or get them to do something else, I turned on him and shouted in exasperation, "Are you *trying* to make me sore at you?" To my great surprise, and his (judging from his voice), he replied, "Yes." It took me a while to understand, or at least to guess, that he had learned from experience that the only way he could be sure of getting the undivided attention of other people, children or adults, was to make them sore at him.

As the year went on, he improved, became only difficult instead of impossible. But he was still a long way from being at peace with himself—the roots of his problem were deeper than I or my class could reach in a year. Our school only went through sixth grade; what became of him later I don't know. Meanwhile, he had taught me something valuable.

At about that time I was beginning to know the interesting but angry and difficult child of a friend. One day I was at their house, talking with his mother about something important to both of us. The boy kept interrupting, more even than usual. I knew by then that children hate to be shut out of adult talk, and tried from time to time to let this boy have a chance to speak. But on this day it was clear that he was trying to keep us from talking at all. Finally, looking right at him, I said, not angrily but just curiously, "Are you trying to annoy me?" Startled into honesty, like the other boy, by a question he had perhaps never really asked himself, he smiled sheepishly and said, "Yes." I said, still pleasantly, "Well, that's okay. Tell you what let's do. Let's play a game. You do everything you can think of to annoy me, and I'll do everything I can think of to annoy you, and we'll see who wins. Okay?" He looked at me for a while—he knew me well enough by this time to know that I would play this "game" in earnest. He considered for a while how it might go. A look at his mother showed that, for the time being at least, he could not expect much help from her if the game went against him. Finally he said, "No, I don't want to play." "Fine," I said. "Then let us have our conversation, and you and I can talk later." Which is what happened.

That was many years ago. From many encounters I have since had with many children, I have come to believe very strongly that children as young as five and perhaps even three are well able to understand the idea of "testing"—doing something to someone else or in front of someone else, knowing they don't like it, *just to see what that other person will do*, and to understand that this is not good. If I thought a child was doing this to me, I would say, "Are you testing me, just doing that to see what I will do?" If the child said yes, I would say, "Well, I don't like that, it's not nice and I don't want you to do it. I don't do bad things to *you* just to see what *you* will do. Then it's not fair for you to do that to me."

I think children are perfectly able to understand these ideas, to see that they are fair, and to act upon them. When they do, it will make our lives together much easier.

OKAY?

When adults want children to do something—put on coats, take a nap, and such—they often say, "Let's put on our coats, okay?" or "It's time to take our naps now, okay?" That "Okay?" is a bad thing to say. Our lives with children would go better if we could learn to give up this way of talking.

The trouble with this "Okay?" is that it suggests to the children that we are giving them a choice when we really are not. Whatever people may think about how many choices we should give children, children should at least be able to know at any moment whether they have a choice or not. If we too often seem to be offering choices when we really aren't, children may soon feel that they never have any. They will resent this and resent even more our not saying clearly what we mean.

By giving what we intend as a command and then saying "Okay?" we invite resistance and rebellion. In fact, the only way children *can* find out whether or not we are offering a real choice is to refuse to do what we ask. It is their way of saying, "Do you really mean it?"

Many adults feel that in saying "Okay?" they are only being courteous. But this is a misunderstanding of courtesy. It is perfectly possible to be firm and courteous while making clear to someone that you are not offering a choice but telling them what you want to happen or is going to happen. When I visit friends, I expect to fit myself into their life and routines, and count on them to tell me what they are. So they say, "We get up at seven o'clock," or "We are going to have dinner at six-thirty," or "This afternoon we're going to this place to do such and such." They are not asking me whether I approve of these plans, just letting me know that they *are* the plans. But they are perfectly polite about this.

Some friends of mine have a no smoking rule in their house. They are in earnest about this. Inside their front door is a sign saying, "Thank You For Not Smoking." But every now and then a guest misses the sign or takes it as a plea and not a command, and starts to light up. My friends gently but firmly inform their friend and guest that if he or she wants to smoke, the porch is the place to do it, but not in the house. No one argues, no one is offended.

Few adults seem to be able to talk to children in this way. In the Public Garden, or airports, or other places where adults and children gather, I hear hundreds of people telling their children to do things. Most of them begin with "Okay?" pleading and cajoling. If this doesn't work, they soon begin to threaten and shout. They can't seem to give a firm request without getting angry first. Then the child is genuinely confused and resentful, doesn't understand why the adults are angry, or what he has done to deserve the shouts and threats.

If a child really resists doing what you want, it may help to say, "I know you don't want to do what I am telling you to do, and I'm sorry that you don't, and sorry that you're angry, but I really mean for you to do it." It doesn't by any means solve all problems, and it may not even stop the child from being angry. But at least it makes clear where things stand. And of course, at such times we must not get angry at the children for being angry with us. We may have a right (as well as the power) to make children obey, but not to demand that they pretend to like it.

JOHN WAS ALWAYS ALERT to the appearance of this dubious word. During the last two years of his life, he went to a great many hospitals and doctors seeking cures or relief from cancer. More than once I'd be sitting near his hospital bed when a nurse would come in and say, "We're just going to roll you over now, okay?" or, "It's time for your medicine, okay?" Sometimes John would shake his head and smile at me, other times he'd offer frustrated glances at the ceiling, and at some point he would just say, "I hate when they say 'okay'!" ∎

TANTRUMS

PEOPLE WHO WRITE about tantrums seldom give any strong sense that the anger of two-year-olds is *about* anything. One might easily get the impression that these little children are swept by gusts of irrational "aggression" and rage as the coasts of Florida are from time to time swept by hurricanes. Instead, I would insist that much of the seemingly irrational and excessive anger of little children—"tantrums"—is in fact not only *caused* by things that happen to them or that are said and done to them, but that these things would make *us* angry if they happened or were said and done to us. Even in the kindest and most loving families, two-year-olds must be reminded a hundred times a day, perhaps by the words and acts of their parents, perhaps by events, by Nature herself, that they are small, weak, clumsy, foolish, ignorant, untrustworthy, troublesome, destructive, dirty, smelly, even disgusting. *They don't like it!* Neither would I. Neither would you.

On this subject, the mother of J, the little boy whom I described playing with my cello, wrote about his tantrums and how they were both learning how to avoid them.

J is great. No naps now which means he is super go-power all day with a huge collapse about 7:30. He has his room all to himself now, and he really likes to hang out in there alone for an hour and a half most days, driving trucks around mostly. I've never seen a kid more into organizing things. He plays with dominoes and calls them either adobes, for building houses, or bales of hay, and has them stacked, lined up, or otherwise arranged in some perfect order; same with the trucks; he'll scream and yell, as per your theory of two-year-old behavior, if you snatch him up from a group of trucks and carry him off to lunch. But if you give him a couple of minutes to park them all in a straight line then he'll come willingly. Your theory (treat them like big people) works out over and over again; brush past him, leave him behind in the snow when you're hustling up to feed the goats and you get a black and blue screaming pass out tantrum. Treat them "Big" and things roll along. Only hang-up is the occasional times you have to take advantage of your superior size and pull a power play. The trick is to learn to avoid the situations that once in a while make that a necessity, like not getting in a rush, and not letting them get so tired they break down completely—like letting dinner be late.

One thing he gets mad about is being left behind by anybody. However, we just went on a trip....I was quite nervous about leaving him with friends as he had been doing his falling down pass out tantrums for our benefit all week whenever anyone went to town without him (in spite of having the other parent on hand). But he just waved bye-bye and went in the house and had a really good four days. As his father said, obviously he would only bother to pull the tantrum bit for us. He was very calm and very full of new games and words when we got him back, and I know he made progress on all fronts as a result of being away from us and with other interesting people.

...Later we were to go on a long trip down the river, so we left him with some friends, but decided at the last minute our boats weren't sufficient to carry us and our gear on that rugged and remote a trip. So we picked up J and just went camping on the river, taking our boat and going on short hops along stretches of the river where the road was. Again he was super and loved being with grown-ups who ate with their fingers and mushed all their food up in one cup just like him. His father wanted him to go in the boat, so he put him in a life jacket then tied a rope between them. J hated that and had all kinds of misgivings as water sloshed into the boat and he got wet and cold, but he didn't complain. Amazingly he just sat there and looked pissed off for about two hours. I think he was so glad to be included that he bore with the misery.

Susan Fitch applies this same sensible and respectful attitude to the often difficult issue of bedtime:

My husband and I have always been concerned with having "our" time so our son, Jesse's (4) bedtime was very important to us. Although he was very cooperative, Jesse did not enjoy the limited time he had with his father between his arrival and bedtime. This left everyone frustrated and unhappy.

One evening while I was reading *GWS* it occurred to me that he was perfectly capable of going to bed when he was tired. The next day we talked about being tired, how much sleep he needed, when to go to bed in order to wake up in time for playgroup, and about our need to talk with one another and have quiet times. The tension evaporated with his father, and he immediately assumed responsibility for getting undressed and brushing his teeth. Because of just this one letting go, our time alone and together follows a natural pattern that seems to satisfy everyone.

I can't help noting that no cultures in the world that I have ever heard of make such a fuss about children's bedtimes, and no cultures have so many adults who find it so hard either to go to sleep or wake up. Could these social facts be connected? I strongly suspect they are.

COOKING AT TWO

Children are so much more capable than most adults realize. I suspect that children get hurt most often when doing things they are not supposed to do, in a spirit of defiance and excitement, rather than when doing something sensible and natural that they do often and like to do right.

The head of a big adventure playground in London once told me that as long as parents could come right into the playground, the children often hurt themselves, doing things to impress, scare, or defy their parents, but that once the parents were told that they had to wait for the children outside the playground (in a spot with chairs, benches, etc.) the accidents stopped.

I asked Susan Price, a parent in Florida how Matt learned to cook at such a young age. She replied:

The stove. What could have become my first battle with Matt. He learned to turn the burners on. I said no, dangerous. Effect, naturally: *fun, interesting, do it all the time.* So I slapped his hand, slightly, grabbed him up, me in tears, was he, I don't even remember, holding him on the couch, what to do, what to do. Slowly it dawned on me. There wasn't a damned thing dangerous about him turning them on. I was always with him, could keep the stove cleared, his hand was way below the flames. What was I afraid of? *If people knew*, of course. So I let him turn them on, watched, kept my mouth shut. He turned them all on, went over to the table, stood on a chair and looked at them (he was so far below the flame he couldn't see them standing by the stove). How old was he? Less than sixteen months. Did this for a while, then a couple of times the next day, and *that was all*, never "played" with them again except to turn one on when he saw me getting a pan out to cook something in. Or after Faith was born to turn them on for himself, when he wanted to cook something. No, one other time when he was much older and his friend was over he thought it was funny to turn them on and see how afraid his friend became.

Why did he not respond to my "No, dangerous!"? Because there was no real fear in my voice. Children *will* respond to you when you say something's dangerous if you really are afraid they are going to get hurt *at that minute*. I read somewhere that you have to teach children to do what you say because if you don't, they could be out in the street and a car coming and they wouldn't get out of the road when you yelled at them to. That's not the point at all. They're responding mostly to the fear in your voice in that situation, not to the fact that you're telling them to do something.

People are always worrying too much about the future, extrapolating out of the present, with children. They think, if I let them turn the burners on now, they'll always want to turn them on.

My guess is that the main reason Matt no longer needs or wants to play with the stove is that *he can cook on it*. It isn't a toy any more, but a serious tool, that he and the grown-ups use every day. Before they know how to drive, and can drive, little children love to sit at the wheel of a parked car turning the steering wheel this way and that. But who ever saw a child doing that, *who could actually drive*? It would be baby stuff. And it would be baby stuff for Matt to play with the stove on which he and his younger sister regularly cook food that the whole family eats.

I suspect, too, that one reason that Matt responds so quickly to strong fear or other negative emotion in his mother's voice is that he doesn't often hear this kind of emotion. Children who constantly hear in the voices of adults the tones of fear, disgust, anger, threat, and the like soon take that tone of voice to be normal, routine, and turn it off altogether. They think, "Oh, that's just the way they always talk." Then, when we try to make them pay attention to some real danger, they no longer hear us at all.

PAT MONTGOMERY LIVED WITH HER HUSBAND JIM in Ann Arbor, Michigan, where Pat has run her well-known Clonlara School for more than thirty years. During a weekend I spent with them, Jim explained to me that one of his hobbies was throwing knives, which he'd learned to do when he was about eight years old growing up in rural Mississippi. His grandfather had a bayonet that he took from a German soldier in World War I, and it became Jim's first, and favorite, knife for him to throw. In his backyard in Ann Arbor were stacks of logs that he used for targets. So I was not surprised when, after being introduced to six-year-old Felix, their grandson, Felix said, "Do you want to see Grandpa's knives?"

When I said yes, Felix and his younger brother, Simon, almost three years old, fetched a bag full of knives that Jim kept in the basement. Jim had been building a fire in his fireplace, while Pat looked on and the boys showed me the knives. They handled them with great care, while telling me to "be careful" as I held each knife, and explained that the edges of the blades were dull but the points were sharp. The young boys demonstrated to me how to find the center of balance for each knife, what makes each knife different from the others, and so on. I was impressed not only with how they handled the knives but also with how Pat and Jim weren't hovering over them, ready to snatch away the knives or fretting aloud, "Be careful!" I also noticed that Pat and Jim did get a bit concerned when the boys started stabbing a cardboard box that Jim was going to use for kindling—and then Jim said, "You shouldn't stab the boxes like that; you should put the point on the box like this and then push firmly." The boys were happy to comply, and they slowly stabbed the box into kindling for a few more minutes before putting away the blades.

Jim then told me that on Wednesdays he'd come home at lunchtime so he could meet with students from Clonlara who want to learn knife throwing. It's hard to imagine, particularly for a city boy like me, that knives can be used safely and enjoyably to develop skill and confidence by young children. After all, the way I was raised, when I see a knife I don't associate it with *Little House on the Prairie*; I associate it with *West Side Story*! Of course, children earlier in the past century were probably far more comfortable using knives and other sharp tools than we can imagine. As Holt notes, children "are so much more capable than most adults realize." ∎

INSTEAD OF GOLD STARS

UNLESS WARPED BY CRUELTY OR NEGLECT, children are *by nature* not only loving and kind but serious and purposeful. Whenever I hear school people say, "The students aren't motivated, how do I motivate them?" I think of the story about Margaret Mead and the Balinese.

This took place in the 1920s, when very few Westerners had ever been to Bali. Margaret Mead was talking to some Balinese, trying to learn about this strange and very different culture. At some point she asked about their art. The Balinese were puzzled by this question. They did not know what she meant by art. So she talked for a while about art and artists in Western cultures. The Balinese considered this for a while. Then one of them spoke. "Here in Bali we have no art," he said. "We do everything as well as we can."

Very young children are like the Balinese. Just about everything they do, they do as well as they can. Except when tired or hungry, or in the grip of passion, pain, or fear, they are moved to act almost entirely by curiosity, desire for mastery and competence, and pride in work well done. But the schools, and many adults outside of school, hardly ever recognize or honor such motives, can hardly even imagine that they exist. In their place they put greed and fear.

But what about people who have taken out of schoolchildren who have been numbed and crippled in spirit by years of "reinforcement," petty rewards and penalties, gold stars, M&M'S, grades, dean's lists? How can unschoolers revive in their children those earlier, deeper, richer sources of human action? It is not easy. Perhaps the only thing to do is to be patient and wait. After all, if we do not constantly reinjure our bodies, in time they usually heal themselves. We must act on the faith that the same is true of the human spirit. In short, if we give children enough time, as free as possible from destructive outside pressures, the chances are good that they will once again find *within themselves* their reasons for doing worthwhile things. And so, in time, may we all.

4

LEARNING IN THE WORLD

ACCESS TO THE WORLD

EVEN IN SUPPOSEDLY "FREE" OR "ALTERNATIVE" SCHOOLS, too many people still do what conventional schools have always done. They take children out of and away from the great richness and variety of the world, and in its place give them school subjects, the curriculum. They may jazz it up with chicken bones, Cuisenaire rods, and all sorts of other goodies. But the fact remains that instead of letting children have contact with more and more people, places, tools, and experiences, the schools are busily cutting the world up into little bits and giving it to the children according to some expert's theory about what they need or can stand.

What children need is not new and better curricula but *access* to more and more of the real world; plenty of time and space to think over their experiences, and to use fantasy and play to make meaning out of them; and advice, road maps, guidebooks to make it easier for them to get where they want to go (not where we think they ought to go), and to find out what they want to find out. Finding ways to do all this is not easy. The modern world is dangerous, confusing, not meant for children, not generally kind or welcoming to them. We have much to learn about how to make the world more accessible to them, and how to give them more freedom and competence in exploring it. But this is a very different thing from designing nice little curricula.

Here is how a family in Washington, DC, opened up the city to their child:

We live in Washington, DC, on Capitol Hill about two miles from the museums of the Smithsonian Institution. Susan and her mother walk there almost every day, observing, playing, meeting people, going to movies, listening to music, and riding the merry-go-round. They see a fantastic variety of nature movies.... They know art and history museums exhibit by exhibit. Susan can drag you through the history of the universe, through natural history, on up to the latest Mars landing. They eat lunch near the water fountain, see the latest sculpture, take pictures of their favorite spots, marvel at the beautiful spring and fall days. They attend mime shows, tape-record jazz concerts, ride the double-decker bus to their favorite "explore gallery" where things can be played and jumped in. Tuition is very cheap, we all have fun, and we all learn a great deal.

Susan lives in a world of marvelous *abundance*; her resources are unlimited. She has not been "socialized" by school to think that education is a supply of scarce knowledge to be competed for by hungry, controlled children. She doesn't play dumb "Schlemiel."...Our home and neighborhood are like a garden full of fresh fruit to be picked at arm's length by all who want to.

She likes to paint, draw, color, cut out, and paste. She compares her work to that in the museum. We give our comments and ideas when requested.

We have hobbies in astronomy and camping. Her father is a pediatrician who enjoys working with her in constructing electronic gear. She has excellent soldering techniques and has soldered many connections in our home-brewed electric computer now used in his office.

It is not just "educated" and middle-class families who can use the city as a resource. In the chapter "The New Truants" in his book *Acting Out* (see Bibliography, subsection Education and Society), Roland Betts writes:

Today's truants are [New York City's] most misunderstood children. They are also perhaps the most enlightened, aware that neither the schools nor the streets have anything to offer them. They fear both worlds. They sense the futility of the jobs that are available even for those who do finish high school.... Most of them are intelligent, sensitive children, far more accomplished in the arts of reading and mathematics than their peers who either attend the schools or lurk outside of them. These truants rarely brush with the law. Their trademark is their solitude.

Randolph Tracey is one of them. He is now (1978) sixteen, but he has not been to school since the last day of fourth grade. He is poor and black.... [He] is a quiet and meek child, honest in his admission to his mother that he has not been to school in years. He was always a good student, but although he was able to read at a level several years above his grade, he had no tolerance for the continuous noise and confusion that characterized his school. Randolph is never with other children, or with other adults for that matter. He has spent the better part of the past four years in the Metropolitan Museum of Art. Although he has patronized all of the city's museums, he prefers the Met, and humbly claims that he is very familiar with each piece in the museum's standing collection. He recalls being cornered there one afternoon by a class of children he had grown up with from the school he should have attended, a class that might have been his own. He hid motionless behind a Minoan vase for twenty minutes until the danger had passed. Randolph draws and paints on his own but derives far more pleasure from seeing and studying art in the museums.

Danny Hartman is another dropout. His life is consumed by drawing and tracing figures from comic books and art books, which he borrows from the public library. He can mimic perfectly the drawings of Leonardo and Michelangelo and the most intricate of Rembrandt's etchings. He stayed in school, reluctantly, until the spring of his eighth-grade year [where] he was discovered by an art teacher who encouraged him to apply for admission to the High School of Music and Art. For three years she saw to it that he attended daily classes in English and math, and she allowed him to work in her room while cutting gym, science, typing, and social studies.…He was lauded for his talents by his fellow students and was in the eyes of his art teacher a "clear genius." His work was extraordinary. The portfolio he had amassed by Christmas of his eighth-grade year was breathtaking.…

But the High School of Music and Art did not admit Danny. His accomplishments on standardized reading and math tests were unconvincing and his cumulative grade-point average was distorted by his many class cuts and subsequent failures.…The day that Danny received word that he had been denied admission to Music and Art was the last day he ever spent in school.

What Mr. Betts means when he says that Danny's record was distorted by class cuts and subsequent failures is very probably that Danny's school, like most schools, gave him failing grades for cutting classes, regardless of whether or not he knew that material or could do the work. If this was so, it means that to punish him for cutting classes *the school lied about his academic work*—an outrageous and I would think, if tested in court, probably illegal practice which is common in schools all over the country.

Another of the truants Mr. Betts describes is a voluminous and expert reader; another, an expert on the geography, flora, and fauna of Central Park; another, an expert on television shows and movies; another, a raiser and trainer of pigeons; another, an expert on New York City's enormous transportation system. All of them have learned how to learn from the city what they want to learn. None has ever had any help or encouragement from any adult, or any way to use or get credit for any part of what they know. How easy it would be, and how much less expensive than running giant schools, and jails for those who won't go to them, to find ways to help and encourage the interests and talents of these children, and many others like them. As far as learning goes, they clearly don't need much help; the best help society could give them would simply be to stop treating them like criminals, so that they could do their exploring boldly and freely instead of furtively. They do need, and would probably welcome, help in finding ways to *use* what they learn—which is, after all, one of the things the schools are supposedly for.

Meanwhile their experience shows very clearly that for all its hugeness and harshness, the modern city is rich in resources, and that children don't necessarily have to have an adult holding them by the hand every second in order to make use of them.

Judy McCahill writes from England about a small child's active way of using the resources of his world:

Last Saturday for something to do, because D was out of the country, I said to the boys, "Let's go to the art exhibit." S and K thought it was a wonderful idea and began discussing what sort of art they would do there and what pictures (of their own) they might bring from home. Startled, I tried to explain to them what an art exhibit was all about and they were genuinely puzzled at my trying to tell them they were just going there to look at somebody else's pictures. Puzzled, but not deterred, S gathered his supplies, two sets of paints, a brush, some paper, and a jar full of water which he handed me to carry; and K made us all wait while he finished a full-color marker pen painting of an army tank.

When we got there, we strolled along the sidewalks near the craft shop that was hosting the exhibit, dutifully examining the works and passing several fully grown and wise-looking artists sitting in portable lawn chairs, all the while S at my heels urging me to find out how he was supposed to enter the show and me ahead of S, stalling.

Finally an old man who works in the shop, who once told me a long story about his difficulties getting home to Cobham one night during the war when London was being bombed, greeted me. I introduced S to him and asked *him* to explain what an art exhibit was. He started to, but then he and his daughter, who also works in the shop, saw that S was ready to do some work and after a good laugh with a couple of customers over it, gave him a couple of nice big pieces of "card" to paint on. He sat on the doorstep of a small office building nearby and painted, while the rest of us strolled through the exhibit again, window-shopped, and ate ice cream cones.

When he had finished, it was a beautiful picture of a black dog, fur flying, running up a hill on a windy day, a glorious sun in the sky. It seemed to reflect his mood of magic. He took the picture into the shop, where the man said he would put it on sale for 50 pence (and confusedly explained about how the artists had to pay rent to the exhibit), and we went home.

A few days later, still full of the experience, S told a friend of mine about it. She promptly went out to buy the picture, and it was gone! When I suggested to S that he go and check to see if his painting had been sold, he replied that he already had, the next day (which of course was Sunday), and the shop was closed.

And that was that. He was too busy doing something else to give it another thought.

LIFESCHOOL

A young teenage reader writes eloquently about how much she learns from that part of her life that is *hers*:

I started going to public school right into the second grade and in every grade up to the sixth I was a straight A student. All the teachers were nice to me and I was praised and praised again for my work and I got good grades for it too and that's what kept me going.

When I left school at the end of sixth grade to be out for two years, I learned a new realization. Grades are not what make you a good person. I have a pretty good memory, so I remembered all the things I had to, to pass the tests that gave me As. But I've learned from experience that when I'm not interested in what I am supposed to be learning, I forget everything. Unfortunately, I wasn't interested in anything that I was doing, so my second- through sixth-grade years of public schooling are pretty much blank.

In the two years without any school contact I learned how to live without grades and not to need someone to tell me "It's good" every time I did something. It got so that grades didn't mean anything anymore. Basically, I learned that grades prove nothing. I also learned a lot of different things that I wouldn't have, if I had been in public schools. Public schools can't offer experience. I learned how to deal with and relate to adults better because I was around them so much—all the kids were in school! I learned many practical skills that I never would have learned in public school.

At first I wasn't so sure about the idea of not being in school but I soon adjusted and found it very fun. When I look at kids my age, it makes me glad that we did what we did. I am capable of doing so many more things it amazes me. And it's all because I had the time to learn, and enjoy while I was learning. So things stuck in my mind and they are still there because I am still doing new things, while these kids are doing things just to "get out" and then forgetting them in the meantime *plus* not enjoying much of it anyhow. Whew!

I have such a neat home and lifeschool! I consider myself to be very lucky to be who I am and to have the parents I have for believing in nonschooling!

Jud Jerome writes about the experiences of his daughter in "lifeschool":

One daughter was twelve when we moved to the farm. She finished that year of school on "independent study," living at the farm, turning in work to teachers back at the city. But when fall came she did not want to enroll. To avoid the law we enrolled her in a "free" school in Spokane, Washington, run by a friend, who carried her on the rolls, though she has not yet, to date, seen that city or that school. She spent most of the first year here at the farm, pitching in as an adult, learning from experience as we were all learning. While she was still thirteen, we went to help another commune, in northern Vermont, with sugaring, and she loved that place—which was very primitive and used horse-drawn equipment—so asked to stay. This was an agreeable arrangement on all sides—and she has lived there now for over five years, except for one, when she was sixteen. That year she and a young man ten years her senior went to Iceland for the winter, working in a fish cannery. The next spring they traveled, camping, to Scandinavia, hiked the Alps, then flew home—coming back with $3,000 more than they left with, after a year abroad.

Last year she wanted to apply for a government vocational program, for which she needed a high school diploma, so went to an adult education class for a few months, and took the test, passing in the top percentile (and being offered scholarships to various colleges). She "graduated" earlier than her classmates who stayed in school. I think her case illustrates especially dramatically the waste of time in schools. She is by no means a studious type, would never think of herself as an intellectual, has always been more interested in milking cows and hoeing vegetables and driving teams of horses than in books, and in her years between thirteen and eighteen moved comfortably into womanhood and acquired a vast number of skills, had a vast range of experiences in the adult world, yet managed to qualify exceptionally by academic standards. By comparison, her classmates who stayed in school are, in many cases, stunted in mind, emotionally disturbed, without significant goals or directions or sound values in their lives.

Children can learn a great deal from many of the "unhappy" experiences from which we try so hard to protect them. One mother wrote:

We had one long experience that gave us a different kind of "social" activity. Right after we were approved to homeschool, my father was taken seriously ill with a stroke, so when he had recuperated enough, he was put in a convalescent home for therapy. Because the boys and I were free, we would go in each day to visit him. (They would not have been excused from school for this.) But my father was very depressed and the therapist at the hospital had on his record "uncooperative." This didn't give us much confidence, so we went in each day to make sure they didn't give up on him. It was a good experience for the boys as well as me, for whenever the grandchildren would come my father would get undepressed. He would laugh at their antics and then sink back into depression when they left.

So we agreed that we would take our books (it was now September) to the home and stay most of the day with their Pop-Pop. It worked out well, for the boys had a large place to do their work and they could go outside to play whenever they got tired of being in. They would go to the vending machines and get us things, and several times when the home was short-handed because of the "flu" season, we would sort some laundry and the boys would help take it to the rooms. We made it a game and the patients loved having the boys come into their rooms and talk to them.

At therapy we kept assuring my father that when he could walk well, we'd take him home, so he really worked hard, and the boys and I would cheer him on, and the other patients, with "You can do it, Pop-Pop. Hurray!" "Great, Pop-Pop!" The other patients enjoyed us cheering them on and when the therapist saw the positive results from this, he was glad we were there. We saw many patients recover in weeks when the therapist had thought it would take months. We don't hope to have this kind of experience again this year, but it showed us that we *could* take a "sad" situation and turn it into one of rejoicing.

CONTROLLING ONE'S TIME

A mother from Washington State writes about freedom from schedules:

We entered the year with no preconceptions or plan of action. I just figured life would go on, and so it has. We go to bed each night and wake up each morning, the day passes and the necessary work gets done. I know that I live in a healthy environment and that I continue to grow as a person, and I trust that is so for my children, as well, though I haven't been "monitoring" their "progress," nor can I point to any tangible proof of "achievement."

About ten days a month I go to the city to work in a printshop. It is my habit, generally, to wake up early and spend an hour or two quietly planning my day according to what needs doing and what I feel like. But on my "work" days I find it very difficult to "get into" that kind of contemplation. Such a large chunk of the day is already planned for me. If I go to work several consecutive days, by the fourth or fifth day I feel very removed from the core of myself, and find it much easier to contemplate doing what at other times would seem irresponsible to me. I seem to have less energy for recycling, conserving fuel, paying good attention to my husband and children, etc. *When I abdicate the responsibility for structuring my own time, a certain moral strength seems to be lost as well* [Author's emphasis]. Who can guess at the degree of personal alienation we as a society cause our children by structuring so much of their time for them? I am beginning to think the greatest harm is not in the "what" or the "how" of this structuring, but in the very fact that five days out of seven, nine months out of twelve, six hours out of the center of those days, we remove from children the responsibility for their time. Perhaps it is not even the length of the time that is crucial, but simply the fact of the interruption. I know from my own experience that even a small interruption— a dental appointment, say, or a meeting or lecture I have to give—can halt the flow of my own creative energies for a length of time much greater than the interruption itself. Once I change from active to passive participant in structuring my time, a certain numbing takes place so that it is much easier to stay passive, "killing time" until the next prescribed activity, like fixing dinner or whatever.

I have noticed that the only periods of real "boredom," when the children complain of having nothing to do, are on days when a chunk of time has been planned *for* them. There is certainly nothing wrong with planning things to do together, but I have grown wary of too much planning *for*, and of removing it from its natural niche in the unique pattern of a particular day to an artificial projection into the future of anonymous days: "Every Tuesday we will…"

I have never known how to "stimulate" the children. I know that as a parent I should be raising my children in a "stimulating" environment, so that they will not be "dulled" or "bored," but what is more stimulating: a roomful of toys and tools and gadgets, bright colors and shiny enameled fixtures, or a sparsely furnished hand-hewn cabin deep in the woods, with a few toys carefully chosen or crafted, rich with meaning, time, and care, and intimate with the elements of the earth? The only world I can show them, with any integrity, is my world.

Perhaps that is why field trips were such a disappointment for us. We started off in the fall doing "something special," i.e., "educational field trip," once a week. After about a month we all forgot about taking these trips. They were fun, certainly interesting, but I think we were all sickened by the phoniness. Everyone knew the only reason we all trooped into the city to the aquarium was because Mom thought it would be a "good experience." Of much more continuing interest and, probably, greater educational significance in the truest sense, are the weekly trips into town to do the errands—to the bank (where we all have accounts and are free to deposit and withdraw as we please), the post office, grocery store, Laundromat, recycling center (source of income for kids outside of parents), drugstore and the comic book racks—and the evenings at the library and swimming pool. Those things are real, things I would do even if no one joined me, that just happen to be important activities for all of us.

When I am trying to "stimulate their interest" in something, the very artificiality of the endeavor (and rudeness, really—I have no business even trying) builds a barrier between us. But when I am sharing something I really love with them because I also really love them, all barriers are down, and we are communicating intimately. When they also love what I love—a song, a poem, the salmon returning to the creek to spawn—the joy is exquisite; we share a truth. But our differences are also a truth. Common thread and fiber we share, but not the whole piece.

And so I do my work each day, work which is full of meaning for me, and offer to teach it to them: cooking, sewing, splitting wood, hauling water, keeping house, writing, reading, singing, sailing on the lake, digging in the garden. Sometimes they are interested, sometimes not. But if I were to try to "stimulate" them, sugar-coating various tasks, making games of various skills, preaching, teaching *me* to them, they would not have the time—great, empty spaces of time—in which to search deep within themselves for what is most true about them.

And neither, then, would I.

Many parents have written to us about the feelings of liberation that go with unschooling and unscheduling. Gail Myles and her family moved to an island to unschool their children:

I never expected the boys to express any appreciation for this experience. I figured they might be sitting at a lunch with some business friends when they were thirty and mention the year. What I couldn't have predicted is that they would see the difference so soon. They learned to dig clams with the clammers of Maine, the salt of the earth, in forty degrees below chill factors; they lived through situations where everyone takes responsibility for the lives of each other; they came to like and understand opera because it was available to us through Texaco broadcasts, an interest none of us had prior to this;... and probably the best thing they learned was to get along with themselves and each other. They had to, because there was no one else, and if you want something from someone you have to give in return. That should take care of this "social life" garbage. To feel your worth in an adult world side by side with hardworking people, is there a better reward? I don't think so. They even had tears at departing from this small coastal community they knew as "in town."

My rewards were beyond measure. No yellow monster took my favorite friends away every morning; when they were exposed to a new vocabulary word I could use it pertinently in everyday happenings; if we wanted to know molecular theory we could work from 9 A.M. to 4 P.M. till it clicked; everything they were exposed to in Calvert Curriculum was learned by all; they spent early evenings putting on operas they made up, shows for Dad's pleasure were presented, sometimes taking three days just to prepare the staging. We read books, books, and books till 1 A.M., and no one had to be up at 6:30 for the monster.

An additional reward was the result of the history, literature, mythology, and architecture we were exposed to; we went to Athens, Greece, in April, a trip we would never have been interested enough in taking or felt a need to take if "doors" hadn't been opened to us. Bud came to love the Parthenon and had to see it. Tim was a walking encyclopedia on mythology and gave Jack and me the tour in the Archaeological Museum, and Mike was our history guide—we didn't even need a Greek service. Mike is also a gifted writer, and after reading his final composition for Calvert the teacher said she wished she could fly up to meet him, said he knew what writing was all about—she wanted to fly to Troy and Greece as his subject was the Trojan War. He had made her *feel* something inside.

I enjoyed the Calvert system. Their writers are excellent and really speak to the kids. It was a personal relationship in which they looked forward to hearing from someone who was writing to them. Letters were scarce and they learned the value of the written word. But I must say we *used* the curriculum to our needs and interests and only took the grading so that the boys would not be denied the credit upon returning to public school. This was completely their choice—they are encouraged to set policies regarding their futures.

The idea I hate most about public schools is that they should have my children all day when I feed, clothe, doctor, transport, and care most for them, and I am denied those hours with them and the sharing of their learning experiences. I cannot reinforce their education if I am denied the subject matter they are exposed to and am only left with tired grumps who eat, do homework, and flop to bed.

REAL-WORLD SKILLS

From the cover story of the April 1980 issue of *Home Educators Newsletter*:

These children [of a homeschooling family] form an exclusive student body as they are each born into the school. They take their places according to ability rather than grade level. They listen to works far above their comprehension, just to be part of the present company. In our own instance, we have one child that keeps all vehicles in top running shape, another who provides milk, eggs, and meat for the table, another who displays beautiful artwork, and another who enjoys gardening.

Katrina spends several hours morning and afternoon doing her farm work, but she is the beneficiary of her own labor, keeps all the records for feed, hay, and other purchases so that she can calculate her profit when animals are sold and what man-hours and money have been expended to gain that profit. I personally am not the least interested in any type of farm work and yet I know that this is developing within Katrina an ability far beyond anything that I could teach her. How much barley will a pig eat in a week, a month, till time for the market? What animals have the quickest turnover? What type of labor hours are necessary to operate a farm? I couldn't answer any of these questions, though Katrina can, and for an eleven-year-old girl I consider that quite an accomplishment. She has a reading assignment just like the other children of 200 pages per week plus a written paper every day. She generally turns in a paper that has to do with her present projects.

It is a rare occasion that I do not get the type of workmanship out of my children that I would get out of some adult. We are presently sectioning off a room in the basement and all the partitions will be built by the children. One startling fact is that John, at age seven, has all his own tools, including a power saw and drill. He builds beautiful miniature log cabins and will be in charge of measuring and cutting boards for the partition project. He is also planning on paneling his own room....

Kevin has repaired all my major appliances since he was kindergarten age. Recently I had to hire a repairman to come and fix my furnace motor, which turned out to be shot and had to be replaced. This repairman hadn't been here for several years, and his first question was "Why can't Kevin fix this?" When he discovered the problem, he knew that the present motor was beyond repair and he went to get another. However, he brought the burned-out one back because he felt that Kevin could use parts from it.

People often ask me how I can tolerate the children doing things that are normally only done by adults, and professionals at that. Well, I watch the children carefully and never expect one to do a job which is over his head. I experiment constantly, finding natural abilities and letting them try their wings in harmless, inexpensive ways. If a child shows an ability in a certain area such as plumbing, I try them out taking apart an elbow and putting it back together without a leak. Next comes faucets, or setting a toilet. Next might come the installation of a shower unit, and finally the child is ready to plumb a bathroom. I would have no qualms about letting my thirteen-year-old plumb my entire house. After all, he wired it for DC electricity when he was only eight. Our daughter Cathy is remodeling her own home now (she's nineteen), and she has done all her own plumbing, plastering, wallpapering, and carpentry. Matter of fact, that's how she helped pay for her college education. She worked as a carpenter in an all-male shop!

Handling money is one of the most useful real-world skills and one that gets distorted for many children. Louise Andrieshyn wrote us from Manitoba about her children and money:

> Heidi and Michael have just bought themselves ponies with their own money. You'll be pleased to learn that Heidi (10) wrote a cheque for hers.
>
> I don't know what other banking practices are like, but at our credit union any child can have a full-fledged account (and *must* be a shareholder in the corporation in order to have an account). Living in the country, we mail-order shop quite a bit and Heidi's cheques have never been questioned. But perhaps the people who receive them don't know her age! I don't suppose they would ever dream that they were accepting a cheque from a ten-year-old. If they knew, I wonder whether they would refuse to accept it or ask for counter-signing?
>
> Since Heidi has a fully personal account, not an "in trust" one, we as her parents are not even allowed to touch her money. We found out the hard way! We went to the credit union to take some money out of her account and they wouldn't let us. They pulled out her file card and showed us her signature saying that only she was able to handle the money in that account. She had signed it when she was 5! I remember distinctly "letting" her sign it, thinking condescendingly how "nice" the experience was for her. Little did I know I was providing her a degree of absolute financial independence.

Another letter shows how a sense of the value of money can start very early:

Thought I'd share with you M's "coming of age" as a consumer. M recently turned three. She received a dollar inside a birthday card sent by one of her friends (a 92-year-old). Last year, when he sent a dollar I took it without even showing it to her and bought her some balloons with it. This year she opened all her own mail and instantly recognized that it was money and that it was a present for her. She was quite pleased and put it in her wallet which until now was only for *playing* "grownup," and had held only small change. She discussed the dollar, and that she could buy something—whatever she wanted—for herself.

Next day when she got a five-dollar bill in another card we made a fuss again. We discussed the difference in value—on our fingers—of ones and fives, and I thought, "This is going great!"

Next day, when she got a card with a check for *ten* dollars, I thought, "Oh, no, this learning experience is getting out of hand." I hoped she wouldn't realize what a check was so I could spirit it away, but she was too sharp. "More money!" she exclaimed. So we explained what a check was, and traded it for two fives. M had previously studied the one and the five and pointed out that there were different men on them and asked their names (she's very into everything having a "name").

Then M asked me what she could buy with all her "moneys." I suggested she look in the toy catalogues. She got very excited over a construction set (Tinkertoy), and I told her she could look for one like it next time we went to town. So next time Daddy went to town M grabbed her purse and went along to shop for her present to herself. When she found her "struction set" and went to the counter to pay for it—her first purchase—Daddy told her to give the woman a Lincoln, expecting her to get back two Washingtons. Drats!—she gave her a Jefferson! M took it right in stride. Perhaps we should have left it alone, but at home Daddy traded it for two Washingtons. Controlling it again.

After she played with the Tinkertoy set for a couple of days, she expressed disappointment that she couldn't build a house with it. She checked the catalogues and zeroed in on a Lincoln Logs set. The next shopping expedition to town turned one up—for a Lincoln and three Washingtons. We pointed out that she'd spent a lot of money and didn't have that much left. I sense that she has a very balanced feel for money, a good sense of its value, so I'm not worried that she'll either hoard the rest or blow it recklessly.

With all this concern with cash, M didn't lose track of the fact that the money was sent as presents from people who love her. We took pictures of M posed with her presents and a big smile to send along with the thank-you notes.

SPEECH AND LANGUAGE IN REAL LIFE

The difference between learning in and from real life and learning in schools is perhaps most important of all in speech and language. Ivan Illich writes about this in "Vernacular Values and Education," in his book *Shadow Work*.

> In most cultures, we know that speech resulted from conversation embedded in everyday life, from listening to fights and lullabies, gossip, stories, and dreams. Even today, the majority of people in poor countries learn all their language skills without any paid tutorship, without any attempt whatsoever to teach them how to speak.[49]

Illich goes on to point out that all over the world many poor people in nonindustrial countries speak more than one language—a goldsmith he knows in Timbuktu speaks *six*—and that on the whole it is only in nation-states that have had several generations of compulsory schooling that we find most people speaking only one language. For in these supposedly advanced nations, people no longer learn their languages from people who talk to them, meaning what they say, in a context of everyday life, but from professional speakers who are trained and paid to say what others have prepared for them. Much is said about how inarticulate today's young people are. I suspect that an important reason is that so much of the speech they hear, on TV or in school, is not real speech but canned speech, prepared in advance and often not even by the speaker. They don't hear many real voices. But it is hearing real voices that makes us want to speak.

A memory. When my sister and I were about four and five, perhaps even less, we visited our grandparents. There was a landing on the second floor, with a railing, through which we could just see down the stairs into the room where the adults sat talking after dinner. After we had been tucked into bed and good-nights said, and the grown-ups had gone back downstairs, we would slip out of bed, crouch down by the railing, and listen to the grown-up voices. We couldn't understand what was being talked about. But the pull of those voices was fascinating. Usually after a while we would sneak back into bed. But one night we fell asleep there by the railing, where the grown-ups found us when they went up to bed. I don't remember what came of this, whether we were scolded or punished and sternly warned not to get out of bed again, or whether the grown-ups said nothing about it.

Since then, I have seen in many other families that it is very hard to keep young children in bed if a group of adults are having lively conversation not too far away. The children will find a hundred different reasons for coming to check out what the grown-ups are saying.

But, some might say, that's all very fine for privileged families that have interesting visitors. But what about most families, average families? The answer is, first of all, that all people are interesting. As Studs Terkel and Robert Coles have shown in their (very different) books, everyone has many good stories to tell. As long as real people are talking, not just people on TV, children will want to hear their voices and see their faces, and will learn much from them.

I FIRST MET IVAN ILLICH in the mid-nineties. More than once, I heard Ivan say how much he learned as a young boy simply by sitting under his grandparents' table in their house in Vienna, listening to their conversations. We can't measure such informal learning, but as these stories indicate, people do learn important things about and in the world differently than they can in a conventional school classroom. ∎

5

LIVING AND WORKING SPACES

SCHOOL OR CLUB?

TO A PARENT WHO WROTE about joining a few other parents in forming their own school, I said:

Thanks for news of your school. One piece of heartfelt advice. People sending their kids to your school must be made to understand that if there is something they think those children *must* be taught or *must* learn, basics or whatever, it must be *their* responsibility to do that teaching, and to do it in their own home—or at any rate, away from the school. The school must be a place where people come together to do the things that interest and excite them most. Otherwise, you will be torn to pieces with arguments about whether the school should teach reading or arithmetic, or teach it one or four hours a week, or whatever. Believe me, I speak from the bitter experience of many people.

And this would be my very strong advice to any group of unschoolers who want to start a school as a way of escaping compulsory attendance laws, or giving their children a place to meet and be with other children, or for whatever reasons. Okay to have rules which say, more or less, no fair hurting or bothering other people. Every human society has these, and children expect them and understand them. But the school must not try to *compel* learning. If it does, people will argue endlessly and furiously about what kinds of learning must be compelled. This has happened to small alternative schools again and again.

Nancy Plent, a mother in New Jersey, wrote about this:

> One more thing I did want to say is about the other mothers I'm meeting. None of us worry about social adjustment stuff; we all know that kids can keep occupied with friends of all ages and with their own interests. But every one of us feels that our kids need more kids. They are feeling "different" and left out, no matter what their situation. E often greets a sunny day with, "Boy, it's a great day to ride green machines! I'll call Tommy and…oh, he's in school today." No big thing, maybe, but it happens often, to all of our kids, and we worry about it.
>
> For this reason, the talk always comes around to "maybe if we started some kind of school." We know it is a problem without an answer right now, but we bat it around wistfully all the time anyway. I can only see an answer when we find more people doing it, convince more people that they should do it. I'm giving it all I've got.

It would be a fine thing if in any community there were more places for children, and indeed people of all ages, to get together and do various kinds of things. I talk about what such places might be like in early chapters of *Instead of Education*, and even more in an appendix describing a remarkable place called the Peckham Family Center, which existed for a while in a part of London in the late 1930s. (People are trying to organize a new one in Scotland.)

In some ways, the country clubs that rich folks belong to are a much better model of what we want than a school. Take away the eighteen-hole golf courses, the elaborate tennis courts and other facil-ities, the palatial clubhouse, and what's left is very close in spirit to what we are after. You don't *have* to play golf just because you go to the golf club. You don't have to *do* anything. There are certain kinds of resources there for you to use, if you want, but you can spend the day there sitting in a chair and looking at the sky. Why not an inexpensive version of the same thing? A country club without the country—or per-haps a different kind of country, just a little patch of field or woods or whatever is handy.

If we can keep the idea of a family club in mind, we will probably make more sensible choices and decisions.

Some years ago, a good friend of mine, Peggy Hughes, then living in Denmark, decided to make a 16 mm sound film about the Ny Lille Skole (New Little School), a small "school" in which she was working, which I describe in *Instead of Education*. She had done a small amount of black-and-white photography but had never even owned a movie camera, let alone made a film with sound.

In time, working almost entirely alone, with occasional advice from the more experienced, she produced a film, about forty-five min-utes long, called *We Have to Call It School*. I am not unbiased about it; she and I are old friends, I loved the school and the people in it, and for some of the footage I was her sound man. But I think it is the most vivid, touching, and true film portrait of children that I have ever seen. Anyone who likes, enjoys, and respects children will surely be charmed and delighted by it and may learn much from it.

Why should unschoolers want to see a film about school? The answer is in the title. Early in the film is a shot of the children arriv-ing at school in the morning. Over this we hear the voice of one of the teachers, Erik, saying, "We have to call it school. The law in Denmark says that children have to go to school, and if we didn't call this a school, they couldn't come here." But it is not a school in any way that we understand those words. It is a meeting, living, and *doing* place for six or seven adults and about eighty children, ages six through fourteen. It is more like a club than anything I can compare it to. The children come there when they feel like it, most of the time during the winter, not so often when spring and the sun arrive. Once there, they talk about and do many things that interest them, sometimes with the adults, sometimes by themselves. In the process, they learn a lot about themselves, each other, and the world.

The film is important for unschoolers for many reasons, among them this one. What we need in our communities is not so much schools as a variety of protected, safe, interesting *spaces* where children can gather, meet and make friends, and do things together. Such spaces might include children's libraries (or sections of libraries), children's museums (a wonderful one in Boston), children's theaters (children *making* the drama, not just watching it), children's (or children's and adults') arts or craft centers, adventure playgrounds, and so on. One such space was the Peckham Center. Another such space could be something like the Ny Lille Skole. It's not a matter of copying it exactly, but of catching the spirit of it.

GREENHOUSE

Beth Hagins writes from Illinois about still another child space, the best of the lot, because it is not primarily for children at all, but has its own real and serious work.

We are working to create a biological research setting for children in the south Chicago area. It's a large solar greenhouse that we have built with people in the black township of Pembroke, Illinois. It's a very rural, low-income community. The quality of life is superbly suited to growing without schooling.

I don't know how to describe the place without sounding like a grant application. I've been "learning" there for the past four years, largely being taught by the older people. They've taught me how to grow, how to make compost, how to conserve, how to slaughter, how to cooperate. I've never been happier learning anywhere. It's even helped put my own formal academic instruction in perspective...(Kindergarten through PhD).

The greenhouse manager is a 67-year-old man who's been selling and growing all his life. Our experiments are economic and biological. We are raising laying hens, getting eggs, saving chicken manure, growing worms, fertilizing starter plants, and watching our chickens and plants *flourish* in all the sunlight. We would love to have a few children to work with. We are working to get a few local children involved actively, but it is always more exciting for them to have friends from outside the area coming to learn, too.

...It's funny. As I think back on school, the one thing that I feel most molded by was the reward structure for getting As. Apart from a B in sociology as a sophomore in college, I don't think I got anything but As since fourth grade. I discovered I could get As in anything, although I am to this day not very quick on my feet in terms of thinking. I suppose that the As were what opened doors for me, got me into more exciting learning situations—like regional orchestras, national debate forums, and other kinds of special "larger than life" experiences that can stimulate and impress if they do not intimidate. I don't know enough about the deschooling movement to know if this kind of larger association of children is possible. We hope to be able to do something like this with the greenhouse experiments, and to introduce the children to some of the schooled, practicing experimenters who nonetheless share the values of the deschoolers. Many of the solar societies are organized and powered by very wonderful scientists and researchers who would like the opportunity to work on a limited basis with children outside a formal school context.

SPACE UNLIMITED

Harold Dunn of Oregon writes of the hazards of calling any kind of children's space a "school," and about traveling in Mexico with children:

My primary interest is in building nonschool alternatives for kids. Two years ago, when I still believed that Free Schools were the answer, I started a mini-school, with five kids and two adults living with me in my home, a converted school bus parked way out in the Oregon woods beside a small lake. Tuition was free, teaching nonexistent, curriculum based on survival since we had less than $100 a month for all eight of us to live on.

Two of the boys, aged 14 and 15, had spent much of the summer out at my place, always busy and creative in their play. They dreaded the return to public school in September, so we called ourselves a school and just continued on as we had all summer. Only it didn't work out. They became bored, restless, and complained they weren't learning anything.

It took me quite a while to realize that since they were now in "school," they expected somebody to *do* something *to* them. It didn't matter that all summer they had been exploring new realms and expanding their limits with no adult supervision. Now they demanded to be told what to do. Somebody was supposed to learn them something, or else it wasn't a real school and no damn good after all.

I realized then how much we had destroyed for these two boys just by calling ourselves a school. Of course, the destruction happened gradually during all their previous schooling, as they were conditioned to believe that learning is a passive thing, and that school is where it happens.

The three other kids in our school, age 5, 10, and 12, had never been to school, so had no preconceived ideas of what to expect. What a joy it was to watch them explore the world and themselves. Their greatest treasure was my library card, which allowed them to read hundreds of pages each day. They never seemed to get their fill of books, yet they still had energy to cook, bake, chop wood, wash dishes, and clean house. The two oldest girls did far more than their share of the work needed to sustain us all—because they *wanted* to. They were alive, eager, and incredibly inventive. They saw the whole world as open to them, because nobody had taught them there were things they couldn't do.

In a month's time, M (12) went from being a virtual nonswimmer to being the first kid to pass the "Mountain-Man Test," a challenge I had put up to a group of boys that hung out at the lake all that summer. The test consisted of swimming out to the middle of the lake (about 100 yards), alone, at midnight, and diving to the bottom (12 feet), bringing back some mud to prove it. Several boys had tried it, but they all chickened out, even those that were much better swimmers than M. But she stuck with it, working hard to overcome her fears. (It's *dark* down in that lake at night.) And the night she passed the test she announced that since she was now the only member of the Mountain-Man Club, she was changing the name to Mountaineers!

The incredible contrast between these girls, who had no previous schooling, even in free schools, and the two boys so conditioned by their years of public school dogma, was a powerful lesson for me. For many years, I had dreamed of starting a new kind of free school, run entirely by the kids themselves, rather than controlled by the parents or the teachers, as is usually the case. Finally my dream had come true, only to teach me its own absurdity. Any kids truly free to run their own school exactly as they see fit, will immediately declare a permanent vacation, and that will be the end of it. They may get together as before, and do the same things, but they won't call it school unless you make them—and then *you're* running the show, and that's not freedom, even if you're doing it, as I was, "for their own good" to keep them out of public school.

FARM SPACE

An article by Jerry Howard in *Horticulture* tells about a food-raising space in a rich Boston suburb:

> Bill McElwain, a Harvard man who had taught French, run a Laundromat, and become a discouraged farmer, moved to the prosperous town of Weston, Mass., and saw a lot of fertile suburban land going to waste, on the way to and from his work in Boston (rehabilitating houses in the South End).
>
> He saw suburban teen-agers with few alternatives to football, tennis, drama or boredom, and he saw poor city people paying more for food in Roxbury than he was in Weston. (Bill surveyed the cost of twenty-five identical items in both areas and counted a 13% difference.)
>
> In April 1970, Bill began with borrowed hand tools and donations of seed and fertilizer. With a handful of dedicated helpers, he cultivated almost an acre; the produce was trucked into Roxbury and distributed free to a children's food program and a housing project. There, residents collected donations that found their way back to the farm.
>
> Within a year, Bill was hired as project director of the new Weston Youth Commission. In 1972, he convinced the town to buy the farmland. He ignited a small but dedicated cadre of supporters, including enough people in the volunteer government to insure the continued support of the town. More kids got involved with the farm, and with the proceeds from the vegetables (now sold in Boston for a nominal $1 a crate) he paid workers a minimum wage. The town put more money and equipment into the project, and by 1975, the farm was growing as much as 100 tons of produce a year. About 25% of this was sold locally; the rest went into Boston.
>
> Bill McElwain was fifty years old when the town bought the farm. He is still project director for the Youth Commission, despite his cavalier view of keeping fiscal records, and he still writes a column for the

Weston Town Crier, in which he proposes dozens of other activities for the young to take part in.

One fall, for instance, Bill counted 600 maple trees along Weston roadsides. In a year and a half, he and a crew built a sugarhouse near the junior high school (using pine boards milled from local trees); scrounged buckets, taps, and evaporating equipment; and produced a cash crop of 250 gallons of grade A maple syrup. There was cider pressing, orchard reclamation, firewood cutting, crate making, construction of a small observatory, and an alternative course at the high school with regular field trips to Boston's ethnic neighborhoods, and to rural New Hampshire.

Virtually all his plans, large or small, have these common ingredients: they provide young people with paying jobs that are educational, socially useful, and fun; they operate on a small scale, need little capital, and use readily available resources, preferably neglected ones; and they bring a variety of people together to solve common problems in an enjoyable context. Building community is one of Bill's more crucial goals, and he'll seize any opportunity—planting, harvesting, "sugaring off," a woodcarving workshop, or May Day—to bring folks together for a festive occasion.

MANY HOMESCHOOLERS TRY to run family businesses out of their homes as a way to make it all work, but this is often no less stressful and, sometimes, more financially burdensome than trying to balance a traditional job with homeschooling. However, homeschoolers tend to be more entrepreneurial, and home businesses as a primary or secondary source of income are probably more common among homeschooling families than the general population. I personally know computer programmers and organic farmers, symphony conductors and general contractors, who figure out ways to arrange their schedules to allow for homeschooling in their lives, and many others would be able to, as well. Children at any age can be involved in discussing how they spend their time. Goals and schedules will emerge as the discussion occurs, and this will be an ongoing, not a one-time, process, because goals and schedules do change, particularly for young people. Think of this as a strength of homeschooling: There is more time to have these talks and to listen to children's observations. Lessons can be compressed and expanded as needed, performance can be evaluated in dynamic situations, and families can take a break or vacation whenever needed. Homeschooling families can have a different rhythm than families that listen to the beat of school (more about this in Chapter 11). There are many ways to make homeschooling work once all parties see learning as an activity that may sometimes involve classes, rather than as just "classroom activity."

Children have always been welcome at the Holt Associates offices, but after John died and staff members started having families, the offices, at times, just teemed with kids. We usually worked while the children played, though sometimes they'd ask if they could help pack books, answer phones, stuff envelopes, or stamp letters. They'd work alongside us for a while, and then either drift into a new activity or conversation with a friend or, sometimes, they'd ask for more work when they completed a task. Sometimes one or two kids would walk into my office and ask questions about what I was doing; sometimes they'd just play hide-and-seek in my office, while I pretended not to see them. However as the kids became older, ages eight to twelve in particular, they wanted to have their own space for play or privacy. We allowed the younger ones to ride small bikes in our basement storage area, and the older ones to create a clubhouse in the back-issue storage room.

If you came into our office in those days, you would see evidence of children everywhere. Our walls were filled with their drawings and projects, and the air would sometimes be filled with their games and talk; during good weather we found it useful to pay a colleague to take the kids to a nearby park so we could work quietly or hold important meetings without interruptions. Seeing a child sitting on their mom's lap while she read a book to him or her during a break was a common sight in those days, and something we encouraged. Many of the delivery people who came to our office would wonder aloud if they were delivering to a day-care center instead of a place of business! Yet, somehow, all the work that needed to be accomplished got done. It wasn't the most efficient and cost-effective way to run a business, but it was a lot more interesting than your typical office, particularly if you liked being around kids.

As the children got older, many staff members found that they were involved in serious schedule conflicts, picking up and dropping off the older ones at classes and meetings all around town during business hours. Sometimes staff members pooled their homeschooling driving, so our office often became a hub for pickups and drop-offs for kids, particularly the older ones. Sometimes teens scheduled meetings or workshops with adults they wanted to learn with in our office during business hours, which worked just fine. We had enough office space to accommodate such events.

My three girls, in particular, enjoyed playing with makeup and doing dress-ups, so our office had a good stash of costumes, plastic jewelry, and accessories stored in an old toy chest near the shipping area. Phil Cranshaw, my father-in-law, who worked as our shipper/receiver, once was teasing the girls by taking a big feather boa out of the chest and wearing it while he packed orders, refusing to give it back to them because he "looked so good with it on." The girls loved seeing "Papa Phil" wear the boa while he worked, and there was much laughter to be heard. However, when the UPS man made his delivery that day, he caught sight of Phil prancing before the girls with the boa around his neck. Just as Phil started to explain what was going on, the UPS man stopped him with this remark: "Don't apologize. I shouldn't be surprised by anything when I come to this place!" ∎

6

SERIOUS PLAY

I N THIS CHAPTER, PARENTS give us a few glimpses of the ways in which children use play, fantasy, make-believe, poetry, song, drama, and art as a way of exploring and understanding the world. This is an important part of their life and growth. People have done some persuasive studies to show that children who are good at fantasizing are better both at learning about the world and at learning to cope with its surprises and disappointments. It isn't hard to see why this should be so. In fantasy we have a way of trying out situations, to get some feel for what they might be like, or how we might feel in them, without having to risk too much. It also gives us a way of coping with bad experiences, by letting us play and replay them in our mind until they have lost much of their power to hurt, or until we can make them come out in ways that leave us feeling less defeated and foolish.

For a healthy and active fantasy life children need time, space, and privacy, or at least only as much companionship as they choose. Obviously school, or any other large-group situation—day-care center, nursery school, play group, and the like—does not allow much of this. Perhaps worst of all, they are usually under the eye and control of adults who, even if they will allow children a fantasy life, feel they have to watch it, understand what it means, judge it, make use of it. It was for just this reason that a well-meaning and quite highly praised book, written about ten years ago, called *Fantasy and Feeling in Childhood*, seemed and still seems to me deeply mistaken. The gist of it (and there may well be many books like it) was that if we, that is, people who work in schools, paid enough attention to the fantasy lives of children, we could learn to understand them and bend them to our own purposes.

This would be a great mistake and a great wrong. Instead, we should be content to watch and enjoy as much of children's fantasy lives as they will let us see, and to take part in them, if the children ask us to and if we can do so happily and unselfconsciously. Otherwise, we should leave them alone. Children's fantasy is useful and important to them for many reasons, but above all because it is *theirs*, the one part of their lives which is wholly under their control. We must resist the temptation to make it *ours*.

We must also resist the equally great temptation to think that this part of children's lives is less important than the parts where they are doing something "serious"—reading, or writing, or doing schoolwork, or something that we want them to do—or to think that we can only allow them time for fantasy after all the important work is done, as we might give them a little piece of candy after a meal. For children, play and fantasy are part of the main courses of the meal. Children should be able to do them, not just in what little tag ends of time remain after all the "important" work is done, but when they are most full of energy and enthusiasm. We talk these days of "quality time." Children need quality time for their fantasy and play as much as for their reading or math. They need to play well as much as they need to read well. Indeed, we would probably find if we looked into it that children who are not good at playing, dreaming, fantasizing, are usually not much good at reading either.

At any rate, here are some nice accounts of this part of the lives of children.

FANTASTIC WORLDS

A mother writes about the world her son created:

> But at the same time we are, deep inside, ready to "un-school." I am absolutely convinced of its rightness. My problem is my children, especially the older one (10). After five years of schooling he has made it palatable and even enjoyable by creating a world within a world there with a couple of his friends. The schoolwork is no problem; he goes so that he can get together easily with 2 or 3 other boys for playing baseball or whatever. Also, their world contains its own society of "weepuls"—scores of Ping-Pong-ball-sized fuzzy creatures of different colors with big feet and tiny antennas. For almost a year they had their city covering our 20' × 12' sun porch (forced to be dismantled because we are remodeling). I haven't read *Gnomes*, but doubt if it could be a more complete study than these kids have with weepuls: the cast of characters, layers of their society, their soccer and football fields, space-ports and ships, disco, museum, school, movie theater, transportation system, all made in detailed miniature with great care and skill; their diet of only bananas and banana juice, their death by contact with water, and so on. When J went on a scout trip to the snow, the weepul King Eeker went with him on skis made out of tongue depressors. The weepuls go to school and hide in the desks until break time when they come out and make school their place and the boys can do what they want with and through them. Homework and boredom are put up with for the chance to meet A and K and play with weepuls.

Candy Mingins, a teacher, writes about a similar game called Atlas:

The family didn't have much money, and did have plenty of German thriftiness—hence the children were not swamped with plastic toys and gadgets....They had to create their own play, so C and his brother and two sisters (all older) played this ongoing game (invented mostly by his brother) for 8 years or more. It was a game of the World. Each child had tribes of people made from: toothpaste caps glued to marbles (the Lilliputians); Hi-Q game pieces (the Microscopians); used Magic Markers with toothpick swords and aluminum foil shields (the Sudanis); cooking oil bottles decorated with paper (the Criscoeans); etc. The tribes fought battles in the garden, conquered territories, kept maps and records, held art shows, had a newspaper, and had their own languages and money systems.

It was an ingenious invention of play, which the children created entirely by themselves, and which lasted through time, always encompassing new interests and ideas as the children grew.

COPS AND ROBBERS

A mother writes about a perennial child's game and her own memories of it:

Nobody ever told me not to play guns. But, when I was a kid, and the gang played cops 'n' robbers, I had a problem because I couldn't "die." Some kid would shoot me, and I would want to fall down and die, but somehow I couldn't, and I would just stand there and look dazed. And if I shot somebody, he would just ignore me because he knew I hadn't really killed him.

After I grew up and had kids of my own, and they had taught me *how* to play cops 'n' robbers, I realized that I had been a very schizoid child, very uptight, totally lacking in spontaneity, frozen out of the

NOW—and playing guns is a kid's way of getting really "with" other kids and into a very fast-moving, action-packed *present*.

My observation (of about 15 years watching such games) is that only very free-spirited kids can play a really good game of cops 'n' robbers, and that many games of cops 'n' robbers are ended by a child who *does* have feelings of violence and cruelty and causes an "accident" to happen in which someone is hurt. Usually that child wants to put an end to the game because of jealousy—he *can't* share in the fun; not because he has been excluded by the others, but because he isn't capable of playing.

I don't think "playing guns" usually has anything to do with guns, violence, hostility, or cruelty; it is a game of awareness. Feelings, other than joy, get in the way of awareness, and you can explode your feelings by experiencing the sound of the cap exploding in a cap pistol, for instance.

In playing guns, I believe it goes like this: If I am *aware* of you first, I can shoot you, and you have to die! If I get surprised by you, then I KNOW you are more aware than I am because *you* surprised *me*, so I've got to die. I just give up all awareness (falling in the process) until I feel a surge inside me that says I'm ready to be born again—MORE alive than before! Sometimes you and I catch each other at exactly the same time, and then we have to battle it out—Bang! Bang! Pow! Pow! I got YOU! NO you didn't, I got you FIRST!—until we both know that one of us has bested the other. One of us must die and be born again!

If, instead, one of us gets MAD—then the game quickly ends.

Oh, I love a good, noisy game of cops 'n' robbers!

I am an old fossil of almost forty who couldn't play guns now to save my soul, but at least I still remember that I learned something from some kids a long time ago.

I'm trying to *tell* you something that can only be experienced, which tells me that I'm a fool. So, my suggestion is that you find a free-spirited kid (maybe you have one in your home?) and see what you can learn from him.

I believe that it's best to learn to look at the spirit—the feelings expressed—in what your child does and see through the material object. After all, a child can express his feelings of cruelty and hostility when he pets the dog, and he can express his joy and delight when he shoots his gun. If your child is a joyful child and he WANTS a gun, I think you can trust in his joy, because the Bible says the things of this world are perishable, but the things of the spirit are everlasting, and I, personally, think kids are born knowing this.

Even if a child uses his toy gunplay to drain off his anger and hostility, without hurting anything or anyone in the process, what's the harm in it? My husband says he can remember having those feelings when he played guns as a kid (whereas I never saw such feelings expressed when our kids played guns). He said he thought it was a good thing that he had that outlet, as he had a very unhappy home.

Theo Giesy, a Virginia mother of four, had this to say:

Darrin and Danile were introduced to guns by a friend K when they were 2 and 4, respectively. K was 4. One of them would stand on a hassock, the others would shoot him and he would die very dramatically. Then someone else would climb up to be shot and die. K died most dramatically and was most fun. This was repeated as fast as someone could climb up, always with high spirits, fun, and friendliness. Darrin immediately wanted guns and built up quite an arsenal. Shortly after that we moved from California to Michigan. Without K the game changed entirely. Now Darrin and Danile would play house. She would stay home and take care of their babies (her dolls and his dolls) and he would ride the scooter to go off to the woods with his gun to hunt a bear to bring home for them to eat. (All imagination—no one we knew was a hunter.) Darrin was then 2½. At the same time when Darrin was really angry, he never thought of guns. His expression of violence was "I'll throw a shoe at you." Guns were part of the world of fun and imagination and had nothing to do with real violence. The "death" of K and Danile and Darrin had nothing to do with hurting anyone.

I thought of that often the next year when Darrin's best friend was not allowed to have guns and they were not allowed to have guns at nursery school. So they built guns out of Tinkertoys or snap blocks. Parents who forbid guns are neither preventing violence nor gunplay and parents who allow guns are not encouraging violence.

HOMEMADE STORIES

The mother of a two-year-old boy told me that she had made up a story in which he was the hero, and all the other characters the animals on their small farm. He loved the story. Later she wrote it down and sent me a copy, saying, "You may find it a bit cute but a five-year-old boy wondered—in a whisper—all the way through, 'Is it true?'"

Children, whether in city or country, are more likely to be interested in stories in which they play a part, and which are full of things drawn from their everyday life. Parents, or other people who know the children well, are the ideal people to make up such stories. Even if they are not very polished, such stories are likely to be much more interesting than most of the stories in books for little children.

A. S. Neill, at Summerhill, used to make up stories for the children there, in which they were the leading characters, chasing or being chased by various spies, crooks, and villains. And as many know, *Alice in Wonderland* was made up for the real child who was the Alice in the story. So, take a shot at making up stories for your children. As with everything else, as you do it you'll get better at it.

Here is part of my friend's story:

PIG IN THE BED
On Tuesday last week a strange thing went on;
Jack came home early and his parents were gone.

He knew right away that something was up
When he took a look at his friend the pup.
(He was drinking a Coke, taking sips as he spoke.)

"Hey Jack! Look out! Better step aside.
The horse and her colt are going for a ride!"
Jack turned around when the pickup truck
Made the sound that it makes when it's just starting up.

The horse put it in gear and sputtered past,
Then before she started going too fast,
She yelled, "Sorry, Jack, to be taking your car,
But it's been a long time since we've gone very far."

Jack stared, then he wondered, then he said, "OK,
But will you try to get back by the end of the day?"

He shrugged and went on down to the kitchen,
But when he got there it was full of his chickens!
"Just fixing a little midday treat.

We get awfully tired of old corn to eat,"
Said the hens as they mixed and blended and baked
Until they came up with banana spice cake.

Everywhere Jack looked in the house, he found animals—even in his
bed! How to get them out before his parents came back? Then he hit on
the solution:

"I've got it!" said Jack, and he started to scream:
"Up in the barn there's chocolate ice cream!"
The chickens took wing, the pig climbed out of bed.
The cow left the tub and the goats quickly fled.

Up the road the horse was parking the truck.
Jack ran to the freezer. "Whew! I'm in luck!"

He got out two gallons of chocolate ice.
"Plenty for everyone! As long as you're nice."
He passed it out fairly to all on the farm,
To the pig in the pig pen and the cow in the barn.
"Thank heavens you knew just what to do,"
Said the dog, passing his plate. "May I have some too?"
"Certainly," said Jack. "But what will mom say
When she sees I ate two gallons of ice cream today?"

Most parents, whether on a farm or in a city, could spin such a homemade epic. It doesn't need to scan or rhyme as well as this—the children who see themselves in the story won't be fussy.

REQUIEM FOR A TURTLE

Small children when left on their own love to make up their own songs and chants. One mother told me about a chant that her daughter, when two years and nine months old, had made up one day while swinging on the swing, and seeing something disappear with a crunch into the mouth of her cat. The chant went like this:

Oh, we went downtown…
Downtown my mother
and Mary Jean went.
We saw some pretty turtles,
some pretty little turtles.
Yes, we did. O yes we did!
Pretty, pretty little turtles…
They wiggled and wiggled,

They wiggled their heads,
They wiggled their legs,
And their tails they wiggled, wiggled...O!

My mother buyed me
Two little turtles
Two little turtles *and*
One little turtle made
The *other* little turtle
Not lonesome...O!
He was s'posed to make him
Not lonesome...O!

Did he make him not lonesome? NO!
He climb out, out...
He fall on the ground...O!
Oh, oh, oh, OH!
He climb out
Over and over AGAIN!
I just can hardly believe it!
Poco-cat
Ate him all UP!

However, it turned out later the cat *hadn't* eaten the turtle, who was found under the child's bed.

A VERY YOUNG ARTIST

A father writes about a "precocious" artist:

We have one of the happy stories about unschooling. Before M was born, we had decided not to send her to school. We moved to the

country thinking it would be easier there. Now I realize it might sometimes be more difficult.

We were lucky. The teacher and school board of our local school, where I am janitor, have been tolerant and helpful. The teacher is one of the good ones. M goes once a week on a day of her choosing. Any more than once a week, she thinks, would be awful. One defense that we have thought might help if we are given any trouble about not going to school is that she is bilingual and does learning in her other language at home. (There are laws protecting bilingualism in California schools.) M's mother is Japanese.

THIS SITUATION HAS CHANGED OVER TIME. California and other states passed "English-only instruction" in public schools starting in 1998, but in 2016 the educational tide turned again and restrictions on bilingual education were lifted. Speaking only English or being bilingual in the classroom do not have to be mutually exclusive. Teachers and students both need options when things aren't working rather than ensuring by law that only one method can be used. ∎

M began to draw when she was 6 months old. Everything she did was treated as important art. By the time she was one year old she could draw better than anyone around her. Knowing that she could do something better than anyone, even better than the ever-competent giants around her, emboldened her strokes. In other areas it gave her the confidence to try something difficult, then to continue until she could do it well.

At one year of age, she was given an easel and some tempera paints. On her second birthday she got nontoxic acrylics, the medium she has preferred since. She enjoyed painting so much that she began calling herself an artist.

We became curious about other children artists so we checked out

the children's art scene in San Francisco where we were then living. We made the surprising discovery that M is a child artist who does not paint children's art. Her work would look absurdly out of place in a show of children's art. Especially so since she began using acrylics because it is always assumed that children's art should be done with watercolors. For obvious reasons acrylics are easier to use than poster paints or tempera but they cost more. I know people who make 5 or 6 times my subsistence wage who tell me they can't afford acrylics for their children. What this really means is that they think children can't do anything worth that much.

Probing deeper in this direction via an understanding of adultism might begin to explain what I mean when I say that much of what is known as children's art is an adult invention.

In all the contacts we have had with the children's art establishments in San Francisco and Tokyo we have had nothing but unpleasant experiences. They are amazed but they are even more skeptical. I think they are hoping she'll turn out to be the 40-year-old midget in one of your books. [Author's note: This refers to an episode in *Escape From Childhood*.] Finally we know they are the enemy. We avoid them, scorn their nonsense books on children's art ("Children will generally not be ready to paint before they are 5 years old"), frown back at the saved missionary smiles they are in the habit of turning on their flock. When they used to say M's work was very good for her age I asked them if they would say Picasso's erotic drawings, done in his latter years, were good for his age.

It is recognized that children have their original imagination destroyed in the socializing process and that as adult artists they must struggle to regain it if they are to create an original vision. There must be some way for people to grow up without losing this although it rarely happens. The most obvious thing to do is to stay out of school and maybe to prevent their exposure to phony children's art. One indication of what might have happened to M if she had been forced to go to school full-time is that when she draws at school her drawings are stiff and uninteresting. They are like children's drawings are supposed to be, cute and easy to patronize. She also prints her signature on them like the other children do. She has always signed her name in cursive and has used nothing but cursive at home since she learned it when she was 4 years old. She's 7 now.

M's conversations about what was going on in the paintings while she was doing them were so interesting that I decided when she was 4 years old to get some of her old paintings out to talk about them with her. She enjoyed seeing her treasures again. About the same thing she said originally was repeated but more concisely. She called them poems. During her fifth year she began writing her poems and stories by herself. One of her 4-year-old poems about a painting described what she imagined she did when she was wandering around the world with us five years before she was born: "When I was in Mama's stomach it was very dark so sometimes I wanted to get out. From a secret door I was looking out of Mama's stomach through her navel. Everywhere Mama went I was watching from my secret door. Each time I looked out she came to a new town. I saw the whole world. That's the place I was born."

With his letter the father sent me some reproductions of M's early work, five paintings done between the ages of twenty-six and thirty-eight months. They were printed in Japan, perhaps by some museum in connection with a show on children's art. I am guessing, but they look like the postcards of paintings that one can buy in museums. The paintings themselves are stunning. Three of them would stop you dead in your tracks if you saw them in an exhibition of "adult" art. The colors, the shapes, the drawing, the design, the underlying idea of the paintings, are extraordinary.

I am ready to believe that M is an exceptionally talented child.

But that is what I felt when I first heard four- to six-year-old children, students of Suzuki in Japan, playing difficult music by Bach, Vivaldi, among others, in perfect time and tune. Perhaps other children might do work of equal beauty and power if their talents were taken seriously and given scope.

7

LEARNING WITHOUT TEACHING

MUCH OF THE MATERIAL IN THIS CHAPTER could have gone into Chapter 4, "Learning in the World." I put it here to make a different point. There I was talking about children (and others) learning outside of school. Here I am talking about them learning without teaching—learning by doing, by wondering, by figuring things out, and often in the process resisting teaching when well-meaning adults try to force it on them. A letter from Judy McCahill in England aptly describes this kind of learning:

> I do have the worst time explaining to people how I teach the kids. The trouble arises from the very basic concept, which most people can't grasp, that the kids actually teach themselves. I find it impossible, both timewise and because of my live-and-let-live nature, to give any sort of formal lessons. Recently I thought I would begin giving myself systematic lessons in basic science so that I could teach the kids better, but after three days that failed because I always seemed to have something more important to do than study. So, I

continue with my major technique of just answering questions as well as I can and helping the kids to ferret out information when they want it.

It interests me, though, how quickly the kids latch on to my *real* enthusiasms and, without anybody intending anything, begin to learn. Last summer I visited the Tate Gallery (a big art museum in London) with a girl who had just finished a year-long course in the history of art. She infected me with her enthusiasm, I attended a slide-illustrated lecture that day, and I examined incredulously the calendar of (free!!!) events the Tate had set up—all sorts of lectures, films, special exhibitions, and guided tours.

I've only been back to the Tate once since then, but I brought home a couple of books and gloatingly circled all the events I would attend if I could. (Next week I am going to a performance of *Julietta* by the English National Opera which is connected to a film and lecture on Surrealism at the Tate.) Last month our 18-year-old niece came to stay with us and she and Colleen have gone to the Tate three or four times. She [Colleen] has checked an art book out of the library (never having been interested in art before). And the boys often page through the books, studying the pictures. We have many discussions arising from what the girls have seen at the Tate; Colleen takes notes on the lectures for my benefit. So something new has entered our life, and it was completely accidental.

NO WORDS TO THE WISE

As many may know, in the Suzuki method of violin instruction, at least as first conceived and practiced, the parents of a child, while it is still a baby, begin to play for it, and often, recordings of the easy violin pieces which it will itself learn to play at the age of three. Kathy Johnson and I have talked often (in letters) about Suzuki. Recently she wrote:

You asked me last December to let you know how my home adaptation of Suzuki violin with my two-year-old daughter is working. I hadn't actually brought home the 1/16-size violin then, but in self-defense had to get her one to keep her from having tantrums when my dad and I played. Her being well into the "No" stage now is living proof of why they don't organize a class of young Suzuki violinists until age three.

But I feel you *can* do more at an early age than merely play the record. With no big fanfare, one day when a tantrum started during our duet, I simply suggested she play her own violin—that little one over there in the corner. She gave me a look as if to say, "Oh yes, but of course!" And before the duet was over, she had figured out how to open the case, get the violin out, and saw the bow upside-down over the strings a few times. She was delighted.

In the past four months, whenever we saw such a gross mistake on her part, either my dad or I (whoever was closer) would *very briefly* reach down and show her a better way to play as we went along. Of course, she had to learn some rules: not to carry her instrument around the house, especially on noncarpeted surfaces, not to handle the bow hair (or it won't make any sound on the strings), etc. We were amazed how fast she learned to respect her instrument. She even keeps the bow rosined!

She hasn't mastered the technique of playing just one string at a time yet, but she has darn good position, and a wonderful time developing those long full bows.

We were amazed when out-of-town relatives came to visit and our *shy* little daughter brought out her violin to squawk on the strings in front of a roomful of adults. We were all proud—but not as proud as she was! I think the important thing my dad and I learned very quickly was to recognize that moment when she needed help, capitalize on it briefly, then leave her alone to experiment. Praise is used, but in not much greater amounts than Dad and I praise each other. We play for enjoyment. I think she does, too.

She won't stand for a "lesson." Help that is a few seconds too long or in the wrong tone of voice brings loud "No-No's" followed by her putting her violin away and being angry. At this age, there's a fine line between happiness and tears. When she wants, if she wants, we'll see an expert.

A mother writes about another child resisting teaching:

My daughter (3) is in the kitchen teaching herself addition and sub-traction on the Little Professor Calculator—a machine I don't really approve of—and every time I give her a gentle hint, she flies into a rage, but when I leave her alone and watch her out of the corner of my eye, I see her doing problems like 3 + 5 = 8!

Years ago I went to a meeting of Catholic educators, where I heard a talk by a wise, funny old man who had been teaching all his life. One thing he said made us all laugh and has stuck in my mind ever since: "A word to the wise is *infuriating*!" Yes it is, because it is insult-ing, and little children pick up this expression of (often loving and protective) distrust or contempt, even when we're not conscious of sending it.

Some years ago, I was reading aloud to a small child, as yet a nonreader, perhaps three or four years old. As I read aloud, I had the bright idea that by moving a finger along under the words as I read them I might make more clear the connections between the written and the spoken words. A chance to get in a little subtle teaching. With-out saying anything about it, and as casually as possible, I began to do this.

It didn't take the child very long to figure out that what had begun as a nice, friendly, cozy sharing of a story had turned into something else, that her project had by some magic turned into *my* project. After a while, and without saying a word, she reached up a hand, took hold of my hand, and very gently moved it off the page and down by my side—where it belonged. I gave up "teaching" and went back to doing what I had been asked to do, which was to read the story. A father writes:

It is not possible for an inquisitive child to delve deeply into dinosaurs without wondering about, and learning, how big they were (measurements), how many roamed a certain area (arithmetic), where they lived (geography), what happened to them (history), etc. And, after daddy's knowledge of dinosaurs was exhausted, which happened pretty quickly, a lot of reading was necessary. In short, it simply isn't possible to learn a lot about dinosaurs or anything else without along the way learning and using knowledge and skills that are intellectually prerequisite. After all, the reason that we call "the basics" by that phrase is that they *are* basic, and to worry that a kid will learn just about anything without learning and using the basics is like being worried that he might decide to build a house starting with the roof.

It's hard work, of course, for us to adjust ourselves to the kids' interests. They wake up every morning curious but, alas, rarely curious about the particular topics that we might be prepared to talk about or might prefer that they be curious about—that's when temptation rears its head and must be suppressed. It's a waste of time and quickly degenerates into intellectual bullying to try to sidetrack a kid onto topics *you* think he should be learning. Of course, going along with the kids' interests may, as it recently did in our family, find you subjected to six straight days of inquiry into space exploration. But, if you will just be patient and observant, the time comes when the kid, because *he* realizes that it's pertinent to learning about his primary interest, will, almost offhandedly (but it sticks), add rocket thrusts, multiply fuel loads, distinguish ellipses from circles, etc. Keep your mouth shut when you are not needed and be ready to help when you are. The kid will learn.

Perhaps the reason that so many adults—including, I confess, myself—find it hard to refrain from "helping" kids is that it wounds our egos to see how well they get along without us! How can that dumb kid of mine learn so much without a smart fellow like me to teach him? We try in effect to horn in on the kids' sense of pride in accomplishment and, all too often, particularly in schools, we succeed. The results are psychologically and intellectually catastrophic for the victims.

Another father writes:

I have read the books you have written, and between them and Bob (4), I've found, for me, the best way to teach is by example, and the best way to learn is by doing. (Bob continually tells us, "I don't want to know that" when we try to teach him something he doesn't want to learn.) Linda and I are impressed how quickly he picks things up, but what impresses me the most is his ability to just sit and think. I never knew young children did that until Bob showed me. He also repeats and repeats things until he has them. We put him to bed at 9 P.M., and often at 11 we can hear him talking to himself as he goes over things he wants to get straight. This is how he learned the alphabet and how to count to 129. That's his favorite number and he counts to it over and over and over. Somehow, he has picked up the idea that a number means a quantity of objects, and I am amazed he has learned that level of abstraction so quickly and completely.

I've tried to let Bob and David learn what they want to at the rates they set, but sometimes it is hard not to teach. There is one story I enjoy, simply because it was the only time I've been successful at teaching when Bob wasn't interested. When Bob was learning to count, he asked me what comes after 113. I didn't answer his question, but instead asked him what comes after 13. Well, he got mad because that's not what he wanted. I remained stubborn and he finally said, "14 comes after 13, what comes after 113?" very indignantly. I immediately said, "114." At first he was disgusted because I didn't answer his question the first time, but then he understood what I had just done. He broke out in a big grin and covered his face. We like to trick each other, and I had just gotten him.

One summer I was visiting an eight-year-old friend and her mother. They lived in a little house on a small side street, really more an alley. Cars seldom come through so kids can play there safely. In one part of the street there are high board fences on both sides, which makes it a good place for small ball games. My young friend and her friends often play their own version of baseball here. For a bat they use a thin stick about three feet long. The ball is a playground ball about six inches in diameter. The rules fit the space perfectly; with that stick, no one can hit that ball over those fences.

The day I arrived, after dinner, she asked me if I would pitch some batting practice. I said, Sure, and we had about forty-five minutes' worth in the alley. Next morning after breakfast she asked again, and we had about an hour more. Some of the time she very kindly pitched to me. I was amazed to find how hard it was to move that squishy ball with that skinny stick.

The point of the story is that in all this I did something about which I felt quite pleased, that I don't think I could or would have done even five years ago. In our almost two hours of play I did not offer *one word* of coaching or advice. The words were more than once on the tip of my tongue, once when she tried batting one-handed (she did better than I thought she would), once when she tried batting cross-handed (she gave it up on her own), and now and then when she seemed to be getting careless, not watching the ball, etc. But I always choked the words back, saying to myself, "She didn't ask you to coach, she asked you to pitch. So shut up and pitch." Which I did.

Nor did I give any praise. Sometimes—quite often, as a matter of fact—when she hit a real line drive, I let out a word of surprise or even alarm, if it came right at me. Otherwise, we did our work in silence, under the California sun. I remember it all with pleasure, and not least of all the silence. I hope I can be as quiet next time.

A mother in Ontario describes an extraordinary day in which she and another mother let the children lead the play:

Last fall we had a school group meeting [of children who on most days were learning at home] twice a week. Mostly two- to four-year-olds and mostly girls with one five-year-old girl and a six-year-old boy. Altogether there were about twelve children. It was quite a delightful group.

This is the day I remember best from that time. We began painting, and working with clay, and playing in the yard in front of the house. As lunch time neared, we decided to have a picnic in the little pine forest. (This was one of the favorite nice weather activities.) The little pine trees are about twelve years old and a wonderful size for little people to climb and create fantasy worlds within.

As we were eating, I noticed some tiny green plants growing within the browns, reds, oranges of the fall leaves. I looked closer at the little plants and suggested that the children near me help me look for the various tiny plants growing around us. We found my favorite spring greens—sorrel and peppergrass—and some clover and a couple of plants none of us were familiar with. We nibbled the greens and were pleased with our discovery.

Soon the wonderful game of "roaring lions in the forest" began. The other mother and I sat to rest for a while. One child (3) stayed with us looking at the plants. She was a very quiet child and often stayed by herself very absorbed for long times with her interests while all the others very easily related and played and talked with each other. Sometimes I wondered if she wanted help getting to know others, if she was lonely and frightened in her solitude. But from observing her I'd decided she was actually quite happy on her own a lot. She almost never talked at school, but I knew she could talk because I'd heard her talk to her older sister quite freely. So when she began talking to me about the plants I was delighted. We looked very slowly at many little plants and she pulled some out to look at the roots. Then she looked at the different levels of dead leaves—the brand new, bright crunchy ones were pushed away by her delicate finger, next there were softer brown ones, then black matted ones, then dirt. We talked throughout this examining of the magic of plants and earth.

When that was complete, we moved off to join the others who led us through the pines to the edge of the swamp—cedars and black gooshy mud and water. Someone took shoes and socks off and within a very short time all shoes and socks came off. There was a great deal of splashing and stamping and singing and joy. Someone fell down and got his pants mucky. (I thought—What are his parents going to think?) They were obviously having way too much fun to stop them. Soon all clothes were being taken off and put on the moss under the cedars. And the jolly dance continued. The little girl I described earlier was joining right in with all the others looking quite radiant. One child stayed back from the muck and the wet. He didn't seem disturbed by the others dancing in the muck, but obviously it didn't appeal to him. Exploring the swamp went on until it was time to dry off, get dressed, and go home.

I thought about that day and wondered how most of the parents would have responded. Some might not have allowed the naked water play—others probably would have. Some probably would have felt there wasn't much happening that day as much of it was spent on a long walk. But I was glad that the other mother who was there was as willing as I to follow the little people on their adventure and I loved that day!

FINDING OUT

A three-year-old has moved into a new house and has played in the sunshine on the new roof. He goes downstairs to supper and when he comes back steps into a changed and darkened world. With a wondering glance he says, "The big shadow is all around." Another three-year-old sees a thin cloud float across the moon. She watches intently, then says to herself, "Like ice, like ice."

This child's vision, quoted in a Colorado (Boulder) magazine called *Outlook*, is echoed by Hanna Kirchner, writing in Poland about the work of the physician Janusz Korczak:

He always stressed that by means of learning the everyday expressions from the obscure language of adults, the child tries to fathom the mystery of life. The child's fragmentary and incomplete knowledge of the world, welded together by imagination, creates a specific "magic consciousness" which, as has been discovered in the twentieth century, exists among children and primitive people and may be associated with the origins of poetry.

She then gives this wonderful quote from Korczak's book *How to Love a Child* (not yet translated into English):

[One child says], "They say there is one moon and yet one can see it everywhere."
"Listen, I'll stand behind the fence and you stay in the garden."
They lock the gate.
"Well, is there a moon in the garden?"
"Yes."
"Here too."

They change places and check once again. Now they are sure there must be two moons.

And yet they figure out, sooner or later, and *by themselves*, that there is only one moon.

And Theo Giesy tells this nice story:

When Danile was 6 or 7, she was lying in my bed thinking about money and wondering how $1 would divide among 3 children. She thought about it a while and said, "You could break it into dimes and give each one 3, that leaves 1 dime, you break that into pennies and give each one 3, and I get the extra penny." That was all her own, I made no comments or suggestions.

When I first taught fifth grade, before I had "taught" the children anything about fractions, or even mentioned the word, I used to ask them questions like this: "If you had three candy bars, and wanted to divide them evenly among five people, how would you do it?" Most of them could think of one or more ways to do this. But after they had "had" fractions and learned to think of this as a problem that you had to use fractions to solve, most of them couldn't do it. Instead of reality, and their own common sense and ingenuity, they now had "rules," which they could rarely keep straight or remember how to apply.

Since to so many people "learning" means what happens in school, or what is supposed to happen, I would rather use other words to describe what we humans do as a natural part of our living. "Finding out" seems to fit pretty well. Here, a reader talks about this continuous process:

I am almost a caricature of the congenital unteachable. It may have been something I picked up from imitating my father, for I notice he shares the trait to this day. He is very quick to learn, but utterly resists being taught.

I began to see how much this unteachability pervaded my life when I began about a year ago to see how much of my childhood I could remember distinctly. Probably the extreme example was learning to play the piano. I am told that I started banging away on the family upright at about age four. One day my dad got tired of the noise and said something to the effect of "If you're going to play, why don't you play *something*?" Well, I quit until my parents left the house, and when they came back that afternoon I was already picking out tunes. In a year I played "Silent Night" at church Christmas ceremonies.

So much has been like this. I started drawing at about four, also holding the pencil the wrong way. People said that I would never be able to draw that way. After selling dozens of paintings and drawings, I still hold it that way—I don't like the other way, as it produces a more unsteady hand for me. When, at about twelve, I wanted to write books, my dad gave me an old Royal and left me alone. I learned to type at good speed with one right-hand finger.

Then there were swimming lessons, which almost permanently made me hate swimming. A couple of years afterward, when I *wanted* to swim with my friends, I jumped in and swam as if I had always done so.

I taught myself auto mechanics on my first car, after being told for years that I was low in mechanical ability. I became a good carpenter's apprentice in two months, building one and a half houses with just one carpenter working at the same time. I surprised them all (except my parents—who had been listening) when I switched from an undergraduate education in pre-law to master's work in engineering, putting to rest the old thing about how artsy-booksy types cannot cope with numbers.

How did I get through schools? Only one way—by taking the offensive. Way back around fifth grade, my parents supplied us kids with the *Golden Book Encyclopedia*. I lapped up each book as it came home from the supermarket. Not long after that I was tested for reading at school and was found to be reading five years ahead of my grade. What is more, the *Golden Book Encyclopedia* gave me two invaluable things which freed me from much of the meaningless work the schools had cut out for me. One, I acquired from the encyclopedia a working familiarity with many aspects of science, history, geography, and art— such that I still "leaned on" this knowledge during exams as late as, say, tenth grade. Moreover, it taught me an understanding of how the world works, so that I could figure out what I did not actually know.

I recall what I did in fifth grade to free up more time to study airplanes, which I was then immersed in as a subject. The teacher wanted us to come up with five new words a week which we were supposed to define as a vocabulary lesson [Author's note: as if anyone ever learned words this way]. Trouble was, words did not come to me at this steady pace. So, one day, I reached into the dictionary for two hundred-odd words and did a year's assignments in one bored stroke. Then I went back to gobbling up new and historical words as part of the new book I was writing on airplanes.

When I went back to grad school, I again entered on the explicit understanding that I would take some required courses and do some required research for the chance to be allowed hunks of free time to pursue an area that no one at the school even understood. It worked. So well, in fact, that I literally walked into a job working with the guy who my previous research had shown to be tops in the field.

And now I find some strange truths. With the top-notch people that make up our company, *what counts is the ability to teach oneself* [Author's emphasis]. As my employer puts it, "Though we may seem to know a lot around here, we succeed because we start out by admitting our ignorance, and then setting out to overcome it."

This points up one important idea, the "need to know." People often say of me that I "know" a great deal about this or that; but often

I have only average knowledge or less. In any given context, however, I can identify what I need to know next, and self-reliance has taught me to immediately acquire the knowledge in ways which do not essentially differ from one case to the next. Thus it occurs to me that if people recognized knowledge as being important *only in relation to actual goals*—narrow or broad in scope—rather than being some kind of unquestionable goal in itself, they might better know how to go about acquiring it.

I know more than a few individuals who share my experience. Their existence assures me that a market exists for free schools offering not "teachers" but *the resources necessary for self-teaching*.

THE SHORT, HAPPY LIFE OF A TEACHING MACHINE

When the Santa Fe Community School was just starting, a young inventor, who hoped to market one of the "teaching machines" then in fashion, lent one of his models to the school. It was a big metal box, that sat on top of a table. Through a window in the front of the box, one could see a printed card. Beside the window were five numbered buttons. On the card one might read something like this: "An apple is a (1) machine, (2) animal, (3) fruit, (4) fish, (5) musical instrument." If one pushed button #3, a little green light went on above the buttons, and a new card appeared behind the window. If one pushed any of the other buttons, a red light went on. Like most teaching machines, it was only a fancy way of giving multiple choice tests.

On the day the inventor brought the box to school the children, aged five through eight, gathered around to see how it worked. The inventor showed them how to use it, and for a while the children took turns pushing the buttons and answering the questions on the cards. This only lasted a short while. Then the children began to say, "Open the box!

We want to see inside the box!" Someone opened up the front panel, showing the cards, mounted on a revolving drum. Beside each card were five little holes, and a metal plug to stick into the hole matching the "right answer" to the question on the card.

The children considered all this a minute, and then fell to work— *making cards*. After a while they all had some cards to load into the machine. Bargains were struck: "I'll play using your cards if you'll play using mine." One child would load up the machine with his cards and put in the answer buttons, then another child would come and take the test, then they would trade places. This went on for perhaps a day or so, all very serious.

Then, so the friend told me who was teaching there at the same school and saw all this, the game began to change. There was much loud laughter around the machine. The teachers went to see what was going on. What they saw was this. A child would load the machine, as before, and another child would take the test. Up would come a card saying something like, "A dog is a (1) train, (2) car, (3) airplane, (4) animal, (5) fish." The child taking the test would press button #4, the "right answer," and *the red light would go on*. The child who had made the card, and others watching, would shriek with laughter. The child being tested would push the buttons, one by one, until he hit the "right" one and the drum turned up the next card. Then, same story again, another right answer rewarded with the red light, more laughter. When one child had run through all his rigged cards, the other would have a turn, and would do exactly the same thing.

This happy game went on for a day or two. Then the children, having done everything with the machine that could be done with it, grew bored with it, turned away from it, and never touched it again. After a month or so the school asked the inventor to take his machine away.

This little incident tells us more about the true nature of children (and so, all humans) than fifty years' worth of Pavlovian behaviorist or Skinnerian operant conditioning experiments. Maybe Psychologist and

Pigeon is a good game, for a while at least. But all human beings soon want to play Psychologist; no one wants to be the Pigeon. We humans are not by nature like sheep or pigeons, unquestioning, docile, happy to work the machine as long as it lights up its green lights or rolls out its food pellets. Like these children, we want to find out how the machine works, and then *work it*. We want to find out how things happen, so that we can make them happen. That is the kind of creature we are. Any theory of learning or teaching which begins by assuming that we are some wormlike or ratlike or pigeonlike creature is nonsense and can only lead (as it has and does) to endless frustration and failure.

LEARNING A NEW LANGUAGE

Young children who come into contact with people who speak more than one language will learn to speak all of those languages, usually without much trouble. Older people, who have a great deal of trouble, are amazed by this. To explain it, they invent fancy theories about children having a special aptitude, or their brains being somehow different from adults'.

The real explanation is simpler. The child, who in his home speaks language A, but meets outside the home other children who speak language B, does not in any way set himself the task of "learning language B." In fact, he does not think of himself as "speaking language A," or indeed any language. He just speaks. He tries to understand what people are saying, and to make them understand what he wants to say, and the more he does this, the better he gets.

Now, all of a sudden, he meets some people whom he can't understand at all, and who can't understand him. What he wants and tries to do is understand those people, at least a little, *right now*, and to make them understand him, at least a little, *right now*. That is what he works at, and since he is smart, tireless, ingenious, not much discouraged by difficulties, and not at all worried about "failing" or looking foolish, and since he gets instant responses to tell him whether he is understanding or being understood, he very quickly gets good at it.

His parents think how wonderful it is that he is learning language B so quickly. But he is not trying to do that. He would not understand what it meant to "learn a language," and would not know how to do such a task even if people could explain to him what the task was. He is just trying to communicate with those people he meets.

After my father had retired from business, he and my mother began to spend the winter half of each year in Mexico. My father, who had been—just barely—a good enough student to graduate from a "good" college, told himself sternly, and kept telling himself for six years and more, that he ought to "learn Spanish." My mother, who had not gone to college and had been a poor student—she had always been terribly nearsighted, but beyond that was bored to death by the tasks of school—could not have cared less about "learning Spanish." What she wanted, like little children, was to be able to talk to these people around her, who were not at all like any of the people she had ever known, and who interested her very much. She had always had a small child's keenness of observation and sharpness of mind, and now, like a young child, she began to try to talk to the people around her, to ask the names of things, to ask *how* to ask the names of things. The people she talked to, enchanted as people always are by someone who makes a real effort to speak their language, talked back, showed her things and told her their names (as they did to me when I visited), gently corrected her mistakes in pronunciation or usage, not so that she would speak "correctly" but only so that she would be better understood, and helped her in every way they could. The result was that very soon she could talk easily and fluently with people on many subjects.

At the same time, my father, who thought of himself as trying to "learn Spanish," which meant to learn to speak it correctly, so that *then* he could talk to the people around him, never learned more than twenty or so words in all the years he lived in Mexico. Now and then my mother tried to get him to say a few words to the people he met. He couldn't do it. He was struck dumb by his school-learned fear of doing it wrong, making a mistake, looking foolish or stupid. He backed away from all these human contacts, telling himself all the while that he really ought to learn Spanish but was just too old, didn't have the aptitude, and so on.

LEARNING MUSIC

The October 5, 1977, issue of *Manas* magazine quotes this interesting fragment from the book *Piano: Guided Sight Reading* by Leonard Deutsch:

> The famous Hungarian and Slovak gypsies have a centuries-old musical tradition. This colorful folk has brought forth numerous excellent instrumentalists, notably violinists. They learn to play much as an infant learns to walk—without teaching methods, lessons, or drills. No written music is used. The youngster is merely given a small fiddle and *allowed to join the gypsy band* [Author's emphasis]. He gets no explanations or corrections. He causes no disturbance, for his timid efforts are scarcely audible. He listens: he tries to play simultaneously what he hears, and gradually succeeds in finding the right notes and producing a good tone. Within a few years he has developed into a full-fledged member of the band with complete command of his instrument.
>
> Are these gypsy children particularly gifted? No, almost any child could accomplish what they do. The band acts as teacher talking to the pupil in the direct language of music. The novice, by joining the band, is immediately placed in the most helpful musical atmosphere

and psychological situation; thus, from the beginning, he finds the right approach to music activity.

In contrast, an extremely intelligent and capable friend, not at all daunted by most forms of learning, and a lover of music, once told me that she wished she could read music, but that ever since she had been taught music in school, the task had seemed hopelessly mysterious, terrifying, and impossible. I asked her if she could think of any special part of it that seemed harder than the rest. Like most people in that position who are asked that question, she made a large gesture and said, "All of it. I just don't understand *anything* about what those little dots mean on the page." I asked if it was the rhythm or the pitch that seemed most mysterious. After some thought, she said, "The pitch." I then said (there was a piano handy), "If you like, I think I can show you in a few minutes how to find any written note." She agreed. Within half an hour she was very slowly playing, by herself, a piece out of a beginning piano instruction book.

Five things made it possible for me to help her find out how to do this. (1) It was her idea, her interest; *she* wanted to do it. (2) I was at all times ready to stop if she wanted to. She knew I would not, in my enthusiasm for teaching, push her into the confusion, panic, and shame into which eager or determined teachers so often push their students. (3) I accepted as legitimate and serious both her anxiety and her confusion. Even in the privacy of my own mind, I did not dismiss any of her fears or questions as silly. (4) I was ready to let *her* ask all the questions, to wait for her answers, and to let her use my answers as she wished. *I did not test her understanding.* I let her decide whether she understood, and if not, what to do about it, what question to ask next. (5) I was not going to *use* her to prove to her or myself or anyone else what a gifted teacher I was. If she wants to explore written music further, fine. If she wants to ask me for more help, that's fine too—though even better if, as I suspect, she can do it without my help. But if, having proved to herself that she *can* figure out what notes mean, she doesn't want to do more of it—well, that's fine too.

In an article entitled "Violinist Par Excellence," in *Music Magazine*, February 1980, a great violinist talks about teaching:

Nathan Milstein says his own family in Odessa was not particularly musical. "They became musical eventually," he laughed. "But I don't think a musical family makes much of a difference." His mother wanted him to play violin not because she was musical, but because, as he said once, she "wanted to calm me down and she thought the violin would do it."

Later, he taught his younger brother how to play the cello. "It wasn't difficult. If somebody's smart and knows music, he can do it. I could teach him because I played the same family of instrument: violin, cello, it's the same, only you put your fingers further apart. People exaggerate everything."

Like many artists, Milstein suspects that even the role of teachers is exaggerated. "A teacher doesn't help much. Not many teachers do. Young people often think that if they go to a teacher, the teacher will tell them how to play. No! Nobody can tell you. A teacher may play very well in one way, but his student might not be able to play as well if he is taught to play the same way. That's why I think that the teacher's business is to explain to the pupil, especially the gifted ones, that the teacher can't do very much except to try to open the pupil's mind so that he can develop his own thinking. The fact is that the pupils have to do it. They have to do the job; not the teacher."

Looking back, Milstein admits that none of his teachers were particularly helpful in this way. "But you see," he explains, "I was always very curious and experimenting. Instinctively I thought that if I will not help myself my teacher will not help me."

…The worst teachers, in Milstein's opinion, are those who are not performers themselves. "Performers can give students more than any professor who is in the Curtis Institute or in the Juilliard School," he says vehemently. "Because you can only give something to a young person from your own experience. Teachers who don't perform, who never studied for a career, how do they know? I know of famous teachers in America that are ruining young people. Ruining!" By contrast, Milstein does not think that a very gifted person will be ruined by not having a teacher.

SELF-TEACHING

A teacher in Vancouver writes:

I saw an interesting thing this past week. I was down at a little storefront place called the Community Computer Institute (a small business which rents time on computers—the little personal ones—for very good rates: they also have self-teaching programs which you can use to have the computer teach you how to use the computer). While I was there an older man and a young boy, about 11, came in and were looking around. The kid was fascinated and the man was a little perplexed and amazed, "They're finally here…my, my…." However, the kid began to show the man some games on one of the simpler computers and within a few minutes both were engrossed in a major "Star Trek" game. After the game the kid explained some rudimentary principles of programming to the man, who by this time was very interested.

So was I, because here was a classic example of a teaching/learning situation between two people without regard for age, roles, or formal structure. I felt very good watching this whole episode and wondered what kind of things we could invent to facilitate this kind of thing happening throughout the city. I tried to explain this to some of the teachers I work with and they just ignored me. "That's not real learning and it just gets in the way of teaching them math skills." Here was an 11-year-old kid who had taught himself more about computers than I know, just by hanging around this place before it officially opened (so they let him use the computers for free) and by reading simple articles about programming. And they tell me that it's not real learning!

A mother writes more about "real learning":

The best thing I wanted to share with you is that E is reading. I was prepared to see him a nonreader still at the age of 10, 12—who could tell? He was fascinated with the shapes of letters on his father's truck when he was two, picked out letter shapes in sidewalk cracks, read short words on signs, played games with beginning sounds (his idea, not mine), and generally always liked words.

Getting from that stage to actually reading books left a blank in my mind. If he didn't want me to help him, didn't sit down and work at it, how was he going to read beyond the shopping center signs stage? It must be at this stage that school people nervously rush in with methods and phonics rules, and at times I had to stop myself from doing the same. Teaching habits die hard. He knew so much! But he wasn't pulling it all together, wasn't even interested in opening a book to see if he could read the whole thing. I was dying of curiosity to see if he could, but I kept biting my lip every time a "lesson" threatened to come out.

He started about three months ago curling up with a comic book in the magazine section of the supermarket every week. Sometimes he'd buy one, and after we read it to him once, he'd take it off to a corner and study it for a while. He began "reading" them in bed. I knew something was happening because he got very quiet at these times, never asked me what a word was, and never made comments on the pictures. It became clear to me that reading was a private thing to him. After a while, he picked out easy books for bedtime reading and offered to read them to me. There were very few words he didn't know, and I'll never know how he learned the others. But it doesn't matter. He did it because he wanted to. I just hope I can keep on resisting all the pressures to do otherwise and let him set his own priorities.

One of our readers tells us about his brother's learning:

My brother is an electronics technician, by trade, and an electronics whiz by vocation. While still a teenager he *taught himself* all the mathematics, language, etc., necessary and built many complicated things—an oscilloscope, a computer, etc. He is now making a lot of money (I am not!) as a skilled technician (I am not!) while continuing to develop his own very creative ideas in electronics in his free time, with his own equipment, at home.

TEACHING VERSUS LEARNING

In "Vernacular Values and Education," a chapter in his book *Shadow Work*, Ivan Illich wrote of a man he had visited:

This man…had ceased to be a parent and had become a total teacher. In front of their own children this couple stood *in loco magistri*. Their children had to grow up without parents, because these two adults, in every word they addressed to their two sons and one daughter, were "educating" them—they were at dinner constantly conscious that they were modeling the speech of their children, and asked me to do the same.[50]

Volume 3, numbers 5 and 6, of *The Home and School Institute Newsletter* talks about things people can do with children at home. At first glance, many of them seem very sensible and pleasant, things that many loving and observing mothers have been doing for years.

BEDROOM—READING

Dress Me and Body All (vocabulary builders). There are words that attach to clothing—shirt, blouse, sock, shoe, etc.—and there are words attached to body parts—foot, arm, head, knee, etc. The bedroom is a fine place to learn these words; say the words aloud as clothes go off parts of bodies, print the words on large pieces of paper and label clothes in closets and drawers.

Well, yes, perhaps. It all depends on the spirit in which this is done. If you like babies and little children, and on the whole, I do, it is fun to talk to them about the things you are seeing or doing together. In *How Children Learn* I said that many mothers (or other adults) getting a small child ready to go out might say something like:

"Now we'll tie up this shoe; pull the laces good and tight; now we'll get the boots; let's see, the right boot for the right foot, then the left boot for the left foot; all right, coat next, arms in the sleeves, zip it up, nice and tight; now the mittens, left mitten on the left hand, right mitten on the right hand; now comes the hat, on it goes, over your ears." This kind of talk is companionable and fun, and from it the child learns, not just words, but the kinds of phrases and sentences they fit into.

But I'm afraid that the real point of this, that the talk *was* companionable and fun, a way for the mother to express in words some of her love for the child and pleasure in its company, may have been lost. In this mother's voice, as I hear it in my mind's ear, I can hear tones of pleasure and excitement, the words matching the action, perhaps a sympathetic grunt as she tugs at a stuck zipper or pulls on a boot, the whole thing underlined with many an affectionate squeeze or pat. This is not at all the same thing as saying, as we put on the child's coat, "Coat! Coat! Coat!" so that the child will "learn that this is a coat." The difference is between talk which is done for the pleasure itself, with learning only a possible and incidental by-product, and talk which has no purpose other than to produce learning.

From what I read elsewhere in this *Home and School Institute Newsletter*, it looks as if they have fallen solidly on the wrong side of this line:

> *Subject Bounce.* Over a fast breakfast or a sit-down dinner, play this "talk" game that prepares children for putting their thoughts into writing. Toss out a subject, start with simple ones that children know about—summer, friends, breakfast, school. The child then comes up with a statement about it; examples, "Summer is the best season," or "Friends like the same things you do." As children build sophistication, their subjects and statements get more sophisticated, too.

Awful! Reading this, I understand and share the real horror that Illich felt at his friend's dining room table. Years before I began teaching, I spent an evening with parents of young children in a home in which nothing was said or done without some kind of "teaching" purpose. Every word or act carried its little lesson. It was nightmarish, the air quivered with tension and worry. I could not wait to leave.

Life is full of ironies. I wrote *How Children Learn* hoping to help introduce the natural, effortless, and effective ways of learning of the happy home into the schools. At times I fear I may only have helped to bring the strained, self-conscious, painful, and ineffective ways of learning of the schools into the home. To parents I say, above all else, don't let your home become some terrible miniature copy of the school. No lesson plans! No quizzes! No tests! No report cards! Even leaving your children alone would be better; at least they could figure out some things on their own. Live together, as well as you can; enjoy life together, as much as you can. Ask questions to find out something about the world itself, not to find out whether or not someone knows it.

THE PRICE OF TEACHING TRICKS

Dr. Gregory Bateson, one of the most learned and creative intellectuals of our time, who in his life studied and wrote a great deal in anthropology, psychology, and other fields, summed up much of his life's work and thought in the book *Steps to an Ecology of Mind*. In one chapter, discussing the difficulties of communicating with dolphins and other animals, he says,

> [There are] very special difficulties in the problem of how to test what is called the "psychology" (e.g., intelligence, ingenuity, discrimination, etc.) of individual animals. A simple experiment...involves a series of steps: (1) the dolphin may or may not perceive a difference between the stimulus objects, X and Y. (2) The dolphin may or may not perceive that this difference is a cue to behavior. (3) The dolphin may or may not perceive that the behavior in question has a good or bad effect upon reinforcement, that is, that doing "right" is conditionally followed by fish. (4) The dolphin may or may not choose to do "right," even after he knows which is right. Success in the first three steps merely provides the dolphin with a further choice point....
>
> Precisely because we want to argue from observation of the animal's success in the later steps to conclusions about the more elementary steps, it becomes of prime importance to know whether the organism with which we are dealing is capable of step 4. If it is capable, then all arguments about steps 1 through 3 will be invalidated unless appropriate methods of controlling step 4 are built into the experimental approach. Curiously enough, though human beings are fully capable of step 4, psychologists working with human subjects have been able to study steps 1 through 3 without taking special care to exclude the confusions introduced by this fact.[51]

In other words, as a rule, when psychologists ask a human subject to do some task, and the subject does not do it, they tend to assume it is because he cannot do it. This makes it quite easy for subjects, especially if they are people from whom the psychologists expect little, to fool their testers. In *Dibs In Search of Self,* Virginia Axline tells about a very capable six-year-old boy who had been able to make a number of experts in such matters think, wrongly, that he was autistic, illiterate, and all but incapable of speech. In *The Naked Children*, Daniel Fader tells of some black students in a Washington, DC, junior high school who by their behavior and test scores had tricked their teachers into thinking, again wrongly, that they could barely read, could not speak Standard English, and indeed could speak little English of any kind.

Bateson goes on to say:

> Let me now consider for a moment the art of the animal trainer. From conversations with these highly skilled people—trainers of both dolphins and guide dogs—my impression is that the first requirement of a trainer is that he must be able to prevent the animal from exerting choice at the level of step 4. It must continually be made clear to the animal that, when he knows what is the right thing to do in a given context, that is the only thing he *can* do, and no nonsense about it. In other words, it is a primary condition of circus success that the animal shall abrogate the use of certain higher levels of his intelligence.[52]

My uncle by marriage, Grove Cullum, an officer in the US Cavalry, expert horseman and lover of horses, made this point more bluntly. One day in conversation I happened to make some remark about horses being intelligent. "Goodness, no," he laughed, "they're not intelligent. If they were, they'd never let us ride them."

In 1959 or so, teaching fifth-graders in a very exclusive private school, which with rare exceptions would not even admit children with IQs of less than 120, I wrote, "School is a place where children learn to be stupid." I could see it was so, but didn't know why. What was it

)out even this very high-powered, child-centered, "creative" school, that made children stupid? I came to feel, as I wrote in *How Children Fail*, that it was fear, boredom, and the confusion of having constantly to manipulate meaningless words and symbols. I now see that it was that, but far more than that, the fact that *others had taken control of their minds*. It was being *taught*, in the sense of being trained like circus animals to do tricks on demand, that had made them stupid (at least in school).

On the basis of much experience, Bateson says this is true of all creatures, and I agree. The elephant in the jungle is smarter than the elephant waltzing in the circus. The sea lion in the sea is smarter than the sea lion playing "My Country, 'Tis of Thee" on some instrument. The rat eating garbage in the slums is smarter than the rat running mazes in the psychology lab. The crawling baby, touching, handling, tasting everything it can reach, is smarter than the baby learning, because it pleases his mother, to touch his nose when she shows him a card with NOSE written on it.

The most important question any thinking creature can ask itself is, "What is worth thinking about?" When we deny its right to decide that for itself, when we try to control what it must attend to and think about, we make it less observant, resourceful, and adaptive, in a word, less intelligent, in a blunter word, more stupid.

This may be the place to answer a question that by now many people have asked me: What do I think of baby training books—teach your baby this, teach your baby that, make your baby a genius? I am against them. The tricks they tell parents to teach their babies to do are not necessary, not particularly helpful, and if continued very long, probably quite harmful. The trouble with teaching babies tricks, even the trick of reading, is that the more we do this, the more they think that learning means and can only mean *being taught by others to do tricks*, and the less they want to or can explore and make sense of the world around them in their own ways and for their own reasons.

I don't doubt for a second that the experts in teach[...] can indeed teach them an impressive variety of tri[...] still quite young. But this has little or nothing to do with [...] or the capacity for it. Intelligence, as I wrote in *How Children Fail*, the measure of how much we know how to do, but of how we behave when we don't know what to do. It has to do with our ability to think up important questions and then to find ways to get useful answers. This ability is not a trick that can be taught, nor does it need to be. We are born with it, and if our other deep animal needs are fairly well satisfied, and we have reasonable access to the world around us, we will put it to work on that world.

8

LEARNING DIFFICULTIES

DISABILITIES VERSUS DIFFICULTIES

I HAVE INCLUDED THIS SHORT CHAPTER, which may someday be part of a longer work on this subject, for several reasons. In the first place, parents who teach their children at home may find now and then that some of them do things like writing letters or spelling words backward or showing some confusion about right and left. Such parents should not become alarmed, or assume that something serious is wrong with their child, or that they must throw the whole matter into the hands of "expert" specialists. In the second place, parents who have already sent children to school may be told that their children have such problems. Such parents, again, should not panic and should be extremely skeptical of anything the schools and their specialists may say about their children and their condition and needs. Above all, they should understand that it is almost certainly the school itself and all its tensions and anxieties that are causing these difficulties, and that the best treatment for them will probably be to take the child out of school altogether. In the third place, parents should resist the general claim on the part of schools that only they are competent to teach children because only they are able to tell which children have learning disabilities and if so, what must be done about them.

To school people and others who talk to me about "learning disabilities," I usually ask a question something like this:

> How do you tell the difference between a learning *difficulty* (which we all experience every time we try to learn anything) and a learning *disability*? That is to say, how do you tell, or on what basis does someone decide (and who is the someone?) whether the cause of a given learning difficulty lies within the nervous system of the learner, or with things outside of the learner—the learning situation, the teacher's explanations, the teacher him/herself, or the material itself? And if you decide that the cause of the difficulty lies within the learner, who decides, and again on what basis, whether or not that inferred cause is curable, in short, whether anything can be done about it, and if so, what?

If any readers ask these questions of schools, I would like very much to know what answers they get. I have never received any coherent answers to these questions. What I usually get instead are angry insistences that learning disabilities are "real," that is to say, built into the nervous systems of children. Here are some of my reasons for thinking they are not, and instead, what may be some of their true causes, and what we might sensibly do about them.

NOBODY SEES BACKWARD

A few years ago a national magazine ran a full-page ad for some organization dealing with so-called learning disabilities. At the top of the ad, in large letters, were the words, SEE HOW JOHNNY READS. Then a photo of an open children's book printed in very large print, large enough so that people reading the ad could read the book. The story was "The Three Little Pigs." But many of the letters in the story had been shifted and turned around in odd ways. Some were upside-down or backward. Sometimes two adjacent letters in a word had been put in reverse order. Sometimes an entire word was spelled backward. Then, beneath the photo, again in large letters, the words THINK HOW JOHNNY FEELS. Then some text about all the children suffering from "learning disabilities" and all the things the organization was doing to cure or help them.

The message was plain. We were being asked to believe that large numbers of children in the United States, when they looked at a book, saw something like the photo in the ad, and so, could not read it. Also, that this organization could and would do something about this—it was not clear just what—if we gave it enough support.

I looked again at the children's book in the photo. I found that I could read it without much trouble. Of course, I had two advantages over this mythical "Johnny": I could already read, and I already knew the story. I read it a bit more slowly than I ordinarily would; now and then I had to puzzle out a word, one letter at a time. But it was not hard to do.

This was by no means the first time I had heard the theory that certain children have trouble learning to read because something inside their skins or skulls, a kind of Maxwell's demon (a phrase borrowed from physics) of the nervous system, every so often flipped letters upside-down or backward, or changed their order. I had never taken any stock in this theory. It failed the first two tests of any scientific theory: (1) that it be plausible on its face; (2) that it be the most obvious or likely explanation of the facts. This theory seemed and still seems totally implausible, for many more reasons than I will go into here. And there are much simpler and more likely explanations of the facts.

The facts that this theory set out to account for are only these: certain children, usually just learning to read and write, when asked to write down certain letters or words, wrote some letters backward, or reversed the order of two or more letters in a word, or spelled entire words backward—though it is important to note that most children who spell words backward do not at the same time reverse all the individual letters.

I was too busy with other work to take time to think how to prove this theory wrong. But for a while I taught in a school right next door to what was then supposed to be one of the best schools for "learning disability" (hereafter LD) children in New England. I began to note that in that particular learning hospital no one was ever cured. Children went in not knowing how to read and came out years later still not knowing. No one seemed at all upset by this. Apparently this school was felt to be "the best" because it had better answers than anyone else to the question, "Once you have decided that certain children can't learn to read, what do you do with them all day in a place which calls itself a school?" Later, when I was working full-time lecturing to groups about educational change, I had other contacts with other LD believers and experts. The more I saw and heard of them, the less I believed in them. But I was still too busy to spend much time arguing with them or even thinking about them.

Then one morning in Boston, as I was walking across the Public Garden toward my office, my subconscious mind asked me a question. First it said, "The LD people say that these children draw letters, say, a P, backward because when they look at the correct P they *see* it backward. Let's put all this in a diagram.

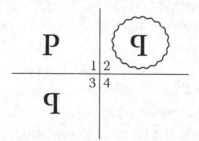

"In space #1 is the correct P which the child is asked to copy. In space #3 is the backward P which he draws, because (we are told) this is the way he sees it. All right; in space #2 we will put what the child supposedly sees when he looks at the correct P in space #1." (The wavy line represents perception.)

Then came the $64,000 question.

"Now, what does the child see when he looks at the backward P in space #3, the P that he has drawn?"

I stopped dead in my tracks. I believe I said out loud, "Well, I'll be d——!" For obviously, if his mind reverses all the shapes he looks at, the child, when he looks at the backward P in space #3, *will see a correct P!*

So our diagram would wind up looking like this:

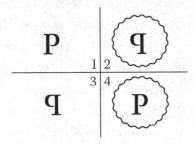

This imaginary child, if he did what the LD experts say he does, would look at P#1, see P#2, draw P#3, and *looking at that, see P#4.* What he had drawn would not look *to him* like what he was trying to copy. He would think to himself, "I made a mistake," and would draw his P the other way around. At least, he would do so if, as the LD people claim, his drawing was an accurate copy of what he perceived. Even if his mind reversed every shape it saw, *a backward P would still look backward to him*! To put it still more broadly and fundamentally, we cannot tell by looking at the shapes people draw whether or not they perceive shapes backward, *since they would draw the same shapes in either case*!

So the "perceptual handicap," "he-draws-backward-because-he-sees-backward" theory, goes down the drain. It does not explain what it was invented to explain. Nor does it explain anything else—this event, the child drawing the letters backward, is all the evidence that supports it. Why then does this obviously false theory persist? Because, for many reasons, it is very convenient to many people—to parents, to teachers, to schools, to LD experts and the giant industry that has grown up around them—sometimes even to the children. The theory may not help anyone learn to read, but it keeps a lot of people busy, makes a lot of people richer, and makes almost everyone feel better. Theories that do all that are not easy to get rid of.

But then, why does the child draw the P backward? If he is not, as I have shown, reproducing the shape that he perceives, what is he doing?

The answer is plain enough to anyone who has watched little children when they first start making letters. Slowly, hesitantly, and clumsily, they try to turn what they see into a "program," a set of instructions for the hand holding the pencil, and then try to make the hand carry out the instructions. This is what we all do when we try to draw something. We are not walking copying machines. When we try to draw a chair, we do not "copy" it. We look at it a while and then "tell" our hand to draw, say, a vertical line of a certain height. Then we look at the chair again, then back at the paper, then "tell" our hand to go halfway up the vertical line, and from that point draw a line of a certain length in a certain direction. Then we look back at the chair for more instructions. If, like trained artists, we are good at turning what we see into instructions for our hand, we will produce a good likeness of the chair. If, like most of us, we are not good at it, we will not.

In the same way, the child looks at the P. He sees there is a line in it that goes up and down. He looks at the paper and tells his hand, "Draw an up and down line," then draws it. He looks back at the P, then tells his hand to go to the top of the up and down line and then draw a line out to the side. This done, he looks back at the P, and sees that the line going out to the side curves down and around after a while and then goes back in until it hits the up and down line again. He tells his hand to do that.

As you can tell watching a little child do this, it may take him two or three tries to get his pencil all the way around the curve. Sometimes the curve will reverse direction in the middle, and that will have to be fixed up. Eventually he gets his line back to the up and down line.

At this point, most children will compare the two Ps, the one they looked at and the one they made. Many of them, if they drew their P backward, may see right away that it *is* backward, doesn't look quite the same, is pointing the wrong way—however they may express this in their minds. Other children may be vaguely aware that the shapes are not pointing the same way, but will see this as a difference *that doesn't make any difference*, just as for my bank the differences between one of my signatures and another are differences that don't make any difference.

In thinking that this difference doesn't make any difference, the children are being perfectly sensible. After all, they have been looking at pictures of objects, people, animals, and so on for some time. They know that a picture of a dog is a picture of a dog, whether the dog is facing right or left. They also understand, without words, that the image on the page, the picture of dog, cat, bicycle, cup, spoon, and so forth, stands for an object that can be moved, turned around, looked at from different angles. It is therefore perfectly reasonable for children to think of the picture of a P on the page as standing for a P-shaped object with an existence of its own, an object which could be picked up, turned around, turned upside-down, and the like. Perhaps not all children feel this equally strongly. But for those who do, to be told that a "backward" P that they have drawn is "wrong," or that it isn't a P at all, must be very confusing and even frightening. If you can draw a horse, or dog, or cat, or car pointing any way you want, why can't you draw a P or B or E any way you want? Why is it "right" to draw a dog facing toward the left, but "wrong" to draw a P facing that way?

What we should do, then, is be very careful *never* to use the words *right* and *wrong* in these reversal situations. If we ask a child to draw a P, and he draws a T, we could say, "No, that's not a P, that's a T." But if we ask him to draw a P, and he draws one pointing to the left, we should say, "Yes, that's a P, but when we draw a picture of a P we *always* draw it pointing this way. It isn't like a dog or a cat, that we can draw pointing either way." Naturally, there's no need to give this little speech to children who never draw letters backward. Indeed the chances are very good that children who start off drawing certain letters backward would, as with errors in their speech, eventually notice the difference between their Ps and ours and correct it, if we didn't make such a fuss about it. But if we are fainthearted and feel we have to say something about backward Ps, it ought to be something like the above.

However, I strongly suspect that most children who often reverse letters do not in fact *compare* shapes. Like so many of the children I have known and taught, they are anxious, rule-bound, always in a panicky search for what the grown-ups want. What they do is turn the P they are looking at into a set of instructions, memorize the instructions, and then compare the P they have drawn against the instructions. "Did I do it right? Yes, there's the line going up and down, and there's the line going out sideways from the top, and there it's curving around and there it's coming back into the up and down line again. I obeyed the rules and did it right, so it must *be* right."

Or perhaps they may try to compare shapes, but are too anxious to see them clearly. Or perhaps, as with anxious people, by the time they have shifted their eyes from the original P to the P they have drawn, they have forgotten the original P, or dare not trust the memory of it that they have. This feeling of suddenly not being able to trust one's own memory is common enough, and above all when one is anxious. Now and then I find myself looking up a phone number two or three times in a row, because each time I start to dial the number I have the panicky thought, "Did I remember it right?" Usually I can only break out of this foolish cycle by saying to myself, "Right or wrong, dial it anyway." It usually turns out to be right. But I can understand how a certain kind of self-distrusting person (by no means rare) might go through this process a great many times. I am sure that many of the failing students I have taught have had somewhere in their minds the permanent thought, "If I think of it, it must be wrong."

It is possible, too, that a child, making up a set of instructions for his hand, might try to use the ideas of Right and Left, but with some of the confusions I will talk about later in this chapter, so that "right" when he was looking at the P might mean the opposite of "right" when he was drawing it. The fact remains that whatever may be children's reasons for drawing letters backward, there is no reason whatever to believe that seeing them backward is one of them.

STRESS AND PERCEPTION

We can tell a good deal about the competence of a particular group of experts by the kinds of research they do or do not do.

In World War I we first began to see evidence that prolonged anxiety, stress, and fear can have great destructive effects on the human nervous system. The trenches were a kind of satanic laboratory of stress. More soldiers than ever before lived for much longer times than ever before in cold and wet conditions, with the constant threat of death, often under continuous heavy bombardment. As a result, many suffered a disorder that doctors called "shell shock." Some became totally blind, or deaf, others became paralyzed, shook all over, lost all control of their muscles and limbs. The authorities first suspected faking, but it was soon clear that these soldiers were not faking. The only cure for these ailments, which in many cases looked like physical disorders, was to take these men away from the stress of the battle front. After some time in a safe and calm place, they regained to varying degrees their sight, hearing, and use and control of their limbs. Many were even able to go back to the front.

In World War II this happened again. Many of the British troops who spent days on the beaches at Dunkirk, under continuous bombardment from both guns and planes, broke under this stress in exactly the same way. The doctors of World War II called their condition "psychoneurosis." The cure was basically the same—to remove the afflicted men from the scene of stress and danger.

In the years since then, all kinds of other evidence has begun to accumulate that stress can cause what seem to be physical disabilities. In my own work I began to see, not only among the children I taught but also in myself as I struggled for the first time to learn a musical instrument, that anxiety could make it much harder for people to think, to remember, or even to see. In *How Children Fail* I described how one day, under pressure, I totally lost for a short time the ability to see meaningfully. Five years later, in *The Lives of Children*, George Dennison described, in the most painful and almost clinical detail, the effects of stress and fear on one of his pupils.

So it was reasonable to suppose, when educators began to claim that some children might be having trouble learning because of "perceptual handicaps," that they might look for possible connections between such inferred handicaps and children's fears and anxieties. As far as I have been able to learn, very few of them have yet done so.

Not long ago I was one of many speakers at a large conference of specialists in learning disabilities. Before more than a thousand people I reviewed the evidence for a connection between anxiety and perceptual or other learning disorders. I spoke of the medical experience of two world wars and of my own experience as a teacher and as a beginning learner of music. Then I asked for a show of hands in response to this question: "How many of you have heard of—only heard of, not done—any research on possible connections between perceptual handicaps in children and their anxiety, however measured? How many have heard of any research to find whether and to what degree lowering measurable anxiety in children might lessen the incidence of perceptual handicaps?"

In that roomful of over a thousand experts in this field, *only two peo-ple* raised their hands. What the others may have known, I do not know. But only two raised their hands.

I asked what they knew. One told me of research I had long known about, done by a man who, at least until very recently, had no degree in psychology and no standing whatever in the educational "estab-lishment." He had found high correlation between children's anxieties and perceptual handicaps, and that lowering the anxieties did indeed greatly lower the incidence of such handicaps. (He also found that diet was highly important.)

The other man who raised his hand did not speak. But later, he wrote me a letter. He is, and has been for some time, a professor of education at a leading university in the very city in which this conference was held. He too had suspected the kind of connection I talked about. He then had worked out a way of teaching reading that he thought might lessen this anxiety, had used this method to teach a group of students officially labeled "perceptually handicapped," and had found that after quite a short time in his class, in the opinion of their regular teachers, his students were much less "handicapped" than they had been before. This, I would add, in spite of the fact that his classroom was nowhere as stress-free as others I have known, or as he himself might have made it if he had not been under pressure to show some fairly quick results.

There were other questions I have asked at other places and times, but did not think to ask there. When I first heard that boys were sup-posed to be four or five times as likely to have "perceptual handicaps" or "learning disabilities" as girls, I asked in a letter published in a national magazine whether any research had been done to look for possible connections between this four- or five-to-one ratio and the sex of the teacher. I have yet to hear of any. And it would surely be interesting to see what connections there might be between the incidence of "percep-tual handicaps" in children and the measurable anxiety *of their teach-ers*. But again, as far as I know, no such research has been done.

Meanwhile, we have every reason to be extremely skeptical of the expertise of people who fail or refuse to ask such questions.

One more note about the LD conference. On one of the many tables displaying books and pamphlets were copies of a newsletter published by a leading LD association. Reading one, I came across a most extraordinary sentence in an article by a former president of the association, who said that LD professionals should firmly insist that the causes of these disabilities were always neurological. She admitted that so far there was little evidence to support this idea. Then she added these remarkable words: "We must not take the absence of evidence as the evidence of absence." In other words, just because there is no evidence to support our theory doesn't mean that we shouldn't continue to push it.

THE "SEEING-BACKWARD" HYPOTHESIS is no longer used to describe dyslexia, and there is much evidence that dyslexia is not a neurological problem to be treated with medication. Nonetheless, John's call to first consider the learning environment instead of genetics when dealing with learning difficulties is still not considered much in US schools. Children who are overly energetic or difficult should not be drugged as the primary or preferred way of helping them cope with learning difficulties in school.

Further, prescriptions for Ritalin, Adderall, and other stimulants used to treat attention-deficit/hyperactivity disorder (ADHD) have significantly increased in the United States compared to other countries. "While the global prevalence of ADHD has remained stable for the last three decades, an increase of 26% was seen in ADHD diagnoses in US children ages 5 to 11 between 2007 and 2016, with an increase of 123% during the same period among US adults."[53] ∎

RIGHT AND LEFT

M ANY ADULTS GET UPSET and anxious about right and left. If a child writes a letter backward, or reads off some letters in the wrong order, or does anything else to suggest she is confused about right and left, adults begin to talk excitedly about "mixed dominance" and "perceptual handicaps" and "learning difficulties." The child is quickly labeled as "having a serious problem." Specialists (if the family or school can afford them) are called in and told to take over.

A child once asked me a question that not only completely surprised me, but also suggested that when children are confused about right and left, the reason may not be in them but in us, the adults, and the way *we* talk about right and left. In short, the child's confusion may make sense, and if we only understood that, we might easily straighten it out.

I was in an early elementary classroom, working with some children in a corner of the room. I needed something in my desk and asked a child please to get it for me. He said okay, and asked where it was. I said, "In the top right-hand drawer." There was a pause. Then he said, "Whose right hand, mine or the desk's?"

For an instant I was baffled. Then I saw, and understood. When he looked at the desk, it was as if he saw a living creature looking at him. So I said, "*Your* right hand." Off he went, brought back what I had asked for, and that was that.

Later, I thought that many young children must be animists, seeing objects as if they were living creatures. I wondered how many of them might have had that same question in their minds, without ever asking it. And if they didn't ask it, how did they ever learn the answer? Probably from experience. They went to the desk, looked in *its* right-hand drawer, found nothing, looked in *their* right-hand drawer, found what they wanted, and so learned which was meant, like the infant I described in *How Children Learn*, who at the table asked people to pass the salt, pepper, butter, and so on, so that by seeing what was passed she could find out what those words meant.

But some children might not interpret the desk experience in that way. They might assume that the adult had made a mistake about the drawer. Or they might think that they themselves had made a mistake about which was right and which was left. The kind of children who worried about mistakes, because their parents or teachers worried, might be particularly ready to blame themselves for any confusion.

Only recently, as I began to think more about this, did I realize that our adult rules about right and left are even more confused than I had thought. Thus, when we ask a child to get something out of our right-hand coat pocket, we mean the coat's right hand, not the child's. When we talk about the right headlight of a car, we mean the car's right. But the right-hand entrance to a house is *our* right hand, not the house's. We adults talk sometimes as if things were people, and sometimes as if they were not, and there's little rhyme or reason in the way we do this. Why should a car or boat or train have its own right side, but not a house?

In the theater, of course, the confusion about whether the audience's or the actors' right or left is meant led people to invent the notion of "stage right" and "stage left" to mean the right or left of the actors as they looked at the audience.

Under photos of groups of people, we see, "Reading from left to right, Jones, Smith, Brown, etc." A child being shown such photos might hear someone say, "That's me over on the right." Our right as we look at it? Or the right of the group? So the people on the right are *really* on the left, and vice versa. Some children might see this as more of the world's delightful nonsense. But other children might think in panic and terror, "Why don't they make up their minds which way they want it? How do they ever expect me to get it straight?"

We might well ask, how do any of us ever get it straight. Most of us learn it the way we learn the grammar of our language, which is so subtle and complicated that (I am told) no one has yet been able to teach it to a computer. Early on children learn that the words *I, you, she,* and so on refer to different people depending on who is saying them. Not an easy thing to figure out, when you come to think about it. Yet no one ever explains that to them. Nor do they say to themselves, as they grow up, "*I* refers to the person who is talking, *you* to the person or persons talked to, *we* to both of them together, and *he, she, they, or it* to the people or things talked about." They just use the words that way, and it works.

In the same way, most children don't think to themselves, "Cars, boats, coats, trains, planes, all have their own right hands, while books, photos, desks, houses do not." They just learn from experience which is which, and they don't worry much about the contradictions, just as most French children don't worry about why a house should be feminine and a building masculine, or a coat masculine and a shirt feminine.

In short, most children master the confusion of right and left because they never become aware of it, any more than I did until just a few days ago. Others may become aware of the confusion but are not troubled by it and don't feel any need to set it right or make sense of it—it's just the way things are. But some children are philosophers. They examine everything. They expect and want things to make sense, and if they don't, to find out why not. Still others are threatened and terrified by confusion and paradox, above all, by seeing people act as if something made sense when it obviously doesn't. At some deep level of their being, they wonder, "Am I the one who's crazy?"

I suspect that most of the children who have persistent trouble with right and left in school or in life are of this latter kind. After a few right-left mistakes, which they make only because they have not yet learned our crazy right-left rules, they begin to think, "I must be stupid, I never can figure out right and left." Soon they go into a blind panic every time the words come up. They work out complicated strategies of bluff and avoidance. When people ask about right and left, they learn to get other clues—"You mean the one by the window?" (Since this chapter first appeared as an article in *GWS*, many adults have told me about the tricks and devices they must rely on to keep from mixing up right and left.) In general, they assume that there is something wrong with them.

If this is true, what might we do about it? One thing we should *not* do is to set out to "teach" the rules of right and left. Most children have always figured out right and left without much teaching, other than being told when very little, "This is your right hand," "This is your left foot," and the like. Let them go on learning it that way. But if a child seems to be confused or anxious about this, then we can begin to make the rules more explicit. We can say, "I mean *your* right hand, not the desk's," or "I mean the *coat's* right hand, not yours," perhaps adding, "I know that sounds a bit crazy, but that's just the way we say it, don't worry about it, you'll get used to it."

EAST AND WEST

Thinking about right and left brought back an old memory. Years ago a teacher of geography told me of a most interesting and surprising discovery. Teachers who teach young children about maps and directions find that some pick it up quickly. But others, when shown a map and asked to point east, act like the children I described in *How Children Fail*—wave their hands in all directions while carefully reading the teacher's face for cues, watch their smart classmates, bluff, fake, wait it out, and so on. Most teachers let it go at that, thinking, "Good students, bad students, you get all kinds."

But somewhere along the line, a teacher noticed something. A few children, shown a map and asked to point east, almost always pointed wrong, *but always in the same direction.* Looking into it further, investigators found that a small percentage of people, some children, some adults, had a strong sense of direction. It was as if they had a compass in their minds or as if under their feet the ground was everywhere marked with direction lines. Whether their compass and direction lines were correctly labeled, whether the east they pointed was in fact true east, my informant did not tell me. But, asked to point a given direction, they always pointed the same way.

My mother had that kind of sense of direction. Driving without a map on strange, winding, suburban roads, when the rest of us had long since lost our bearings, she always knew about where we were, which way we were headed, and which way we needed to go to get where we wanted. An inborn gift? Perhaps, though it can probably be learned. At any rate, for children with such a gift, the question "Which way is east?" can only mean "Which way is *true* east or *world-east*?" If we understood this, we could make the distinction (which we ought to make anyway) between *world-east* and *map-east*. Once children understood the relation between maps and the territory being mapped, which we could help them see by making maps of their room, the house, the yard, the block or neighborhood, and so forth, we could then ask questions like "If you were here"—showing a point on the map—"and began to walk east, show me on the map where you'd be going." Or we could take the walk first, and then see on the map where we had walked. After doing this a few times, a child would be able to show map-east, map-north, and the like.

I talked to a teacher friend (math) about this. He laughed and said that when he was a child he thought for quite a few years that north, world-north, was straight up, and world-south straight down, since all the maps he had seen were in school, on the walls. In time, he figured it all out for himself, *by* himself.

Recently these musings about east and west have led to a new thought. Suppose there were some people who thought that right and left, like east and west, referred to something in the world itself, in short, that right meant world-right and left meant world-left. How could they ever figure out, from our talk about right and left, which was which? One minute world-right would seem to be this way, the next minute that way. We can hardly imagine their confusion and, probably, terror. Most of them would soon decide that they were just too stupid to figure out what seems so easy for everyone else. Yet they, or we, might quickly clear up all that confusion by just asking a couple of the right questions.

What to do if children seem to have these confusions? Above all, keep calm. If children show confusion about right and left, don't panic, give them plenty of time to work it out for themselves. Some small things we could do might help. When we first start telling children which is our right hand and which our left, it would probably be a good idea for us to be facing the same way, the children standing in front of us or sitting on our lap. At some point, facing the same way, we might both hold a toy in our right hand, and show that when we are facing the same way, the right hands are on the same side, but that when we turn to face each other, the right hands are on the opposite side. It would probably be better not to talk much about this as we did it. Just show it now and then, as another interesting fact about the world.

Beyond that, we should not assume, just because children do know that this is their right hand and this their left, that they understand all about right-hand drawers and coat pockets—all our strange rules about right and left. For some time, when we talk about such things, we should be sure to point out which side we mean. If the child seems to take all this in stride, we don't need to say anything and would be wiser not to. But if the child seems unduly puzzled or anxious about this, then we could make the right-left rules more explicit.

9

CHILDREN AND WORK

ON FINDING ONE'S WORK

IN HIS BOOK *Growing Up Absurd*, Paul Goodman asked (italics his): "But *the question is what it means to grow up into such a fact as 'During my productive years I will spend eight hours a day doing what is no good.'*" Later, in an essay printed in a collection of his works entitled *Nature Heals* he wrote:

> Brought up in a world where they cannot see the relation between activity and achievement, adolescents believe that everything is done with mirrors, tests are passed by tricks, achievement is due to pull, goods are known by their packages, and a man is esteemed according to his front. The delinquents who cannot read and quit school, and thereby become still less able to take part in such regular activity as is available, show a lot of sense and life when they strike out directly for the *rewards* of activity—money, glamour, and notoriety....
>
> It is disheartening indeed to be with a group of young fellows who are in a sober mood and who simply do not know what they want to

do with themselves in life. Doctor, lawyer, beggar-man, thief? Rich man, poor man, Indian chief?—they simply do not know an ambition and cannot fantasize one. But it is not true that they don't care; their "so what?" is vulnerable, their eyes are terribly balked and imploring. (I say "it is disheartening," and I mean that the tears roll down my cheeks; and I who am an anarchist and a pacifist feel that they will be happier when they are all in the army.) [54]

Paul Goodman was writing here about poor boys. But even in the more hopeful 1960s it was just about as true of affluent youth. In those days I was often asked to speak to high school assemblies, mostly in rich suburbs of big cities. What I almost always talked about was the difference between jobs, careers, and work. A job, I said, was something that you did for money, something that someone else told you to do and paid you for doing, something you would probably not have done otherwise, but did only to get the money. A career was a kind of ladder of jobs. If you did your first job for a while, made no mistakes and caused no trouble, whoever gave you that job might give you a new job, better paid, maybe slightly more interesting, or at least not so hard-dirty-dangerous. Then, if you did that job okay for a while, your boss might then give you a slightly better job, and so on. This adds up to what is called "a career."

By "work" I meant and still mean something very different, what people used to call a "vocation" or "calling"—something which seemed so worth doing for its own sake that they would gladly choose to do it even if they didn't need money and the work didn't pay. I went on to say that to find our work, in this sense, is one of the most important and difficult tasks that we have in life, and indeed, that even if we find it once we may later have to look for it again, since work that is right for us at one stage of our life may not be right for us at the next. I added that the vital questions, "What do I really want to do? What do I think is most worth doing?" are not one that the schools (or any other adults) will often urge us or help us to ask; on the whole, they feel it is their business only to prepare us for employment—jobs or careers, high or low. So we will have to find out for ourselves what work needs to be done and is being done out there in the world, and where and how we will take part in it.

As I said these things, I looked at the faces of my hearers, to sense how they felt about what I was saying. What I saw, and usually heard in the question periods that followed, made me feel that most of these students were thinking, "This guy must have just come from Mars." Work worth doing? Work that you would do even if you didn't need money, that you would do *for nothing*? For most of them it was not just impossible, it was unimaginable. They did not know, hardly even knew *of*, any people who felt that way about their work. Work was something you did for external rewards—a little pay, if you were like most people, or wealth, power, fame if you were among the fortunate.

Among all the young people I talked to, there was never, anywhere, a hopeful, positive, enthusiastic response to what I said. I cannot remember even one among all those students, the most favored young people of the (then, at least) most favored nation in the world, who said or later wrote to me, "Mr. Holt, here's what I am interested in and care about, how can I find a way to work at it?"

FINDING TRUE WORK

I was on my submarine, the USS *Barbero*, heading west for Pearl Harbor, when we first heard the news about the atomic bomb. I knew enough to know that before long any country that wanted could and would make them. It seemed clear to me that the only way to prevent the worldwide spread of nuclear weapons, and in the end nuclear war, was to have some sort of world government. When we came back to the United States in October to "mothball" our sub, I tried to find any other people who might be working in some way for world government. By the middle of the following summer I decided that I had to find a way to do this work full-time. I went to the three world government organizations to ask for a job. Two had nothing. The third had nothing at the moment, but said that in the fall the young man working in their mailroom would be going back to college and that I could have his job for $35 a week. I said I would take it. In the fall I began work, making up and sending out packages of literature, stamping the mail, keeping the membership card files, running the Addressograph machine, and doing any other odd jobs that turned up. One day I was told that the Junior Chamber of Commerce in Bayonne, New Jersey, had just asked for a speaker, on a day when all our other speakers were busy. Would I do it? I gulped and said I would. It was the first of about six hundred speeches that I was to give for the organization. Later I left the mailroom and began to work as a "field organizer," traveling about, giving speeches and trying to start local chapters.

In 1952 I left the organization, spent much of the next year living and traveling cheaply in Europe, and came home, thinking that I might try to go into farming, since even then I was very interested in what we now call ecology. My sister, who had been trying without success to persuade me to be a teacher, did persuade me to visit a small co-ed boarding school, the Colorado Rocky Mountain School, that John and Anne Holden had just opened in Carbondale, Colorado. Since the school planned to do much of its own building and food raising, she thought I might be able, while working and being paid, to learn many things I would need to know if I did go into farming. Thinking, "It can't hurt to look," I went to the school two weeks after it had opened and spent a day there, living the life of the school, going to some classes, talking to the students, helping some of them with their work, and playing soccer with them.

I liked it. My insides sent me the same message they had sent years before, when for the first time I went down into a submarine: "Right now, this is the place for you." Next day, just before I left, I said to John Holden, "You know, I like it here, and I'd like to stay and work here." He made what some might have taken as a rather negative reply: "Well, we'd be glad to have you, but the trouble is, we haven't any place to put you, and we haven't any money to pay you, and we haven't anything for you to do." In return I said, "Well, if you get some sort of roof over my head, I don't much care where you put me, and if you're feeding me I can probably live without money, for a while at least, and I'm pretty sure I can find something to do." It was an offer he couldn't refuse. He laughed and said, "If you're willing to come out here on that basis, come ahead."

Two weeks later I was back. For a month or two I lived in a little building, once a granary, that they were turning into an infirmary. I slept on a cot near a table saw, stepped over piles of sawdust to get to it, lived out of my suitcases. I found plenty to do. I began cooking breakfast for the school every day, tutoring individual students in economics, trigonometry, reading, and coaching soccer. When another teacher left to get married, I took over her room and salary (about $1,750/year). By the next year I was teaching regular classes in English and math and was the school business manager. A year later they hired a full-time business manager, but I then started teaching French as well as English and math. I taught there four years, worked hard, had a good time, learned a great deal.

The point of these stories is that many of the people who are doing serious work in the world (as opposed to just making money) are overworked and short of help. If a person, young or not so young, said to them, "I believe in the work you are doing and want to help you in any and every way I can, and I'd be glad to do any kind of work you ask me to do or that I can find to do, for very little pay, or even none at all if you can give me room and board," I suspect that many of them would say, "Sure, come right ahead." Working with them, the newcomer would gradually learn more and more about what they were doing, would find or be given more interesting and important things to do, might soon become so valuable that they would find a way to pay her or him. In any case, he or she would learn far more from working with them and being around them than in any school or college.

A FALSE START

I have a close friend whom I have known since he was in high school. His marks were good, his parents had money, so when he finished high school he naturally went to a "good" college. Since English had been his best and easiest school subject, he majored in English. Four years and $20,000 later he had his BA degree. What next? Well, his marks were still good, he still had time, his parents still had money, so he went to a "good" graduate school to get a PhD in (now necessarily) English. During these years we remained good friends. One day, when he had completed all the course requirements for a PhD and was finishing his thesis, I asked him, "When you get through with all this stuff, what are you going to do?" The question seemed to surprise him. After a pause, he said, "I don't know, teach English in some college, I guess." I said, "Is that what you really want to do?" This question surprised him even more. After another pause he said, "No, not particularly, but what else *can* I do?" That surprised *me*. Is that what a PhD is supposed to do for you?

He began to teach English at a small state university, in the Western mountain country he loved. He soon found that his students were at college only to get the ticket, and they were not in the least interested in anything he had learned and wanted to teach. All they wanted to know, and very politely asked, was, "What do we have to do to pass the course?" This took all the point out of teaching. For a while he tried to put in his class time, collect his paycheck, concentrate on the farming, hunting, fishing, hiking, camping, and skiing that he really loved, and not worry about his students and what they liked or didn't like. It didn't work. He stuck it out for some years, every year hating it more. Finally he quit. Today, after some difficult years, he is a carpenter and small builder and contractor, doing careful and skilled work in a town where there is enough demand for it to keep him busy. He has found his work. But it still seems too bad to have spent fifteen years of his life and $40,000 of his parents' money just to find out that he didn't want to be an English professor.

TODAY, THE AVERAGE COST to get a bachelor's followed by a PhD in English at a public in-state college now would be more than $150,000. If you want to get that degree at a private college, you can expect to pay at least three times more.[55] ∎

Even then, he was fortunate in having enough money behind him so that he could run the risk of leaving his job and looking for work worth doing. Most people can't. A young woman about to graduate from a school of education once said to me, "Well, I've learned two things here, anyway—that I don't like children and I don't like teaching." I asked why she went on with it. She said, "I have to, I've spent too much time and money learning to do this, I can't turn around and start learning to do something else."

Ten years ago many students used to ask me whether they should go to, or stay in, or go back to college. I used to say, and say now, that a college degree isn't a magic passkey that opens every door in town. It opens only a few, and before you spend a lot of time and money getting one of those keys, it's a good idea to find out what doors (if any) it opens, and what's on the other side of those doors, and to decide whether you like what's on the other side, and if you do, whether there may not be an easier way to get there.

GROWING UP, PERHAPS NOT ABSURD

How much it can mean to a young person to feel that there is work worth doing out there in the world can be seen from these excerpts from letters from a Massachusetts high school senior. During the summer after an unhappy and unsuccessful year in eleventh grade, she wrote:

> I developed a very negative attitude about school but I was still very distressed and concerned about my performance in school. I was still very interested in learning but in the classroom I found learning very dull. I was enrolled in classes in which everyday attendance was mandatory, but I began cutting classes. I was not alone. A whole crew of us used to hang out in a dingy girl's room. The school doesn't have a lounge so this room had to do. Well, my whole school year was a disaster. I dropped out of all my classes except for two when the 4th term rolled around. I scheduled these classes for the morning and so I could leave the school before 11:00 nearly every day....
>
> I was studying my third year of Spanish but I dropped out at the end of the third term because I could not learn in an atmosphere which I felt was hostile (toward me).
>
> ...I often resorted to smoking marijuana during school. It broke up the monotony of a school day. Pot didn't interfere with my studying. I found I could concentrate remarkably well while I was high. But I must say it totally ruined my attitude, especially when it came time to decide whether or not I should go to the next class.
>
> ...My relationship with my family suffered....I was going around with older kids outside of high school....My parents felt these kids were responsible for my attitude change. Perhaps they were to some extent. A few of them had dropped out of high school and none of them went to college except for one kid who stopped going after two years. They didn't seem to be headed anywhere....

Well, here I am. I hope to go on to college yet with my high school record I don't know. Kids have a tendency to goof off during their senior year. I am going to have to work hard to make up for last year's mistakes. But…I feel alienated in school, at home, and even with my "friends."

…I would like to know if you have any suggestions. I am interested in ecology, conservation, English, writing, history, gardening, photography (I don't have a camera, though), silver jewelry making (I have already completed a beginner's course), alternative energy sources (solar energy especially).

In reply, I suggested that during the summer she visit the New Alchemy Institute in Woods Hole, Massachusetts. The New Alchemists, as they call themselves, are a group of people led, or perhaps I should say assembled, guided, directed, inspired, and coordinated by John and Nancy Jack Todd, who are trying to find ways in which human beings can live, in modest comfort, in a gentle, stable, and enduring relationship with the earth. The institute is a small experimental farm and research facility, in which people experiment with solar greenhouses, fish-farming, intensive food raising, tree raising, windmills, composting, biological pest control, worm raising, among other activities. As small as it is, it seems to me to be one of the most important groups of people working anywhere. It is not at all an exaggeration to say that the health and happiness of our country, our planet, and the human race may depend a great deal on what they are able to learn there.

At any rate, the student did visit the institute. In December of that same year she wrote again:

My main purpose for writing you is to thank you for your advice. I had written that I was interested in organic gardening and you suggested that I should visit the New Alchemy Institute. Well, my mother and I took you up on your suggestion one Saturday and although I did not get a chance to talk with any of the Alchemists, I thoroughly enjoyed exploring the farm. I went to a seminar on raising earthworms and saw a movie about the present plight of small farmers in this country.

Last spring an article on the New Alchemy Institute was featured in the *Boston Globe*....I brought it into the Alternative School Room to show my friend and Alt. advisor. I also showed him your letter and I must say with no exaggeration the man was delighted....He had not visited the Institute but in spring he may arrange to take a group of Alt. students for a visit....

During the summer I suffered from an extremely bad attitude about school. I wanted to complete my last year of high school by means of a totally alternative learning process. But I decided upon entering school in September that if I was to have a satisfactory academic record for college, I must work within the system. The trip to the New Alchemy Institute made a permanent impression on me and influenced my decision to major in Life Sciences and Agriculture in college. Well, not only did I wish to improve my academic standing for college, but I also wished to prove to myself that I was still capable of being a good student despite my changed attitudes toward a structured and traditional education. Last year's failures in school nearly ruined my self-esteem.

I enrolled in five major subjects (not including physical education) though I needed only five credits and a year of gym to graduate. I'm presently enrolled in an honors Spanish III course, Latin I, Marine Biology and Animal Behavior, Economics, and an advanced placement English course! Believe me, that is quite a change in academics from the previous year. In order to carry this workload I had to quit Alternative School. No one told me that I had to leave the program, but I decided it was best....Well, I've survived and after the first term I had earned a place on the honor roll.

THE MOST DIRECT WAY

An article from *Sports Illustrated* (December 17, 1979) shows how a person can zero right in on his chosen work:

One of the youngest and most successful design teams in contemporary ocean racing [has] Ron Holland, 32, as its equally unlikely chief. Holland failed the most elementary public exam for secondary schools in his native Auckland, New Zealand, repeatedly flunked math (considered by many to be a requisite in yacht design) and has no formal qualifications whatsoever in naval architecture. He even elected not to complete a boatbuilding apprenticeship. Yet today everybody wants a Holland design.

...At 16 he walked out of secondary school—"too academic," he says—and told his mother later. Even then he seemed to know that his future lay in boats. Until a primary-school teacher introduced him to Arthur Ransome's *Swallows and Amazons*, a classic children's tale about a sailing holiday off England's Norfolk Broads, Holland had read nothing. Teachers had sent him to remedial reading classes. But after *Swallows and Amazons* he became a bookworm. He had been sailing since he was seven, when his father bought him a seven-foot dinghy, undaunted by the fact that in his first race he finished fourth and last.

Holland got into the boating industry as an apprentice, and quickly chucked that job because the boss would not give him time off to go ocean racing....

He spent nearly three years working with American designers, first Gary Mull and finally the flamboyant Charlie Morgan.

It was in 1973, after less than three years of intermittent design experience, that Holland changed course again. He left Morgan to campaign his own quarter-tonner, *Eygthene*, in the world championships at Weymouth, England. It was a radical design—based, Holland admits now, on intuition, not "plain arithmetic." *Eygthene* won.

And just in time. With Laurel, whom he had married in 1971, he was living aboard the cramped quarter-tonner. A potential sale had just fallen through. He had no money in the bank.

Ron Holland sets a good example for people trying to find their work. If you know what kind of work you want to do, move toward it *in the most direct way possible.* If you want someday to build boats, go where people are building boats, find out as much as you can. When you've learned all they know, or will tell you, move on. Before long, even in the highly technical field of yacht design, you may find you know as much as anyone, enough to do whatever you want to do.

Of course, if none of the people doing your chosen work will even let you in the door without some piece of school paper, you may have to pay time and money to some school to get it. Or, if you find out that there are many things you want or need to know that the people working won't tell you, but that you can find out most easily in school, then go for that reason. At least, you will know exactly why you are there. But don't assume that school is the best way or the only way to learn something without carefully checking first. There may be quicker, cheaper, and more interesting ways.

Here are some other examples. This from *Solar Age*, December 1979:

At age 22, Ken Schmitt is head of Research and Development for Alternative Energy Limited (AEL), a small new company...which plans to sell [alcohol] stills beginning some time next year....

At 17, he owned a construction company, which "gave me the capital to experiment." Schmitt has experimented with solar energy systems for the last two years. His pilot plant for methanol (wood alcohol) synthesis may be the forerunner of a plant that will produce half a million gallons per day for Los Angeles motorists; and five foreign countries may buy rights to use a pyrolysis process he developed.

And from the *Boston Monthly*, December 1979:

The head of the Boston Computer Society, a group that regularly publishes a newsletter and holds meetings to learn and exchange computer ideas and information, is 16 years old. Technicians for many of the local computer stores are high school students. Computerland in Wellesley has a volunteer expert with a terrifying knowledge of computers who works with their customers in exchange for unlimited computer time—he is twelve years old.

SERIOUS WORK

A family I know has been traveling around the country in a converted bus, staying for a while in towns that interest them or where they know people they like, then moving on. Not long ago the father wrote:

A friend had just become "owner for a week" of a grocery store because the owner needed a vacation. S, the friend, decided he would capitalize on the opportunity and try to get a month's worth of "ownership" out of a week. He hired me to do several electrical and carpentry jobs while the boss was gone. An impression must be made. Many improvements. Check writing power—hire—fire—chief for a day!

We had to be there early and work before the store opened. I shook the kids up at six, we unplugged the bus, and were off. The kids followed me into the store toting tools. S said they could play in the store and the idea of having a supermarket all to yourself carried quite a charge. Supermarkets almost always come fully equipped with people—most of whom are adults. Children who are there are seldom wanted or welcome. They are usually being admonished by mother for handling the sacks of candy placed carefully within their reach by knowing management.

Well, not the case this morning—the store was theirs. They roamed the aisles for a while contemplating the space. Within half an hour everyone felt at home and C sat down with K at a table in the deli and started reading her a book they had brought from the bus.

Soon S arrived in a panic! The fresh juice-making operation in the back room was two hours behind because the shipment of containers hadn't come. A big selling item for the store was fresh-made juices of several kinds, made from fresh produce early each morning. Panic—the crowds would hit and there would be no juice. Money would be lost, good will would slip. Being "owner for a week" S had fewer learning sets than your average supermarket manager so he said, "Who wants a job?" F and G (the boys) were low on funds—"We do." "Wash your hands and come with me." They went back to the little juice factory in the back room and S introduced the new help to the juice man.

I stopped by about half an hour later and saw an amazing operation. I have never seen F and G work so hard with such enthusiasm. F was filling bottles with carrot juice and G was wiping, labeling, and pricing. The juice man was pouring bushels of carrots into a big peeling machine and then on to a grinder and then to a two-ton hydraulic press. Gallons and gallons of carrot juice were flowing and the boys' eyes were wide and their hands were a blur. Before today carrots existed either one every few inches in a row in the ground or in one-pound plastic-wrapped bundles. These machines ate carrots like a giant dinosaur. The pace was intense. The juice man had his routines down pat and the kids picked up the rhythm. It was a dance and you had to keep in step. Commands came in three-word sentences and they were obeyed. No time for discussion or explanation—real work—a real product—a real classroom. Sacks of carrots became 85¢ bottles of juice in minutes. G said, "I don't care if S pays us or not, this is fun."

Three hours later I was done, the store was open, and they were still having fun. Three large garbage cans of dry carrot pulp sat outside the juice room door. F's shirt and pants were orange and drenched. G was restamping a case of bottles he had marked 58¢ instead of 85¢. No hassle over the mistake—just stamp them again. After all, the juice man had to throw out a whole batch of carrots that got to the shredder before they were peeled. Mistakes are part of what people do. Unfortunately, in schools full of desks, they are forbidden.

I was having my breakfast on the bus when they finished and they popped in, each carrying a fist full of three dollars. They had worked harder in that three hours than I had ever seen them work before and they were ecstatic. They had new knowledge, new dignity (they saved the day), and some negotiable legal tender. My prize was to have been there to see it.

From a mother:

J (4) took another quantum leap. We're market gardeners. He asked for and has his own plot, marked off with string (to his specs) for which he raised plants in the greenhouse and in which he's raising radishes for money. This is all on his own, but we try to help carry out his suggestions and ideas. Including when he's asked me to thin his radishes as he was "too tired." However, yesterday while I was working steadily transplanting, he took up a hoe and hoed every part of the garden that needed it *because he saw it needed to be done* [Author's emphasis]. It took about an hour of hard work in which he did as good a job as I. Usually when he does something well I find myself commenting with some praise, but this time it would have been obviously, even ridiculously, superfluous. As if I would tell my husband he was a good boy for working so hard. J was at that time in that enterprise my equal. I was thrilled.

A mother writes from Manitoba:

One of the best times we had in the euphoric first two months out of school, was a marathon session in the biochemistry lab where I work. I had a 48-hour experiment going which had to be checked in the middle of the night. J went in with me the first night and we had trouble with one of the machines, a fraction collector which moves test tubes along under the end of a length of fine tubing which slowly spits out the stuff to be collected. We stayed there until 5 A.M. and J occupied himself almost the whole time with a stopwatch checking the rate of drips from the tubing, the rate of movement of the tubes, and the rate of a monitoring pen on another machine—all work that was necessary for getting the job done—and he revelled in it.

We left the building just as the last stars were leaving the sky. Sheep and cattle were grazing quietly on nearby university pastures. Only the birds provided sound. J was amazed that he had really passed through all the dark hours without sleeping. I thought of all the kids who could not have the kind of exhilaration he had just had because of their confinement to hours dictated to them by schools.

We slept all that morning and went back to the lab for checks during the afternoon and again at night and the following day. J wanted to stay with it right to the end and did. He learned all sorts of things in that short span of time about units of volume and time, about multiplying and dividing, about fractions, about light absorption, magnets, solutions, and probably other things. The same boy had been completely turned off by school math and was regarded by some as "slow" and "lazy."

A mother writes from New Hampshire:

T, A, and I…earn almost all of our money by seasonal orchard work—picking apples 2 months in the late winter. We leave home and work in various parts of [apple country].

…A started picking of her own accord one day when she was 5. She put her raincoat on backwards, using the hood as a bucket to hold the fruit until she emptied into the boxes. She was very proud of herself. She worked all day and picked 3 bushels. The next rainy day we made a quarter-size bucket out of a plastic waste basket and a pant leg. The cloth bottom opened up for emptying like our buckets. T made her a 10-foot ladder (he makes and sells apple-picking ladders). She picked from the bottoms of our trees and we paid her what we earned per bushel before deductions for food and rent.

Now, 5 years later, she has a custom-made half-size bucket and a 14-foot ladder. She works 2 hours or more most days, picking to the same quality standards we use. She keeps her own tally. She pays about half of her own living expenses from her earnings when we're on the crew. She handles the ladder well, picks as much of the tops as she can.

How much to pay her and how much to expect her to work have been areas of confusion. It didn't seem right to continue to pay her, in effect, more per bushel than anyone else by not deducting any expenses. But if we deducted her full expenses, she wouldn't earn anything (yet). So we compromised. Earning money is not her main motivation but she likes to get paid and it seems good for her to have money to spend. If she continues to increase her production, she'll soon be able to pay her full expenses on the crew and have a good amount left over.

In many poor cultures the kids' earnings help support the whole family. We have to earn enough to live on the rest of the year. So it seems possible that as she gets older she might pay her expenses the rest of the year too, or contribute toward things we'll all use. We are not part of a tradition where the kids work a lot or contribute much to the family's survival. And we are not so close to the line that our survival depends upon her contributions. So when we're in doubt we take the more regular (like our own upbringing) course. I believe she's working a good amount of her own accord when we're on crews. She says she wants to get so she's paying all of her expenses on the crews.

I don't believe in compelling kids to study some subject they don't want to, but I do believe in insisting they do some work, in relation to their abilities and the needs of the family. Since they start with a compelling desire to do what the older family members do, this is no problem. Now sometimes she objects to some chores (it's boring, so-and-so doesn't have to). We insist. If you want to be warm, too, you have to carry firewood, too. She seems to see the justice of it and gives in pretty easily.

She helps with pruning, too. She has her own saw and with direction will sometimes prune a whole tree. But it is a harder skill to learn.

I think living on a work crew has been really good for our family. It helped me set limits and encouraged us to accept time away from each other, but still allowed us to be together when we needed it. Very young, A accepted that I had to work and learned to amuse herself very well. I think that kind of solitude is very important for everyone. She became less clinging and demanding and I learned I could choose which demands I would meet. Before crew life I felt I should give her everything she was asking for. As a result of working with her near I learned that she could accept it and *benefitted* when I sometimes let her work it out herself. This led to both of us feeling our own individuality and made our close times closer. And brought my way of being with her into accord with T's way. Her attitude toward work (and mine) have benefitted from the work situation. Most of the crew, most of the time, are working with a willing attitude and there's a lot of enthusiasm that is catching. She works harder and longer with T, who enjoys pushing himself, than with me.

Since I have been the bookkeeper on the last few crews her interest in math has grown sharply. She helps with the payroll and counts out everyone's final net pay. She seems to have a good solid concept of reading and math. She doesn't gobble them up in quantity but when she's interested in something she follows it through.

I wrote in reply:

You wonder how A compares with other kids her age? My guess would be that she compares very well, probably smarter, more self-reliant, more serious, considerate, self-motivated, independent, and honest.

People get smart by giving constant attention and thought *to the concrete details of daily life*, by having to solve problems which are real and important, where getting a good answer makes a real difference, and where Life or Nature tells them quickly whether their answer is good or not. The woods are such a place; so is the sea; so is any place where real, skilled work is being done—like the small farm where Jud Jerome's daughter worked, like your own orchards.

Two summers ago I spent some time working with a small farmer in Nova Scotia, the neighbor and friend of the friends I was visiting. He had a large garden where he grew almost all his own vegetables, had about 20 acres in hay, raised Christmas trees. He also owned wood-lots, from which he cut wood, for his own use and to sell. He was 72 years old, and did all this work himself, with the help of two horses. The skill, precision, judgment, and economy of effort he displayed in his daily work were a marvel to see. The friend I was visiting, a highly intelligent and educated man, no city slicker but a countryman him-self, who had long raised much of his own food and killed, butchered, and cured or frozen much of his own meat, said with no false mod-esty at all that if he farmed for fifteen or twenty years he might—with plenty of luck and good advice—eventually learn to farm as well as this old neighbor.

LEAF GATHERING

Children show me again and again that they love to be really useful, to feel that they make a difference.

Two years ago, as I write this, I began a mini-experiment in urban agriculture. Each fall, when the trees in the Public Garden have lost their leaves, men blow them into big piles and later take them away. While the leaf piles are still there, I collect several garbage cans full and make a packed-down pile of them in the little sunken patio behind my basement apartment. Every day I pour over them the water I use for washing, dishes, shower, and so on, and use the rotted leaves to feed the worms I am raising.

As soon as the leaves were thick on the ground this fall I began collecting. Many early mornings, I put two plastic garbage cans on a small garden cart, took a leaf rake, trundled the cans into the Public Garden, raked up a pile of leaves, and filled the cans, jumping up and down in them from time to time to pack the leaves well down. Then I rolled cart and cans to the sidewalk behind my apartment, dumped the leaves over the wall into the patio, and later gathered them into piles which I packed down with weights.

One morning I collected and piled up more than a dozen loads. Feeling rain in the air, I thought I would make a couple of trips and bring in four more cans full, while the leaves were still dry. When I reached the Public Garden I saw four boys (eight, nine, nine, and ten, as I later found out), gathering leaves and putting them into the now dry sunken pool that surrounds a small monument. They spotted me and rushed over to ask if they could borrow my garbage cans to fill up with leaves, which would be quicker than dumping one armful at a time. I said that was a good idea, but that I needed the cans, because I was going to fill them up with leaves and take them home. What for, they asked. To make them into rich dirt, I said. They thought about this for a moment. Then they asked if they could borrow the "wheelbarrow." I said, Sure, but that when my cans were full I would need it back. They agreed and went off with the cart, which they used to take their leaves to the empty pond. When I was ready I called to them and they brought the cart back. I took the cans home, dumped the leaves over the wall, and went back for more.

This time the boys came over to ask if they could help by loading into my cans some of the leaves they had put in the pond. I said that there were plenty of leaves left on the ground, and that I didn't want to take leaves away from their nice pile. They insisted that they wanted to do it, so I thanked them and said to go ahead. While they filled the cans, I raked up more leaves. Back they came in a few minutes with full cans, all talking and asking questions. I jumped up and down on the leaves inside the cans; the boys were amazed to find how much the leaves packed down. Then I began to fill the cans with the leaves I had raked. The boys asked if they could help me do that. I said, "Sure." As we worked, I told them I was going to use the leaves to feed the worms I was raising. They were fascinated by this. What kind of worms? How many did I have? Where did I get them? How much did they cost? What did they eat? How did I feed them? What did I keep them in? Why was I doing this?

When the cans were full and loaded on the cart the boys asked if they could help me take them home. I thanked them again and said, Fine. With very little arguing, they organized a four-man cart-pushing team. Two pushed, and two stood up at the front corners holding on, "guiding it," as they said. By this time, they were so curious about the leaves and the worms that I decided to show them. They had been told to stay in the Public Garden, but I said that since I lived only a couple of blocks away, we would be right back and I was sure their mothers wouldn't mind. So they pushed the cart to the wall where I unload. One asked me to lift him up so he could see the leaf pile in the patio. I did, and he was amazed to see how big it was. Soon they all climbed or were lifted to the top of the wall and watched while I dumped the leaves.

When the leaves stuck a bit in the can, one of them helped pry them loose. All the while they asked questions about me. What did I do? I said I wrote articles and books. What kind of books? Books about children and school. And so on.

When we went indoors two boys insisted on carrying the empty garbage cans downstairs, while a third pulled the cart up some steps—a hard struggle—and put it away. Then we went out to look at the leaf pile. I found a worm and showed it to them. There was a chorus of "Yuk! Slimy!" But in only a second or two they all wanted to hold one. I also found and showed them some egg cases, and one of them spotted a tiny worm, newly hatched, hardly bigger than a thread. They were fascinated by this, all four talking and asking questions at once. Soon they asked if they could each have a worm. I said, Sure, got one for each, gave each a little hunk of dirt to keep the worm in, some leaves to wrap the dirt in, and a paper bag to carry it.

As we walked back to the Public Garden, they asked about how worms made more worms. I told them that worms were bisexual, boys and girls at the same time, and that any two worms could come together and fertilize each other, after which both of them could produce egg cases. Soon we were back at the monument and their leaf pile. After a bit more talk, I said that I was sorry but that I had to go home and do some other work. I hated to leave these bright, friendly, curious, enthusiastic, helpful children. I loved working with them and showing them things and answering their questions. I think they were just as sorry to leave me. I remember, when they were pulling the loaded cart (which was quite heavy) toward my apartment, one of them said, to the others, not to me, and in the kind of voice that can't be faked, "This is *fun*, doing this!" They all agreed—much more fun to be helping a grown-up do serious (even if mysterious) work than just playing around in a leaf pile. I hope they may have more chances to work with me, or some adult who cares about what he or she is doing. I hate to think of them ever becoming like the bored, sullen, angry, destructive teenagers who hang out every day at the Boylston Street entrance to the Public Garden.

The other day a young person wrote me saying, "I want to work with children." Such letters come often. They make me want to say, "What you really mean is, you want to work *on* children. You want to do things *to* them, or *for* them—wonderful things, no doubt—which you think will help them. What's more, you want to do these things whether the children want them done or not. What makes you think they need you so much? If you really want to work with children, then why not find some work worth doing, work you believe in for its own sake, and *then* find a way to make it possible for children—if they want to—to do that work with you."

The difference is crucial. The reason my work with the leaves and worms was interesting and exciting to those boys was precisely that it was *my* work, something I was doing for *my* good, not theirs. It was not some sort of "project" that I had cooked up because I thought they might be interested in it. I wasn't out there raking up leaves in the hope that some children might see me and want to join in. I never asked them to help, never even hinted; they *insisted* on helping me. All I did for them—which may be more than many adults might have done— was to say that if they really wanted that much to help me, then they could. Which is exactly the choice I would like to see the adult world offer to all children.

VOLUNTEER WORK

A twelve-year-old wrote us about being an office volunteer:

In July 1978 my mother was asked to work at the Childbirth Education Association office. At that time, we had a three-month-old baby named C. So my mother asked me if I would like to go to the office to mind

C while she did her work. But when I went in, it seemed that C slept most of the time except when she was hungry. So I started to do a little work. Mrs. L gave me some little jobs to do. Her daughter R (who is now a very good friend of mine) helped me to get into bigger things. She taught me to make registration packets. Even now I do about 100 a week at home. She taught me to run the folding machine so that we were able to fold the papers for the registration packets and also for the Memo. We enjoyed that a lot. I can even do it better than my mom because she gets the papers stuck sometimes. I also learned what to say when I answered the phone, even though I had a hard time getting "Childbirth Education Association" out in one breath and I sometimes disconnected people instead of putting them on hold.

I can't forget the literature orders. That was the best. We really had fun doing those. Finding the right papers and counting them out. Writing out bills and addressing the envelopes was lots of fun. R and I both knew what literature was there and what wasn't, so we could answer questions about what was in stock better than our moms.

I also had to do the postage meter at the end of the day. I always tried to use Mrs. L's adding machine to figure out the totals, but sometimes I would have to use my brain; then I didn't like it so much.

But it wasn't all work; sometimes R, her brother, and I would play a game or go to the library. I really looked forward to coming in to the office. But soon the bad part came. I had to go back to school. So as soon as I got my school calendar, I sent in a paper with all the days I had off from school so I could come into the office.

Now I am waiting for the summer to come so I can go into the office and help out.

Not long ago in our office we had so many letters from people asking about *Growing Without Schooling*, and about teaching children at home, that we could not answer them all. In the magazine I asked readers if some of them, who could type and also had a cassette tape recorder, would help with this. Many offered to do so, among them the mother of L, a Down's syndrome child. She asked if it would be okay, for the letters she was doing, if L addressed (in handwriting) the envelopes. I agreed. I sent them a tape of letters, which came back soon afterward, the letters typed, the envelopes neatly addressed. Then I sent them a big stack of letters from all over the country, that we had already answered, but that now needed to be broken down by states so that we could send them to people in the various states for a closer follow-up. Along with these I sent a tape of instructions. About this, L's mother wrote:

> L was thrilled with the whole project, and most impressed with being addressed by name on the tape. She took to the sorting and filing with gusto. I hadn't mentioned that this was another part of our "program," again one where I had tried to convince the schools to do something "real." They kept trying to get her to alphabetize on paper, and I wanted them to give her index cards, recipes, etc., or folders. No use. So when we started our planning this year, I had her make up a bunch of file folders, for each course or planned activity, and she puts receipts, brochures, and stuff in them. Also, we keep her papers for figuring out money, arithmetic problems, sentences, etc. Also, since I need some shape for my days and am a chronic list-maker, we'd make up daily schedules (especially so she could go about her work without having to check with me every minute, something she really enjoys— the independence, I mean). These schedules, if more than routine, go into the folders.
>
> So she was already used to that. She made up the folders (with my help in listing the states and assorted abbreviations). The first round, I went through the letters and underlined the state. The second time around I just screened them to be sure there *was* an address and that it was legible, but didn't note them—she figured them out herself.

Anyway, L loves the job, and can't wait to get started, at night even, after supper. All this seems ideal for L's purpose—some work experience, plus the exposure to the filing, alphabetizing, state names and abbreviations, etc., all without any formal "instruction," just doing it—the perfect way, but hard to find, especially for her. [Author's note: In a later letter, she said that L had a paying part-time job.]

10

HOMESCHOOLING IN AMERICA

ONE OF THE THINGS about *Teach Your Own* that I've rediscovered is how much it is not just a polemic and a practical guide for how and why to homeschool, but that it also represents a major attempt to address the political, legal, and legislative issues homeschoolers faced in the early eighties—and are likely to face now and in the future. Holt writes about the need for allies; about how schools and homeschoolers can work together for society's good and how different groups can work together, even though they may have different visions about education, and so on. However, some readers were intimidated by John's lengthy legal descriptions, even though by explaining the intricacies of homeschooling and the courts he wished to demystify the law and not intimidate people with it.

John wanted people to feel that the law was something they could understand on their own, and he spent a lot of time in the original edition describing various federal, state, and local court decisions that uphold the right to homeschool. When he wrote *Teach Your Own*, homeschooling occupied a gray area in the law, and in some states it still does. Contrary to popular myth, there have never been statutes forbidding homeschooling anywhere in the United States. If homeschoolers are taken to court, it is usually for disobeying the compulsory education laws or some charge of educational or child neglect, not for the act of homeschooling. Indeed, some states still haven't a single law regarding homeschooling, whereas others have reasonable laws and some have laws that are restrictive. There is room for disagreement about how homeschooling occurs and how it is described in each state, but teaching your own children is legal everywhere even if it isn't explicitly called "homeschooling."

The best source of information about the regulations and laws regarding homeschooling in your state is an active homeschooling group in your local community or state; I provide advice about getting this information in Chapter 12 and more resources at the end of the book.

I have edited Holt's three chapters dealing with the courts, legal strategies, and legislature into this one chapter to bring it up to date. ∎

N OT LONG AGO I spoke to a large meeting of educators from southeastern Massachusetts. This is fairly affluent country, so the school people there are probably about as well informed as anywhere. At one point I asked people to raise their hands if they had even a rough idea of what was meant or referred to in *Pierce v. Society of Sisters*. I had expected to see perhaps a dozen hands. Not one was raised. But this U.S. Supreme Court decision of 1925 is perhaps the most fundamental of all rulings on this question.

More recently, when I was testifying before the Education Committee of the House of Representatives of the Minnesota legislature, a member of the legislative staff read to the committee a summary she had prepared of court decisions on compulsory schooling. It was not bad as far as it went, but it was at least *two years* out of date. And it left out some very important earlier rulings in favor of homeschool families.

Most judges in family or juvenile courts, where many unschooling cases will first be heard, probably don't know this part of the law either, since it is not one with which they have had much to do.

This means that when we write up homeschooling plans, we are going to have to cite and quote favorable rulings. The more of this we do, the less schools will want to take us to court, and the better the chances that if they do, we will win. Under our adversary legal system, the task of courts is not so much to decide what "justice" is, as to decide which of the parties before them, in terms of existing laws, court decisions, and so on, has the strongest argument. The courts will not do our legal work for us. If we don't cite favorable court cases in our plans or briefs, judges (who may very well not even have heard of them) are not going to put them in their rulings. But once we put before a court an argument or a legal precedent, the court cannot ignore it, but must either agree with it or find a stronger argument to oppose it. Otherwise, it runs the risk that its ruling will later be reversed by a higher court.

Now and then I discover a wonderful book, which I want to recommend to all homeschoolers, only to find that it is long out of print. One such book is *The End of Obscenity* by Charles Rembar.[56] (PF: Used copies and an ebook version are available on Amazon.) It is the best book for the layperson, at least that I have seen, about how constitutional law *works*. I learned an immense amount from it about how judges think, and about how lawyers go about making cases that they think may convince judges.

Rembar was able to persuade the courts to overturn definitions of obscenity that had been established in statutes and upheld by courts for many years. In other words, he was trying to persuade the courts essentially to reverse themselves on an important point of law—something they very rarely do. And by an amazingly ingenious series of arguments he was able to do it.

The chief lesson of Rembar's book is that if you want the courts, or a court, to reverse rulings that have been well settled in law, you have to present them with arguments they (and the courts before them) have not yet heard. You can't go before them and say what has been said before, in the hope that *this* time they will say yes where previously they had always said no. You have to give them a reason for saying yes that the earlier courts did not have.

THE LAW ON SCHOOLING SUMMED UP

Here, in sum, is the meaning of various rulings on schooling:

1. Parents have a right to educate their children in whatever way they believe in; the state cannot impose on all parents any kind of educational monopoly of schools, methods, or whatever. *Pierce v. Society of Sisters* (1925), *Farrington v. Tokushige* (1927), *Perchemlides v. Frizzle* (1978).

2. The state may not deprive parents of this right for arbitrary reasons, but only for serious educational ones, which it must make known to parents, with all the forms of due process. Again, *Perchemlides*; also *Michigan v. Nobel* (1979).

3. A state that would deny parents these rights by saying that their home education plan is inadequate has a burden of proof to show beyond reasonable doubt that this is so. Parents are assumed to be competent to teach their children until proved otherwise. This Assumption of Competence is kin to and part of the general Assumption of Innocence (of the accused) which holds in all criminal proceedings. *State of Iowa v. Sessions* (1978).

4. In order to prove that the parents' education plans are inadequate, the state must show that its own requirements, regulations, and so on are educationally necessary and do in fact

produce, in its own schools, better results than the parents get or are likely to get. *Hinton et al. v. Kentucky* (1978); also *Nobel*.

PARENTS WHO WISH to assert their rights or bring about change would do well to emulate John's broad-minded political tactics. He recognized and sought legal precedent and protection for homeschooling from all over the political spectrum in order to keep the field diverse and vibrant. He worked hard to keep homeschooling from being cast as either a primarily conservative or a liberal issue, angering partisans of all stripes who want to claim homeschooling as "their issue." For instance, conservative homeschoolers often refuse to use arguments that rely on the right of family privacy because they feel this will further entrench *Roe v. Wade* in case law. Liberal defenders of homeschooling often refuse to use arguments about the rights of children not to go to school, for fear that will bring ruin to the public school system. John never hesitates to mention these and many other legal arguments that support homeschooling, both broadly and specifically.

One of the most striking legal points John makes is one most parents aren't aware of, though most children are: if you learn, the schools get the credit; if you don't, the student gets the blame. In short, you can't sue a school for educational malpractice. John explains the situation in the following section. ∎

A DOUBTFUL CLAIM

WE HAVE ALREADY DISCUSSED the claim of the schools that they alone know how to teach children. Most of the time, they make this claim with no reservations whatever. Yet when they are sued in court for not having done what they say they and they alone know how to do, they suddenly become very modest.

A most revealing article on teacher malpractice in the *American Educator*, journal of the American Federation of Teachers, said, in part:

> In 1972, parents of a graduate of the public school system in San Francisco brought a $500,000 suit against the school district charging that after a total of 13 years of regular attendance, their son was not able to read.
>
> During his years in school, according to information compiled on the case, he was in the middle of his classes, maintained average grades, and was never involved in anything which resulted in major disciplinary action. His parents claimed that during their son's years in the public school they were rebuffed in their attempts to get information on the progress of their son, but were assured by school officials and teachers he was moving along at grade level.
>
> Shortly after the youth's graduation, he was given a reading test by specialists who concluded the youth was only reading on a fifth-grade level....
>
> The California State Court of Appeals rejected the parents' claim of the school system's failure to educate their son. The court declared it was impossible for any person, most of all the courts, to set guidelines for "proper" academic procedures which must be followed by all schools and all teachers.
>
> "Unlike the activity of the highway, or the marketplace, classroom methodology affords no readily acceptable standards of care, or cause, or injury. The science of pedagogy itself is fraught with different and conflicting theories of how or what a child should be taught, and any layman might, and commonly does, have his own emphatic views on the subject," read the court's opinion.

The court was, of course, quite right in saying this. But what then becomes of the claim, which the schools make all the time, that they alone know how to teach children? Parents in conflict with schools might find it very helpful to quote those words from the California ruling.

T HIS VERY ISSUE CAME UP AGAIN, but this time in England. In October 2001, Katherine Norfolk, nineteen, and her parents sued Hurstpierpoint College "for loss of earnings, damage to her career prospects, and personal distress" due to poor teaching by her Latin instructor. The first sentence about this case in the *Guardian* reflects considerable anxiety by the schools over this issue:

> Head teachers of private schools urged parents yesterday not to resort to litigation if their children gained disappointing exam results, after it emerged that a Sussex school was being sued for £150,000 by the family of a star pupil who failed to get a top grade in A-level Latin.[57]

The worries are ill-founded I believe, though they indicate considerable insecurity by school officials. As John noted, the courts wouldn't allow the schools to fail in this way for a number of reasons, and I think, in general, the public would side with the schools in a minute on the issue of teacher malpractice. Indeed, I first learned about the Norfolk case in a humor column featuring real news stories entitled "News of the Weird," which shows how seriously much of the public takes this claim. But Holt's point that even high-priced schools can't guarantee that they know best how to teach children is conveniently ignored by educationists, who insist that unqualified, uncertified, and unschooling parents haven't got a clue how to properly teach their own children. ∎

COURT STRATEGY IN GENERAL

A S JUSTICE BENJAMIN CARDOZO pointed out in his enormously valuable book *The Nature of the Judicial Process*, judges, in making their rulings, take into account a number of things—legal philosophy and principle, legal precedent, the will of the legislature as expressed in the statutes, and *the possible or probable social effects of their rulings*. Thus, as we have shown, parents who have sued the schools because their children did not learn anything there have so far been turned down by the courts, on the grounds that this would very quickly lead to a rush of lawsuits that would bankrupt the schools. We may take it as certain that the courts will not in any foreseeable future make rulings which they think will lead to the quick destruction of the public schools or the end of compulsory schooling. If we ask for such broad rulings, we will be turned down.

Beyond that, either in asking for narrow rulings, or speaking of any we may be able to win, we must be careful not to make large public boasts and outcries to the effect that "this means the downfall of compulsory schooling." In the first place, such boasts would be silly; even if the courts were by some miracle to strike down compulsory schooling, a furious majority of the people would quickly reestablish it, by constitutional amendment if they had to. In the second place, even making such boasts would greatly reduce our chances of getting even narrowly favorable rulings from the courts. In the third place, such boasts tend to terrify the schools, who are already far more terrified than they need be, and whom it is in our best interests to reassure.

T HE IMPORTANCE OF JOHN'S REPEATED ADVICE to "think like a judge" when you consider going to court can't be underestimated. I've seen some homeschoolers decide to challenge compulsory school laws with a thin legal strategy, namely that somehow common sense will make the judges "see the light" and rule in favor of homeschooling and against compulsory schooling. Instead, as Holt indicates, judges prefer to rule in very narrow, case-specific decisions. When I hear about a court case of the "will be a major victory for homeschooling if we win it" sort I cringe; after forty years in the field, I've seen victories in our state legislatures for homeschooling, but also more losses and stalemates than clear victories in court cases. Judges tend to think of school and education as an important tool in their kit of remedies, and homeschoolers, no matter how persuasive their respective case, aren't going to wean judges from their reliance on and perception of schooling as a disciplinary tool.

As John puts it, "I see no point in confronting the authorities directly if you can dodge them." When dodging no longer is an option, then appealing to state legislators is often better than going to court. John's legislative statement and his description of the hearing, which follow, are models of how such action can work for homeschoolers. ∎

LEGISLATIVE STRATEGY

E ARLY IN 1980 I was invited by the Education Committee of the Minnesota House of Representatives to testify at hearings they were holding about home education and private schools. I said that I would be glad to and sent them in advance a statement of my position. What I said to them could, I believe, be equally and usefully said to any other state or provincial legislatures giving homeschooling their attention.

The statement:

Time being short, let us not waste any of it in arguments about whether the public schools are doing a good job. Such arguments cannot be settled here.

*　　*　　*

Let me sum up very briefly my position:

1. In terms of both the short-run and long-run interests of themselves and of the general public, the schools would be wise to view the growing home education movement not as a threat but as an opportunity and a potential asset, and, rather than resist it, to support it to the fullest extent.

2. The legislature itself would be wise, in any education laws it may write, to affirm and support very strongly the right of parents to teach their own children, and to make it as easy as possible for the schools to assist them in this effort.

3. To try to do the opposite, that is, to try to make it difficult or impossible for people to teach their own children, would be a most serious educational, legal, and political mistake.

What does the law have to say about all this? Here we must note that "the law" is made up, not just of the laws or statutes, but of the ways in which the courts have interpreted these laws.

According to repeated court decisions, there is here (as in many places) some conflict between the constitutionally protected rights of the parents and the equally protected rights of the states.

The courts have affirmed, in decisions too numerous to cite, that under the police powers delegated to them that several states have a right to demand that all children be educated, and to that end, to write and enforce compulsory school attendance laws.

But the U.S. Supreme Court has also held, first in *Pierce v. Society of Sisters*, and later in *Farrington v. Tokushige*, that while the state may demand that all children be educated, it may not demand that they be educated in the same way, and that, on the contrary, parents have a constitutionally protected right to get for their children an education which is in accord with their own principles and beliefs. The state, in other words, may not have a monopoly in education, either of schools or of methods. The parents have a right to choice, not just in minor details but in matters of significance.

Subsequent decisions in state courts, in Illinois, New Jersey, Massachusetts, and Iowa, among others, have held that this right of parents to control the education of their children includes the right to teach them themselves. In at least one state the courts have held that the burden of proof is not on such parents to show that they are capable of teaching their children, but on the state to show that they are not capable of doing so.

*   *   *

Some other legal points should be made here:

1. The courts, in upholding the right of the states to compel children to be educated, have upheld this on the sole ground that without such education children would be unfit for employment and would therefore become a burden on the state. It follows that when the states say that a given educational program, whether of parents or of a private school, is inadequate, it must be from this point of view and this one only. The courts have never said, for example, that compulsory schooling was necessary so that all children would have some kind of "social life." This is a fringe benefit—if indeed a benefit at all. Therefore the states cannot rule out an educational program on the grounds that it does not give students an adequate social life. In this area the states have no rights, and the rights of the parents are supreme.

2. A Massachusetts superior court held recently that the right of parents to teach their own children is located not just in the First and Fourteenth, but also the Ninth Amendment to the Constitution.

3. A Kentucky district court, in a ruling later upheld by the state supreme court, said that before the state could demand, for example, that all teachers be certified, it had to produce evidence to show that certified teachers taught better than uncertified ones. In the court's words, the state was unable to produce "a scintilla" of such evidence. Nor, in all probability, could any other state. Indeed, it would be easy to show that the most exclusive and academically

demanding and successful schools, to which the richest and most favored people send their children, have on their faculties few if any certified teachers, or graduates of schools of education.

4. When parents in San Francisco, in 1972, sued the schools because, after thirteen years of school their son was reading only on a fifth-grade level, the California State Court of Appeals dismissed the suit saying, "Unlike the activity of the highway, or the market-place, classroom methodology affords no readily acceptable standards of care, or cause, or injury. The science of pedagogy itself is fraught with different and conflicting theories of how or what a child should be taught…" and concluded that it was impossible for anyone to set guidelines for "proper" academic procedures which must be followed by all schools and all teachers. How can the schools, when charged with negligence, defend themselves as they did in this case by saying that no one really knows how children should be taught, and in the next breath say that they are the only ones who know?

The point is that if the legislature tries to prevent or even unduly circumscribe the right of parents to teach their own children, such laws will surely be challenged in the already overburdened courts and will not stand up.

*　　*　　*

Though you may have been told the opposite, such laws are not necessary to "save" the public schools. The number of people who, even if it were easy to do so, would want to take their children out of school and teach them at home, is small. Not many people enjoy the company of their children that much, or would want to give that much attention to their interests and concerns, or take that much of the responsibility for their growth. In places where the schools have gone to court to prevent people from teaching their own children, they have told the courts that if they ruled in favor of the parents they would be "opening the floodgates," "setting a bad precedent," "starting a landslide."

Nowhere have these dire predictions come true, even in communities in which, after much publicity, the parents won their case.

The best way for the public schools to save themselves, if they are in fact in any real danger, is to solve the problems they already have within the walls of their school buildings. In trying to find ways to solve these problems, they may in time be very much helped by what will be learned about effective teaching by people teaching their own children. They will be further helped by many of these children who will choose, as some are already choosing, to go to school part-time for those activities that interest them most. The example of these independent and self-motivated students will have a powerful effect on other students and on the schools in general.

Under present Minnesota law, local school boards have an unqualified legal right, if they wish, to allow parents to teach their children at home. In short, the law, *as it stands*, is sufficient to *permit* homeschooling. The law may allow local school districts and law enforcement authorities, if they so choose, to prosecute any family for trying to teach its children at home, but *it does not require* them to do so, for at least three reasons:

1. Under the law, school districts may define school attendance in any way they wish. School districts in many jurisdictions have instituted different kinds of off-campus study programs (like the Parkway Project in Philadelphia), or work-study or apprenticeship programs, or even programs which required students to travel to other cities or states. In like manner, schools have for generations been able to extend full academic credit to children of families living or traveling abroad, or traveling in this country in the course of business (i.e., families in the circus or theater) and studying from correspondence courses. No one has ever claimed or could sustain a claim that in doing this, the schools were somehow violating compulsory state attendance laws. Now do the schools, in such matters, have to defend their definitions of "attendance"

to any other state authorities; in this matter they have absolute discretion.

2. Under the law, the school districts and/or the state may define private schools in any way they wish. There is—fortunately—no absolute requirement that private school teachers be certified. All that is required is that the "common branches" be taught in the English language. As for hours of instruction, it is worth nothing that when children who ordinarily attend public schools are for reasons of sickness or injury unable to attend, public schools ordinarily send tutors to the homes of these children, so that they will not fall behind in their schoolwork. How much time these tutors spend with the children varies from district to district. My own limited investigation has shown that this varies from as little as an hour and a half a week to a maximum of four hours a week. It would be interesting for the legislature to check school practices on this throughout the state. Many families using materials from the long-accredited Calvert Institute or similar organizations have reported to me that their children are able to do what the correspondence school calls a week's worth of schoolwork in only a few hours.

3. The law as written gives the school board the right to excuse a child from attending school "if his bodily or mental condition is such as to prevent his attendance at school *or application to study.*" But it is undisputed that many children do badly in school, or fail, or drop out altogether, because they are bored, because the school will not permit them to study at their own level, or because the school has no programs that meet their special interests, capabilities, and needs, or because the competitive and/or threatening atmosphere of the school and classroom prevents them from working up to their capacity. In such cases, and others we might well imagine, it would be legally permissible and educationally wise for schools to grant parents of such children, if they asked for it, the right to

educate their children in ways that, being in greater harmony with their interests, temperaments, and styles of learning, would produce more effective results. Nothing in the law as it stands denies school boards the right to do this, or makes them answerable to any higher authority for any exceptions they might grant.

In short, while the law could, and in my judgment should make more explicit the rights of parents to teach their own children, it does not have to be changed in order to permit this. It is only if the intent of the legislature is to make home teaching far more difficult or forbid it altogether that changes in the law are required.

If the legislature wishes to affirm the right of parents to teach their own children, while continuing to exercise its constitutional right to assure that all children are being taught, it could do so very well by passing resolutions which would, in effect, say more or less the following:

1. It is not the intent of the compulsory laws of this state to deny to parents the right to have for their children an education in reasonable harmony with their own deepest concerns and principles, including the right, if they wish, to teach their own children at home.

2. Nor is it the intent of this legislature to authorize any educational authorities to impose on students under their jurisdiction a uniform curriculum, or uniform methods of instruction and/or evaluation. There are and will remain large and legitimate differences of opinion, among experts and nonexperts alike, on the subjects that should be taught to children, on the order and ways in which these are to be taught, on the materials which are to be used, and on the ways in which this teaching and learning are to be evaluated. Only by allowing and supporting a wide range of education practices can we encourage the diversity of experience from which we can learn to educate our children more effectively, and it is the intent of this legislature to allow and encourage such variety.

3. Rather than draw up any set of detailed guidelines to regulate homeschooling, or set up some kind of special administrative machinery for this purpose, we would prefer to leave to the local school districts the responsibility for supervising and assisting home-teaching families according to their own best judgment, keeping always in mind the very general purposes noted above.

May I repeat once more, even if the legislature passes such resolutions or their equivalent, it will be a very long time before as many children are being taught at home as are right now truant every day from the schools of our larger cities.

The legislature, at least if it wishes to make homeschooling no more difficult than it is today, might be wise to write into law what at least one court, in Nebraska, has already affirmed in a ruling, namely, that the laws governing neglect were not intended to be considered as an integral part of the compulsory school attendance laws, and that the charge of neglect, and the probable consequence of removing children from the custody of their parents, is not to be understood as a natural and legitimate penalty for failing or refusing to send the children to an accredited school. Some considerations:

1. School personnel may say that a threat this severe is needed to guarantee compliance with compulsory school attendance laws. But this violates a very fundamental principle of the common law, perhaps nowhere made explicit but very thoroughly understood, that the penalty for an offense must be proportional to the offense. In the light of this principle, no local government would be able, for example, to punish parking violations with prison sentences, on the grounds that without such severe punishment they could not secure complete compliance with the law.

2. When legislators passed laws saying that the state could, for neglect, remove children from the custody of their parents, what they had in mind was children who were starved, or left naked, or were brutally beaten and tortured, or locked in closets, or chained

to furniture. They did not have in mind the children of conscientious and devoted parents whose only crime was that they did not approve of the kind of education offered in the local schools. To lump such parents with gross abusers of children, as schools have quite often already done, is a most serious perversion of law and justice.

3. It should be added that even people convicted of the most serious crimes—assault, grand larceny, manslaughter, even murder—are not automatically deprived of the custody of their families. If and when such criminals finish their sentences, their families and children, at least if they choose to do so, are waiting for them. To say that violent criminals may be fit to raise their children but that people who want to teach them at home are not, is again a serious perversion of justice.

It must be categorically said that if it were true (which I dispute) that the compulsory attendance laws could only be enforced by such severe and cruel penalties—for loving parents, the most severe of all penalties—there would be something inherently wrong with those laws. At any rate, this way of enforcing them, or of settling or rather foreclosing arguments about what kind of education is best for the children, ought in the name of justice and equity to be removed from the schools' hands.

THE ISSUE OF CHILD abuse at home has been raised as a reason to put homeschooled children into public schools, but never so forcefully until now. In 2020, Elizabeth Bartholet, director of Harvard Law School's Child Advocacy Program, began a campaign to ban homeschooling on the grounds that "homeschooling violates children's right to a "meaningful education" and their right to be protected from potential child abuse, [and] keep them from contributing positively to a democratic society." Following up on this broad claim, in 2021, Harvard organized a webinar series of six, one-hour panels of academic researchers and lawyers to address the "Post-Pandemic Future of Homeschooling" and respond to "many important questions about the practice." This webinar continues as I write this section, and so far the panels have been much more thoughtful than the original call to ban homeschooling.

Tara Westover's excellent and moving memoir, *Educated*, is used as a cudgel by Bartholet to show how cruel homeschooling can be. What needs to be stated clearly, and Westover does so repeatedly in her book, is that the neglect and physical abuse she suffered was a result of her father and brother's mental illnesses, and their erratic domination over the family. Some people, including her grandmother, try to rescue Westover from the crazy home she is in, but it isn't easy for children to leave their parents, and it takes her many years before she can make a clean break. Though homeschooling provided a cover story for her parents to keep her home, it was not the cause or reason for her abuse. When child abuse is discovered in public, private, and religious schools—and there are many documented cases—we don't close down all the schools because they are being used as covers for child abuse. It is also striking to me is that Westover notes favorably in her book that her older brother, who also left the family due to their abusive family situation, successfully homeschooled his children.

In addition to being physically abused, Westover's parents' religious beliefs prevented her from attending college, demanding instead that she be a wife and mother. This is also a clear violation of her rights as a person, let alone an American citizen. People have the right to control and direct their own thoughts and learning and to speak them publicly. Holt describes this right as flowing from the First Amendment:

> A person's freedom of learning is part of his freedom of thought, even more basic than his freedom of speech. If we take from someone his right to decide what he will be

curious about, we destroy his freedom of thought. We say, in effect, you must think not about what interests and concerns you but about what interests and concerns us.[58]

To create a law that requires people to attend only government-run schools in order to prevent potential child abuse not only infringes everyone's educational freedom, it also fails to address abuse directly. It merely puts the child in school and closes alternatives to school. This doesn't address children whose abuse is not detected by mandated reporters, nor does it address the physical abuse of children in public and private schools. Instead of using education as a workaround to protect children from abuse, let's grant all children the same protection adults have under the Bill of Rights: adults who are physically beaten by someone have legal recourse to get redress. The real threat of fines and jail keeps many people from throwing punches even when they want to.

However, our society views children as a special exception to this rule of law. Wikipedia notes that, in 1977's case *Ingraham v. Wright*, "the US Supreme Court held that the Cruel and Unusual Punishments Clause of the Eighth Amendment did not apply to disciplinary corporal punishment in public schools....As of 2018, corporal punishment is still legal in private schools in every US state except New Jersey and Iowa, legal in public schools in nineteen states, permitted in eighteen, and practiced in fifteen."[59]

Also, a fair number of parents choose to homeschool because of the bullying or mistreatment their children receive in school. Banning homeschooling only exacerbates that problem.

Another concern about homeschooling is that it undermines democracy because homeschooled children will not learn the skills needed to participate in our democracy. The idea that compulsory, conventional schooling is needed to make proper citizens is fraught with contradictions. For instance, nowhere is it stated in our founding documents that all citizens need to be processed in public schools to participate in our democracy. Finally, to show how civics can be done by children, some alternative schools, such as Sudbury Valley Schools, allow children to completely participate in their school's governance in direct contrast to mainstream schooling.

As I write this we are in the midst of a quarantine and the rise of domestic abuse is more likely, so we need to create protections for children that go beyond school attendance. The pandemic is forcing us to reintegrate children into our lives and schooling is likely to be different for a while. We need all the tools we have as a society to get through this, and homeschoolers have years of experience they can share about living and learning with children. Rather than ban home-schooling, particularly in this time of quarantine, we should be talking about how learning can be conceived and assessed more broadly, and how children should be treated with dignity and respect. ■

WHAT IS TRUE OF THE LAWS OF MINNESOTA, that is, that they permit (though they don't require) any school district to allow parents to teach their children at home, is equally true of the laws of all other states, for at least two and in many cases all three of the reasons given above. I know of no court cases in which the compulsory school attendance laws of a state have been used to restrict in any way the right of local school districts to establish any kinds of academic programs they wish, whether on-campus, off-campus, job-related, independent research, or whatever. As long as school districts have the support of the voters in their districts, they can do what they want. The notion, apparently believed by quite a few superintendents, that one day a state attorney might prosecute a local school superintendent and/or school board for allowing some parents to teach their children at home is absurd.

In the same way, local school districts can, whenever they want and for whatever reasons they want, allow exceptions to the laws about attending school. State laws saying that parents must supply some kind of statement from a doctor put a burden on the parents, not the schools. In other words, they say that unless the parents produce a statement from a doctor, the schools do not even have to consider their request for an exception. They do not mean, and would not be construed to mean, that the schools are forbidden to consider exceptions unless these are supported by a doctor's report.

In my statement to the committee, I suggested that if the legislature wished to give additional encouragement and support to home teaching, they could do so by passing some rather simple and general resolutions. After the hearings, I said in a letter to the administrative assistant that I thought a resolution by the Education Committee itself, rather than the entire legislature, might do almost as well. If school districts merely wish to be reassured that they are not compelled by law to prosecute all home-teaching families, a statement to that effect by the committee would probably give all the reassurance they needed.

The hearings themselves were very interesting. In opening the hearings, the chairman of the committee pointed out that a number of school districts had asked the legislature to "clarify" the law. What this "clarify" meant was soon made clear. Two witnesses, one a district superintendent, the other a county attorney, told about the troubles they had had, trying to prosecute and send to jail and/or deprive of their children a few families that wanted to teach their children at home. They said to the committee, in effect, "Either rewrite these laws, saying in strict detail what is or is not a private school, so that we can easily and quickly prosecute and convict these people, or else do away with compulsory school attendance laws altogether." No doubt school people in many other states will be telling legislators that they must either allow no exceptions whatever to compulsory school attendance laws (except perhaps to rich people), or give up the whole idea.

In my testimony I did my best to persuade the committee that they were not faced with any such choice. To my written statements I added only these points: (1) In more and more jurisdictions, where families had prepared their case with enough care, that is, made up a detailed educational plan, supported by quotes from educational authorities and many relevant court citations, the courts were increasingly ruling in their favor. (2) The movement for home teaching was part of a growing nationwide movement toward greater self-sufficiency and minimized dependence on large institutions, a movement that from many points of view could only be considered healthy and admirable and that in any case was certain to grow. (3) Trying to crack down on homeschooling families would increase, not lessen, the number and complexity of cases before their courts.

In this last connection the young county attorney had said indignantly at one point that one family was only using the Bible as a textbook. I asked him whether he thought he would have an easier time if he found himself arguing in court before a judge about how good a textbook the Bible was. I added that I thought it would not be hard to make a strong case that the Bible was a great deal better textbook than most of the ones used in schools. Did he really want to get involved in such arguments? The expression on his face as I said this suggested that he did not.

I went on to say that the committee had to understand that no matter how the legislature might change the laws, the people who for various reasons were now taking their children out of school and teaching them at home were going to go on doing so, no matter what. They will fight in the courts as long as they can, delay, stall, and appeal, for years if need be. If finally pinned to the wall, they will simply move to another district or out of the state altogether. The one thing they will not do is send their children back to the public schools. Is it really worth spending all this time, energy, and taxpayers' money to fight a battle that is lost before it is begun? The district superintendent, speaking of the bad publicity his district had received while prosecuting one family, had said at one point, "Even when we win, we lose." Did the schools, and the state, really want this kind of publicity?

One member of the committee asked me a question that, in one form or another, I hear at almost every meeting. It goes about like this, "What would you do about a family that didn't know anything, that didn't want their children to know anything, and that only took them out of school because they wanted to exploit their work, etc., etc." I replied by reminding them of an old legal maxim with which I was sure they were familiar—Hard cases make bad law. I said that if we write our laws—as we too often tend to—so as to take care of the worst possible hypothetical case that might arise, we are almost certain to have laws that are long, cumbersome, difficult or impossible to enforce, and far more likely to prevent good people from doing good work than bad people from doing bad. I went on to say that there might well be families like the one suggested, but that these people were the last ones in the world likely to be interested in teaching their children at home. On the contrary, they are only too eager to get them out of the house, and at the end of school vacations say, "Thank Heaven vacation is over, I can't wait to get these damn kids back in school." Committee members smiled; they obviously knew such people.

In closing, I said that there were limits to the power of governments, beyond which they could not go without losing their good faith and credit. A good case could have been made, and had once been made, that as a country we would be much better off if no one drank alcohol. But the Noble Experiment failed; people would not let the government stick its nose that far into their private affairs, and refused to obey the law. The only results were a great increase in corruption in government and general contempt for law.

As nearly as I could tell from their expressions and questions, the committee was interested in and responsive to what I had to say. Only one member seemed clearly angered and threatened by my words. The last question was asked by the chairman himself, "Do you mean that if we want to allow people to teach their children at home, we don't need to make any changes in the law at all?" I assured him that was what I meant.

If any on the committee were not convinced by what I had said about how determined more and more people are to teach their children in accordance with their own beliefs, the next witness must have convinced them. She was a representative of some association for Christian education, and in her testimony she furiously denounced the public schools (as I had been careful not to). Compared to her I must have seemed a most mild and reasonable person. I like to think that at the end of the hearings some of the committee, at least, were thinking, "Maybe Holt is right, maybe we really don't want to spend the next ten years fighting these kinds of people, maybe we'd be smarter to leave them alone and concentrate on doing what we can to fix up our schools." For Minnesota or any other state, it would be the wiser course.

11

HOW TO GET STARTED

"WHAT IS HOMESCHOOLING LIKE?"

THERE ARE AS MANY WAYS to homeschool as there are families who do it. Indeed, many families discover that what helped one child learn to read or do math doesn't automatically help their other children learn, so it is difficult to say, "Homeschooling is like this for everybody…" with certainty. In general, many parents prefer to start teaching the way they were taught, using regularly scheduled classes and textbooks, and gradually adapting their programs to suit their children's interests and abilities. Shifting away from textbooks to primary source materials and real-life experiences, they draw on other mentors or classes in the community. Some families prefer simply to do "school at home," duplicating school schedules and curricula but screening out objectionable content; there are correspondence and private schools listed in Appendices B and C that will sell you curricula and materials for this type of homeschooling. The way my wife and I prefer to homeschool is more the way John Holt describes teaching and learning, which is often called "unschooling." Most families wind up adapting a position in between school at home and unschooling; in any case, the decision on what homeschooling will be like for you is yours to make, and it is not an unalterable one.

Certainly, you can set up your home as a school, schedule it like school, and teach like in school. But the total school-at-home approach may become stifling to you or your kids, or, like many homeschoolers I know, you may prefer to move back and forth between imposed lessons and learning from the incidents of everyday life on a relaxed, individualized schedule. It is also important to remember that homeschooling doesn't have to mean that your kids stay at home all day, with only their parents, using school materials. For instance, several times a week we scheduled our children to be with other friends, typically, but not exclusively, homeschoolers; we reciprocated at other times during the week. My wife ran "The Detective Club," a popular meeting held every Wednesday night at our house for eight children—seven homeschoolers and a friend who attends public school. When our youngest child, Audrey, wanted to learn sleight-of-hand magic (a hobby of mine) we started the "The Magic Club," that also met at our house once or twice a month. This club ran for two years, and we performed close-up and parlor magic as a group at homeschooling events and nursing homes. In return, we made use of field trips, history clubs, drama clubs, and similar activities run by other homeschooling parents. Classes at museums, area library events, religious instruction, and the local gymnastics and dance academies our daughters attended, were among the local resources we used. Indeed, in some states you can probably arrange for your child to take classes in local public schools, as we've been able to do (it never hurts to ask no matter what state you live in). Some homeschooling support groups have listings of members who are willing to help tutor or converse with children who are interested in learning more about their areas of expertise.

Most important, homeschooling allows you to give your children time to explore and think about things on their own. Children who figure out things on their own, for their own purposes, literally *own* that knowledge and can build on it. So, for example, if your child wants to learn more about archaeology and you know nothing about the topic (and perhaps have no interest in it at all), then you can help them by locating books and materials they can read and use on their own; a friendly resource librarian at your local public library can be an invaluable ally in your homeschooling efforts for this reason alone. You can also consider calling local historical societies, museums, and college professors who might be willing to talk to your child, have them visit or volunteer, or simply allow the children to observe what various aspects of archaeology are actually like.

When we moved into our house, after years of apartment living in the city, our oldest daughter, Lauren, then six, liked to dig in our new backyard. She discovered an unusual round stone and showed it to my wife, Day. Day thought it might be a musket ball from colonial times, and this started a flurry of readings and conversations about the colonial era, guns, and archaeology. Day soon found an archaeological dig being done on a colonial American site not far from our house, and she was able to arrange for Lauren to spend a day helping at the site. You needn't feel you must know everything to help your child; again, homeschooling doesn't have to be like regular school and you don't have to be like a typical school instructor. Instead, you can be a facilitator and guide for your children's explorations of areas in which you don't feel particularly well versed.

Madalene Axford Murphy of Pennsylvania writes about how she did this with her son:

> Early on, our son Christian began to reach the limits of his father's and my knowledge in science and math, and it became obvious that these would be major pursuits in his life. At first, I cheerfully expanded my own knowledge, learning along with him, but finally I had neither the time nor the interest to keep up with him. We met this situation in a number of ways.

…We discovered an astronomy group that met one evening a month, and he began to attend meetings. He discovered that one of the founders of the group was giving a twelve-session seminar on astronomy for adults at our local nature center. On the recommendation of the naturalist there (a friend of his), he was allowed to sign up, though he was only eleven. The first evening, he came home with about ten pages of small print that had to be read for the next class. This was not going to be a warm, fuzzy retelling of myths about constellations with a few facts thrown in here and there about planets and such, but rather a no-holds-barred immersion course in technical astronomy. I was concerned, but Christian wasn't. He plowed through the reading and was disappointed when the classes were over. Did he understand everything? No, nor did many of the adults in the class, but words like "parallax" and "gradient" had become part of his vocabulary and he knew a whole lot more about telescopes and the science of astronomy than he had before.

Another group, the Audubon Society, helped open up several aspects of biology for him.…When they started planning their annual Christmas Bird count, Christian and I decided to participate.…One of the society's more active members was a biologist who worked at a nearby fish research lab, and I asked if we could tag along when he went on the bird count. The bird count itself was not a success: periods of freezing rain kept most of the birds out of sight and made me think they were definitely displaying intelligence superior to the humans on that particular occasion…

But the biggest success of the bird count was the friendship that developed between Christian and Bob, the biologist. Bob invited Christian on other bird counts and for the last two years has taken him along as a timekeeper/recorder on an intense five-hour government-sponsored survey of birds. Christian has become quite skilled at identifying birds and is even trying to improve his ability to recognize their calls.

The summer after the original bird count, Christian discovered he could volunteer at the fish research lab where Bob worked, and he ended up working two eight-hour days a week.... Christian learned a lot about lab techniques and about the amount of tedious work required to get accurate results for a study...

All of these biology activities took place during Christian's "high school" years, a time when homeschooling parents and sometimes children often begin to get a bit more nervous about whether they need to become more traditional, particularly if the children are planning on college. Christian did decide to use textbooks to fill in gaps in his knowledge of science, and activities like those I just described made the textbook knowledge real and useful.

Two other parents show the wide range of approaches that can be used in helping children learn math. Carla Stein of Massachusetts writes:

I took 51 pieces of typewriter paper and wrote the numbers 0 through 50 on them. We lay them out on the floor, Candy Land style, in all sorts of loops and turns around the furniture.... Then we took turns hopping along the trail, stepping only on numbers that were odd, or even, or divisible by 3, 4, 5, etc.... This made for silly fun, especially when the jumps got too long. Then they each got a small stuffed toy and tried to toss the toys onto the right numbers, with lots of misses and shrieking, of course.

Sue Smith-Heavenrich of New York writes:

Some time ago my children were doing "math before breakfast"—a sort of game where they ask each other questions while I get out the cereal and juice. Coulter (who's seven) asked, "What's 1 Toby plus 1 Toby?" Toby, four years old, answered, "Eight."

"No, no," responded Coulter. "What's 1 Toby plus 1 Toby?"

"Eight!" answered Toby, with more volume and conviction.

Suddenly it dawned on me that he was right. In terms of age, two Tobies is the same as 2 x 4, which is 8. So as I passed out the bowls, I asked if one Toby was equal to 4 years. "Yes," Toby replied. They then began to create equations using their friends' ages: "Does 1 J (9) – 1 K (7) + 1 I (6) = 1 T (4)?" and so on.

I wonder how often "wrong answers" are simply right answers to different interpretations of a question. If the purpose of math is to use symbols to phrase observations about the world, then we need to give our children time to grow up using the language of math, and exploring it. When they began to talk, we did not demand that they pronounce each word correctly or use proper grammar. So, too, I think mathematical thinking needs to grow naturally.

I grew up hating math. I remember my father sitting down with me each evening after dinner to go over flash cards. I feared getting the wrong answer. And so, as my reading and verbal abilities grew, my math skills remained stuck, as I made tortuous progress through workbook after workbook. I never, ever would have asked my sister at the breakfast table, "What's 1 Sue plus 1 Sue?" I simply avoided all math, believing (as my mom said) that I was "mathlexic."

Perhaps this is why I do not "teach" math to my children. We work out our problems, play games with numbers, and use math as a tool in our daily living. Today, we were sorting potatoes for market and weighing them. This led to all sorts of interesting math problems. The weight of the bowl we were using to hold the potatoes was 1/4 lb. Often we'd get a bowl full of potatoes that weighed something like 3 3/4 lbs. I haven't yet formally taught fractions, but Coulter figured out how much the potatoes weighed, and added different weights together for totals. His comments? "Gee, Mom, this is fun! When are you going to dig more?"

Stories in other homeschooling publications and in the growing number of books about homeschooling will give you a much fuller picture of how homeschooling works for different families, and how you can shape it to fit your own.

No state requires you to be a certified teacher in order to homeschool your kids. You should remember that you are not teaching a class of thirty children but just your own children, something you've been doing for years. The dynamics of classroom teaching and the tutorial approach you can use in homeschooling are completely different. Your children have large blocks of time with you so their questions can arise naturally and often throughout the course of the day. As any parent knows, young children will ask questions if they aren't conditioned to stop asking them. Just because lots of people put their children in school or, if younger, under professional day care, does not automatically mean that certified professionals are better at nurturing children's learning than uncertified parents.

For instance, a British study, described in the book *Young Children Learning*, compared tapes of the conversations of working-class parents with their four-year-old children to those of nursery school teachers with four-year-olds. It revealed that the children who stayed home asked all sorts of questions about a diverse number of topics, showing no fear of learning new words or concepts. The children under the care of professional teachers had much less range of thought and intensity, and they asked far fewer questions.

The Washington Homeschool Research Project's report, *The Relationship of Selected Input Variables to Academic Achievement among Washington's Homeschoolers*,[60] by Jon Wartes, was able to examine this question in some detail. Wartes was able to study a group of homeschooled children whose parents were state-certified teachers and children of parents who were not certified. The results showed no difference in the learning outcomes of children in both groups, leading the researcher to note that this "suggests that contact with a certified teacher is not a necessary component of academic success. Policy decisions that would, as a general matter, require contact with a certified teacher as a condition to homeschool are not supported by this data."

Many private schools do not require their teachers to be state-certified in education, but prefer instead to have teachers who have strong knowledge in the subject they plan to teach. The schools prefer a degree in the field of history for a history teacher, for example, rather than a certificate in education. Why do these schools not worry about certification? Because they know that enthusiasm for teaching, love of the subject matter, and a commitment to children aren't found only in certified teachers. The same is true in homeschooling.

Correspondence schools, such as the Calvert School and the Home Study Institute have been providing home study courses for American families abroad and at home for many decades. Alaska created a Centralized Correspondence Study (CCS) program, which has been in existence for decades. The state mails a correspondence-study program to parents who then administer the materials to their children. There has been no evidence over all this time that homeschooled children using these programs do less well than their schooled peers in Alaska or elsewhere.

Homeschooling can allow learning to take place at more varying paces than the school schedule allows, giving you and your children lots of time to work on things in different ways than those taught in school, along with the time to obtain different results. Some parents find that being on a different schedule than that prescribed by school's developmental curriculum can be unnerving. However, my wife and I don't see ourselves as managing our children's development according to a strict schedule; we are simply nurturing our children, trying to be the best parents we can. In *The Disappearance of*

Childhood, Neil Postman notes how the concept of school-managed child development came to be:

> By writing sequenced textbooks and by organizing school classes according to calendar age, schoolmasters invented, as it were, the stages of childhood. Our notions of what a child can learn or ought to learn, and at what ages, were largely derived from the concept of sequenced curriculum; that is to say, from the concept of the prerequisite....
>
> [T]he point is that the mastery of the alphabet and the mastery of all the skills and knowledge that were arranged to follow constituted not merely a curriculum but a definition of child development. By creating a concept of a hierarchy of knowledge and skills, adults invented the structure of child development.[61]

Homeschoolers who do not use this structure of child development discover that children learn at widely varying rates; for instance, some homeschooled children do not learn to read until they are ten or eleven; others learn at much younger ages. Children in school must learn to read well enough by third grade in most schools or they will be unable to move apace with the increasingly book-oriented schooling at each grade; but when this administrative concern is ignored, it becomes a bit clearer that children can learn to read well at a wider range of ages than school allows. A study by Alan Thomas, *Educating Children at Home*, indicates that late reading among homeschooled children is common. Some children may not learn to read until they are ten or eleven years old, but "as far as could be ascertained, [there is] no adverse effect on intellectual development, self-worth, or even subsequent attainment in literacy." The "late" readers caught up with and soon surpassed the reading level of their schooled age-mates. Dr. Thomas also notes, in contrast to schoolchildren of the same ages, "in common with most other home-educated children, [the late readers] went on to thoroughly enjoy reading."

FIRST STEPS

Broadly speaking, there are three steps you need to take in order to start homeschooling.

1. KNOW YOUR STATE'S LAWS AND REGULATIONS.

To find out what the laws or regulations are in your state contact someone who is currently homeschooling in your area. Local homeschooling groups are usually the best source of precise information about how to fulfill the requirements of the law in your area (see Appendix D). Many state groups have information packets for new homeschoolers that include information about laws and regulations. See the listings for support groups in the appendix to find one in your area.

You can find the actual wording of your state's law under "compulsory education" or "school attendance" in a courthouse or law library, or you can write to your State Department of Education for a copy of the current regulations. In general, some states require you to submit an education plan to your local district, some require you to file simple documents with your respective state's education department, and some allow you to register your home as a private school. Remember, you do not have to be a certified teacher to homeschool in any state.

In addition to being the best source of current information about laws and regulations, homeschooling support groups can help you meet a lot of people at once and can tell you about local activities. Support groups often have newsletters and meetings and sometimes organize field trips, sports teams, writing clubs, book discussion groups—whatever appeals to the families involved.

2. DEVELOP YOUR CURRICULUM.

I need to emphasize that you don't need a packaged curriculum in order to homeschool successfully. You can write your own curriculum based on your family's philosophy of education, change or adapt it as needed throughout the year, and not run afoul with educational authorities. Many private schools have vastly different curricula from public schools. For instance, in schools using the educational philosophy of Rudolf Steiner, usually called Waldorf schools, children aren't taught to read until they've lost their eyeteeth, which is often later than when they would be taught in public school. Many alternative schools, such as the Albany Free School in New York State or the Sudbury Valley School in Massachusetts use no set curricula at all—you can too. Think of the resources available in your community: libraries, museums, historical sites, courthouses, specialty shops, nature centers. Think of adults you know who can share a skill, answer a question, allow your children to observe or help them at work. Think of real-life activities: writing letters, handling money, measuring, observing the stars, talking to older people. These are some of the ways that homeschoolers learn writing, math, science, and history. Talking with other homeschoolers will give you further ideas.

Some families like to have an idea of what is expected of kids in school at various ages. You can ask a local schoolteacher, principal, or school board member for a copy of the curriculum outline for the grade your child would be in; some are happy to share this information, some are not. If you can get a copy of your school's curriculum, use it as a guide but don't make yourself follow it rigidly; one of the biggest advantages of homeschooling is that you don't have to operate exactly as school does or make your child follow the same timetable. Another useful document is the *Typical Course of Study, K–12* (see Appendix A, subsection Homeschooling).

You can also use the *What Your First Grader Needs to Know* series edited by E. D. Hirsch to see what he thinks a "culturally literate" person needs to know at each grade level. Or ask your local Waldorf, Christian Independent, Montessori, Catholic, or other private school for their curriculum outlines to see what they think a "well-rounded individual" should know.

Some families prefer to start out using a packaged curriculum, and you can investigate which one best fits your family's need; I provide some suggestions in Appendix B at the end of this book. You can also find ads for and reviews of curricula in many homeschooling websites and magazines and examine and purchase them at homeschooling conferences. Generally, a correspondence school's assignments can be completed in a few hours a day, leaving time for other activities.

There is no need to spend lots of money on curricula, books, educational toys and videos, and the like. You really need to spend no more than you would ordinarily spend on a child's interests and activities. Homeschoolers often use the library and other free or low-cost community resources. They share or barter materials and skills with one another or with other people in the community. Some families are able to barter for outside lessons and to volunteer in exchange for admission to arts events or museums. Older homeschoolers find that volunteering is a good way to learn from adults outside the family, and it is often less expensive than taking a class or buying equipment.

3. ENJOY YOUR FAMILY.

Don't let your family get lost in your efforts to school your children. It's easy to replace teachers, but not parents. Some parents burn out from homeschooling by trying to be demanding, "professional" teachers for some parts of the day, then sympathetic parents for other parts, and the stress of switching between these two roles becomes too burdensome. Be a loving parent to your children all the time. Teaching and helping our children learn is an inherent part of parenting that we seem to forget we do once we send children to school. We don't need to—though, perhaps, there are situations where one would want to—imitate classroom teacher behavior and techniques in homeschooling. If you want to take a break and walk through the woods because it is a gorgeous day, you can; the curriculum can wait. Something you discover in the woods could become a prompt for further studies, or it will just be a nice walk. If your child wants to finish an exciting book she is reading instead of doing lessons one day, you can permit that. The lessons can be caught up with later. Homeschooling lets us set our own goals and our own schedules. Don't let curricula and schooling become the tail that wags the dog in your home; enjoy your time together as a family. Overscheduling children with courses and activities is an issue for many families, and in reaction some are urging "slow homeschooling" to counter it, based on how the slow food movement was promoted as an alternative to fast food.[62]

Also, try not to compare yourselves too much with other homeschooling families; each is different. Some families, particularly in rural areas, have a slower pace of life and fewer opportunities for museum trips, specialized classes, and so on. They are able to take advantage of their land, homes, and nature in ways urban homeschoolers cannot. Further, some urban homeschoolers may prefer a slower pace of life than their colleagues who lead very active lives; being a homeschooler does not mean you must be plugged into every activity you can find.

APPROACHES TO HOMESCHOOLING

Homeschooling changes and adapts to the needs of the learner, as well as to any special circumstances that may happen in the family (illness, a new baby, new job hours for a spouse, and so on). You do not, no matter what the law is in your state, need to plan out in precise detail what you will do for the entire year. However, you will probably want to have some sort of plan, or list of ideas, at the start.

It is useful for you and your spouse to clarify how you will home-school, not only to answer skeptics' questions about what it is you're doing but also to keep yourselves from becoming rattled when things aren't going smoothly. It is also good to know where you stand philo-sophically so that you can present your home school in the best pos-sible light to school officials who may question your approach. At the same time, it's crucial to remember that homeschooling is flexible. The word *homeschooling* doesn't refer to any one practice; it simply refers to families learning outside of school. Choices you make at the start of the year are not irrevocable. You can—and you very likely will—adapt and change things as you go. You will also have many opportunities to learn from your mistakes, as we have found out in our own homeschooling. Live and learn!

All the books I mention in this chapter and in Appendix A will provide information, sometimes in great detail, as to the various methods of teaching and learning you may choose. For the sake of brevity, I will divide these approaches into two main philosophies:

1. *School at Home.* Families that choose this philosophy usually aren't worried about "why" their children must learn certain things at certain ages; they are far more concerned with how to help their chil-dren learn what they've decided their children should learn. Families with this philosophy of education have a large number of standard-ized textbooks and curricula to choose from, many of which they can purchase from school supply stores or textbook manufacturers. Often these materials can also be purchased in used book stores, at home-schooling "curriculum fairs," and through direct mail. The curriculum determines what and when subjects will be taught, the parent creates or purchases lesson plans to use on the specified days, and the children are regularly tested to see how much of the material they have learned.

A subset of this category is often called the "unit study," "the-matic," or "project" approach. Parents following this approach design a series of projects, field trips, and readings that build on a particular theme and use it to address several subject areas at once. For instance, one can use Thanksgiving time to study the Pilgrim era for history, biology (what food Pilgrims grew), science (how Pilgrims took care of illnesses), math (calculating how big a plot each person could get at Plymouth Plantation), and so on.

2. *Unschooling.* This is also known as interest-driven, child-led, natural, organic, eclectic, or self-directed learning. Lately, the term *unschooling* has come to be associated with the type of homeschooling that doesn't use a fixed curriculum. When pressed, I define unschooling as allowing children as much freedom to learn in the world as their parents can comfortably bear. The advantage of this method is that it doesn't require you, the parent, to become someone else, that is, a professional teacher pouring knowledge into child-vessels on a planned basis. Instead you live and learn together, pursuing questions and interests as they arise and using conventional schooling on an on-demand basis, if at all. This is the way we learn before going to school and the way we learn when we leave school and enter the world of work. So, for instance, a young child's interest in hot rods can lead her to a study of how the engine works (science), how and when the first car was built (history and business), who built and designed the car (biography), and so on. Certainly these interests can lead to reading texts, taking courses, or doing projects, but the important difference is that these activities were chosen and engaged in freely by the learner. They were not dictated to the learner through curricular mandate to be done at a specific time and place, though parents with a more hands-on approach to unschooling certainly can influence and guide their children's choices. Unschooling, for lack of a better term (until people start to accept living as part and parcel of learning), is the natural way to learn. However, this does not mean unschoolers do not take traditional classes or use curricular materials when the

student, or parents and children together, decide that this is how they want to do it. Learning to read or do quadratic equations are not "natural" processes, but unschoolers nonetheless learn them when it makes sense to them to do so, not because they have reached a certain age or are compelled to do so by arbitrary authority. Therefore, it isn't unusual to find unschoolers who are barely eight years old studying astronomy or some who are ten years old and just learning to read.

It is unfair to think that either of the philosophies I present above are mutually exclusive, though to some "school at homers" allowing children to determine what they will study is as distasteful as being forced to diagram sentences can be for some "unschoolers." Try not to let purists of either persuasion get to you. You must do what you are comfortable with; like your children, you, too, will learn and change as you get more experience with homeschooling. You can start out with a package of textbook and "teacher-proof curricula" (that's how some curriculum manufacturers actually refer to their materials) and if that isn't working you can switch to a unit study or unschooling approach. Indeed, you can do a little of each depending on your child's abilities and your ability to juggle different approaches. You may start out highly programmed and gradually loosen up and let your children have more say in what and how they study as you get comfortable with homeschooling. You may start out highly free-form and eventually find your child engaged in a very strict schedule of music or language lessons, Scout activities, and clubs.

You can also involve your children in creating their course of study for the year. Susan Jaffer of Pennsylvania writes:

Last year, at the beginning of the summer, I asked my daughters what I thought was a casual question: "What would you like to learn about this summer?" They began answering me right away, without so much as a pause, and this is what we ended up with: Suzanne, 8, wanted to learn about stories, poems, science, math, art, music, books, people, planting, animals, places, food, colors, rocks, babies, cars, eyes, and electricity. Gillian, 6, wanted to learn about seeds, bones, plants, books, evolution, dinosaurs, and experiments. I tend to think that the fact that I asked them in the summer freed them from the boundaries of school subjects. In any case, I was stunned by the fact that they had so many subjects in mind, and that their lists were right there waiting for me to ask the right question.

I like Susan's phrase about how her kids expressed such wide interests since they were "freed…from the boundaries of school subjects." It reminded me of a comment I heard author Grace Llewellyn make about helping homeschooled teenagers find ways to study subjects outside of school by not always limiting ourselves to school categories. Grace described a letter in *GWS* from a girl who asked her father what a person who studied whales was called. Her father told her such people were called "marine biologists" and she would have to go to college to become one and study whales. Grace pointed out that marine biology is but one way for children and adults to study and work with whales; the family could also encourage their daughter to study whales as an artist, musician, sailor, ecologist, naturalist, and so on. This point is very valuable to remember if you find your children getting frustrated in their studies and you need a new way to approach the material.

Oddly enough, parents who follow alternative education ideas sometimes find that their children desire and enjoy using conventional curricula. One fourteen-year-old girl strongly desired to use a packaged curriculum program to homeschool, which rattled her mom, an experienced unschooler, who had not used curricula with any of her other children. They agreed to try homeschooling with a packaged curriculum, and the girl flourished with it.

A mother from Kentucky, Cindy Gaddis, sums up this issue quite well. She writes:

I declare myself an unschooler even though my daughter Abbey loves workbooks and my son Adam has to be taught most things in a highly structured manner. I say this because I am respecting their need to learn in the way that works best for them. I would declare an older homeschooler who decides to become much more structured in learning an unschooler because she is respecting her ability to know what she needs and wants at each stage of her life.

It is not unusual to feel overwhelmed by the amount of freedom learning at home allows, especially by those who were in school and are now being homeschooled. It often makes sense to let children get used to their newfound freedom gradually, allowing them more private time and space than they probably had before. But, as Susannah Sheffer, an editor of *GWS, writes*:

At some point the need for that break diminishes and kids begin to feel ready for more activity and focus, [and] it can be difficult to know where to start.

One thing I've found useful, when helping kids go through this process, is to make three lists. One list is for things that come easily, things that you would do anyway, whether or not you sat down and made a plan about them. The second list is for things that you want to work on but feel you need some help with—maybe suggestions of ways to pursue the activity, or maybe some sort of schedule or plan regarding it. The third list is for things you want to put aside for a while, things you don't want to work on right now.

The value of these lists, it seems to me, is that they show kids: (1) that they are already doing worthwhile things, and don't need outside intervention for everything; (2) at the same time, it's perfectly OK to want help in some areas, to have a list of things that you want to do but aren't sure what to do; and (3) that it's also OK to put some things aside for the time being. This might be especially important to kids who had bad experiences with particular subjects in school and who would benefit from realizing that they have much more control in their new situation. Fourteen-year-old Marianne was very emphatic, for example, about putting essay writing on list three, because she had had very unpleasant and discouraging experiences with essay writing in school, and for her, at that time, having control meant being able to say, "I choose not to work on that right now."

Marianne's list two was the longest, as I think it will be for many kids, and ultimately this list may be the most important, because it's the one from which ideas and plans can grow. As I said, it's very important to realize that much of what you're doing already has educational value (school doesn't usually give kids credit for the things they willingly and eagerly pursue on their own). But it's just as important for the new homeschooler (or the longtime home-schooler who is looking to make some changes) to realize that it's fine to need help and to ask for it. Suppose a teenager has a vague feeling that she wants to do something with animals, but isn't sure what. That could go on list two. Then, when the lists are made up and you sit down to give each item closer attention, you can begin to think: what kind of work with animals? what kind of help would you need in making that happen? and so on.

The same goes for more traditional academic work. Suppose the home-schooler says, "I want to keep up with the other kids who are doing algebra in school, but I'm just not sure I'm going to do that regularly on my own." Well, that's OK. What would help? Should we look into finding another adult to work with you? Would it be fun to meet regularly with another homeschooler who is working on alge-bra? Or would a schedule tacked up to the bulletin board help you remember that you wanted to work on this each week?

Sometimes people emphasize the lack of scheduling and fixed appointments in homeschooling, because this open-endedness is one of the things that makes homeschooling feel so different to kids who have spent years in school—no bells ringing, no one telling you you have to do math at this time. And it's true that we often want to stress the way in which home-schooling lets kids take advantage of whatever arises...But in stressing these benefits and these ways in which homeschooling is different from school, we may sometimes forget that the most crucial benefit, and difference, is that in homeschooling you have control—which means that you can make schedules, and plans, and appointments, if you want to.

Most homeschooling books and magazines have stories by teens and elementary school–age children about the types of schedules and help they find useful. There are also many examples of how different families schedule their homeschooling in the firsthand accounts that are available in homeschooling periodicals and books.

Each family is different and each child is different, so don't assume that what worked for one child will work for all. The most important thing, besides love, that you can bring to your home school is the trust in yourself to help your children learn and the trust you have in your children to learn in their own way.

You don't have to teach the way you were taught. In addition to materials and good texts that the students can use to learn on their own, many homeschooling families find tutors. These may be professional teachers, but are more likely to be people who are practitioners of what the child wishes to learn. This often puts parents in a teaching role different from that which occurs in schools; they are more facilitators, "askers," travel agents, general contractors, and counselors than instructors doling out lessons. Parents of homeschoolers learn to ferret out learning opportunities for their children, and they can become quite adept at networking through their local support groups, social media, local newspapers, and community bulletin boards. In short, parents do not have to be the sole instructors of their children.

Some homeschooling parents create clubs or learning cooperatives around certain interests their children may have, such as science, rocketry, or theater, and conduct weekly meetings at their homes or in local libraries. Some share their expertise in exchange for money, barter, or no payment at all: a single mother my wife and I know charges families a modest fee for tutoring children in math at her home; another mother offers a free literature class in her home twice a week to ten homeschoolers; both mothers are former schoolteachers, by the way! A father we know who makes his living as an illustrator is teaching an art course once a week in the evening at his house, as a way to share his love of art with his sons and their friends. Ordinary people, using their own resources, can be highly effective teachers when they share their own interests with children who wish to learn from them.

Some homeschoolers create resource centers to be used by large numbers of homeschoolers, for free or for a fee. In London, England, Leslie Barson created the Otherwise Club in her home as a place for children to work together on projects of their own choosing. As her children got older and the club got bigger Barson wanted to reclaim her home. She found a local community center that let her group meet two days a week for two thousand pounds a year; Barson charges a membership fee of one hundred pounds per family, and she has been able to gain charitable status for the group. She writes:

The Club provides the space for workshops and activities for families. We have three regular workshops—drama, pottery, and a science group for younger children—and we run a number of other activities. Past workshops have included country dancing, visits from police dogs and their handlers, and talks by various experts in areas such as math, home education, and health. Recent workshops have included African drumming at several different levels and a workshop on *A Midsummer Night's Dream* and a trip to see the play.... The Otherwise Club has a small cafe which serves a vegetarian homemade lunch and cake as well as tea and coffee. This provides a small amount of funds and serves as a focal point for the community. We also keep a small lending library about alternative education and a large amount of information about activities and exhibitions in London.

Other homeschoolers find and publicize courses and offerings at local museums, historic sites, community centers, and gymnasiums. In Boston, Harvard University's Peabody Museum and the Boston Museum of Science have advertised courses for homeschoolers. Technological advances now allow internet courses for learning everything from jazz improvisation to secondary school courses leading to diplomas; there are also video and audiotape lectures by experts in all kinds of fields that can be borrowed from libraries or from homeschoolers who share the cost and the materials.

Most homeschooling, and certainly the formation and continuation of these clubs and groups, is performed by people not certified by the state as teachers. Participation is neither mandatory nor graded. The participants get what they put into each activity, and should they decide not to learn in these settings, no external failing grade or other penalty will be given. They can come back to these places and learn what they need when they are ready for it, or they can choose, or create, other situations in which they can learn what they wish to learn. These parents and children are not therefore re-creating compulsory public school in their communities, nor are they creating alternative schools; they are creating alternatives to school for their children.

It's important to remember that some children need alternatives to home as well; clearly not every family is motivated to work with their children the way the homeschoolers I describe here are. However, the only place besides home for most children is school, a situation we have created with our compulsory education laws, and often school is not a good place for children either. When neither home nor school is a safe, productive environment for children and teens, the sorts of places that I describe above can be expanded to accommodate them. I doubt we can get people to change compulsory education laws in America, but there is wiggle room in these laws, as homeschooling and many out-of-school programs sanctioned by various school departments demonstrate. By expanding these exceptions to allow children and teenagers to observe real work or engage in it as apprentices, we will help them learn what is needed to do work well. Children also learn how to interact with others to get jobs done, and how to leave work they don't enjoy and find work they want to try; these are skills that are not only not taught in school but actually tend to atrophy in most schools. One typically works in silence in competition for grades and is penalized for sharing information, and one cannot change jobs when it is apparent that one does not have the capacity or interest to continue with a particular course in school and would like to try something different.

Not all activities are obviously educational, but that does not mean they are not important learning experiences for children. As many have pointed out, play is a child's work. Children typically use fantasy play, in particular, not to escape from the real world, but to get into it: when they pretend to be doctors, firefighters, police, and soldiers, they are using their imaginations to explore these roles. My own children often played school when they were younger! People benefit from periods of play throughout life, and some people are able to find or create adult work that often grows out of their childhood play. School is all too often opposed to the spontaneous play of children, a trend that is increasing as schools march to the drums of testing and standardization, and families bounce to the beat of professionalized after-school programs. Homeschoolers need not turn the screws tighter on children in order to make them learn; there is no need to duplicate school techniques in our homes.

RECORD KEEPING

There are two types of record keeping homeschoolers can do: that which is required by the state and that which they want to do for themselves. Of course, there is some overlap, but on the whole, these are very different types of records. States, and in some cases local school districts, vary in the amount and the kind of record keeping they require of homeschoolers. The first thing you want to do is find out what you have to do legally. Some states require testing (but not always every year); some allow parents to choose among testing, keeping a portfolio, or writing up reports; and some states don't require testing or much record keeping at all. No matter what your state's requirements, you can find a way to fulfill them without getting bogged down or worrying more than is necessary about how much your children are accomplishing. In any case, whether or not your state has record keeping requirements, you may find, as many parents do, that you want to keep some kind of record of your homeschooling, for your own peace of mind and for the fun of chronicling your child's growth—just as parents have always saved their children's drawings, stories, projects, and so on.

Katharine Houk, a longtime homeschooler from New York, wrote to *GWS* about several ways to keep records:

> A topic that frequently comes up at homeschooling support-group meetings at the beginning of the homeschool year is record keeping. For those of us whose homeschooling approach is interest-initiated and far-ranging, it can be a challenge to write quarterly reports for submission to the school district, when learning is expected to be pigeonholed into subject areas.
>
> When our family first started homeschooling, the New York State Home Instruction Regulation was not in effect. Homeschooling was permitted, but was handled differently by each school district, with guidelines from the State Education Department offering suggestions

on how to handle homeschooling. Our district gave us a checklist to fill out periodically, and that was the extent of our reporting. But at that time, I kept daily logs of my children's activities, even though I didn't need them for reporting purposes. I was fascinated with their learning processes, and had great fun documenting all the wonderful things they did. Most of their learning was through play; they played intensely, happily, and for hours and days at a time. My challenge was in translating their activities and our conversations and experiences into a form that would fit in the subject area boxes in my log book.

When the need for reporting came along, with the passage of the current regulation, it was easy for us to make that transition; we had already been keeping records. Besides the requirement that as homeschoolers you must keep an attendance record (!), there is no specific requirement for record keeping in the regulation. But I knew that having a written record of our activities would be helpful to me in writing reports. Besides, I was already in the habit of doing it, and enjoyed creating a record of my children's learning.

I used a loose-leaf notebook for each child. In the front were pages that looked like a lesson plan book, with subject areas listed down the left side of the page, and the days of the week across the top of the page. I included Saturday and Sunday, because learning doesn't stop for weekends. In the notebook I also included a place to record field trips and keep photographs, pocket pages for papers, etc. It served us well, and the children enjoy looking back at them, laughing at the spelling in their early writings, and reminiscing about trips and other activities from years ago.

As the children grew older, I grew weary of sifting their learning into subject area categories. Their learning is all of a piece, and it became tedious to chop it up into artificial compartments on a daily basis. Therefore I changed the notebook to include lined paper, where each day I would write a few sentences about what was done that day. At the end of each month, I would make a synopsis of the month by subject area. Then when it came time for a quarterly report, I would have something to work from.

Now that the children are so much older (12 and 15), it is unnecessary for me alone to do all the record keeping. Also, my offspring are such independent learners and I am so busy that often I am not aware of their activities or of what books they are reading. I do jot things down from time to time that I am aware of and that I find especially noteworthy, but I ask each of them to keep their own notebook, and to write down the books they are reading and their activities, plus whatever else they care to put in their journals. This way I am not invading their privacy, and they have a record in their own writing of what they have done. At report time, they share with us the parts of their journals that they want in their reports. Privacy is an important issue, one that is sometimes not taken into account when school districts want to know everything that is happening with our children.

Some families I know use a spiral-bound notebook for record keeping, and store papers in a separate portfolio. Also there are commercially distributed record keeping systems you can purchase....

Whatever method of record keeping you choose, the results will help you in writing reports and complying with assessment requirements, and will be a wonderful chronicle of your children's growth and development.

Some families prefer to use online resources for keeping track of lists and tasks, such as Trello. The tool you use should be one you are comfortable with and that your children can refer to as well. If you want a more detailed presentation about record keeping and evaluations for homeschoolers, particularly for high school, I recommend Loretta Heuer's comprehensive book *The Homeschooler's Guide to Portfolios and Transcripts*. In about fourteen states, as of this writing, homeschoolers must formally write up their curriculum and submit it to their local education authorities. In other states, requirements are less extensive, so be sure to check the homeschooling laws or regulations in your state.

For those states that do require you to submit a curriculum or plan, here are some guidelines. If you purchase a curriculum, that is what you submit. You transfer the program's stated goals and objectives onto whatever forms or documents the local education authorities wish you to submit to them. If you follow your child's interests, as I'm suggesting throughout this book, then it is largely a matter of translating what one is going to do anyway into language the school officials can understand. Here is an example for you to consider, prefaced by Susannah Sheffer:

> In states that require written proposals in the first place (and not all do), the actual wording of the law, the requirements or preferences of the particular school district, and the inclinations of the family itself will all influence what kind of proposal the family actually writes. Some people believe it's better to write a great deal so that the files are thick and the family appears thorough; others believe it's better to give only the minimum required by law and to let the school officials ask for more if they want more. Both approaches are valid. Some families see the fact that they must write a proposal as an opportunity to articulate their own philosophy and goals for the year for themselves as well as for the district; others view the proposal only as something they must do to satisfy legal requirements and would rather keep it as short as possible. Again, both approaches are valid.... Here's a sample of an effective, shorter proposal [for first grade—PF] that Jane Dwinell (Vermont) wrote for her daughter Dana's first year of homeschooling (again, in the legal sense):

COURSE OF STUDY FOR DANA DWINELL-YARDLEY:

1. BASIC COMMUNICATION SKILLS

Language Arts. Topics may include but shall not be limited to the following: Silent and oral reading; listening skills; telling stories; spelling; homonyms; synonyms and antonyms; writing letters, stories, and poems by hand, dictation, or typing; dictionary use for meaning and spelling; encyclopedia use; library skills; use of basic punctuation; use of table of contents and index; and computer skills.

Math. Topics may include but shall not be limited to the following: Count and write by 1s, 10s, 100s, 1000s; addition and subtraction with single and double digits; telling time and using the calendar; value of coins and making change; and meaning of inch, foot, yard.

2. CITIZENSHIP, HISTORY, AND GOVERNMENT IN VERMONT AND THE U.S.

Topics may include but shall not be limited to the following: Current events; town meeting; travel throughout New England and to Florida; national holidays; map reading: World—name and find oceans, continents, our country, our state; U.S.—name and find New England states; Vermont—find Irasburg, Montpelier, Burlington, Newport, Lake Mem-phremagog, Lake Champlain, Lake Willoughby, Lake Morey, Connecticut River, Black River, Barton River.

3. PHYSICAL EDUCATION AND COMPREHENSIVE HEALTH EDUCATION

Topics may include but shall not be limited to the following: Sports—cross country skiing, downhill skiing, sliding, biking, hiking, tree climbing, swimming, gymnastics, badminton, croquet, canoeing. Health Education—basic first aid for cuts, splinters, burns, sprains, and strains; treatment of common cold; care of teeth and regular dental visits; traffic safety; family meal planning and food preparation.

4. ENGLISH, AMERICAN, AND OTHER LITERATURE
Topics may include but shall not be limited to the following: Novels by nineteenth- and twentieth-century British and American authors; American poetry; Greek mythology.

5. THE NATURAL SCIENCES
Topics may include but shall not be limited to the following: Seeds, bulbs, plants, and flowers; common birds; sun, moon, stars, and basic constellations; seasons, weather, clouds; fire and temperature; farm animals—care from infancy to adulthood, slaughtering; maple sugaring.

6. THE FINE ARTS
Topics may include but shall not be limited to the following: Drawing; painting; computer graphics; making clothes and handkerchiefs for dolls and dress-up; attending concerts and plays; listening to music at home (live and taped); singing.

EVALUATIONS

John Holt writes about the value of feedback versus evaluation in Chapter 12, and I won't labor the point here. However, in his book *What Do I Do Monday?* Holt provides some good context about evaluations outside of conventional schooling:

> In the kind of learning I have been talking about there is no place
> and no need for conventional testing and grading. In a class where

children are doing things, and not getting ready to do them sometime in the distant future, what they do tells us what they have learned.

...What sense does an average grade make in a course like English? Do we average a serious writer's best work against his worst? If I assigned a paper, and a student did badly on it, this only showed that this was the wrong paper for him, where he could not show the ability he had. The remedy was to try and give a wide enough variety of choices and opportunities for writing, reading, and talking so that everyone would have a fairly good chance of showing his best talents.

It is not just in English that it makes no sense to figure students' grades by taking an average of all their daily or weekly work. It makes no sense in any subject....

It is not grading alone that is stupid, but the whole idea of trying to have a class move along on a schedule, like a train. Children do not learn things at the same time, or equally easily and quickly.[63]

As you will see, portfolios and other descriptive measures of learning are well suited for homeschooling families who want to get away from grades and gold stars, particularly if they aren't following a conventional school curriculum. In states that require homeschoolers to provide a form of evaluation during, or at the end of, the school year, homeschoolers can often choose from the following evaluation methods:

STANDARDIZED TESTING. This can be provided by the school or, in some cases, you can negotiate to use a third party, such as a guidance counselor, teacher, or mutually agreed-upon proctor, to administer the test in your home. If you feel the school's choice of test is biased against your homeschooling methods and philosophy, you can ask to administer a different test more to your liking. Before doing this, it is wise to consider how and what you will be teaching your children; if you are following a school curriculum and periodically giving your children tests, then they are probably ready to take these standardized tests. If you have created an individualized study plan for your child, and you do not use standardized testing during your homeschooling year, but your school is forcing standardized tests on you, then it is wise to do as they do in school: obtain previous editions of the test, spend some time teaching the subject matter that you see is on the test, and practice taking the test with your children.

PORTFOLIO ASSESSMENTS. This, combined with a yearly progress report, is how my wife and I handle evaluations of our children for our local district. A portfolio is an extension of the refrigerator magnet: a place where you save and date your children's work. The difference is you want to save a lot of this stuff and sift through it later to find significant pieces of achievement or indications of development for school officials, such as the two-page report on "The Real Pocahontas" our daughter Lauren (then nine) did, or problem solving, such as a series of math problems, with her self-corrections, that Alison (then six) did. We also save workbook pages (our children sometimes ask for workbook pages just to see if they can do the same stuff their schooled friends do!), lists of books we buy or check out from the library to read to them or that they read themselves, and brief journal notes about significant events, such as a trip to Plymouth Plantation when Lauren and a friend helped bake bread and make candles "the real way" by spending all day in one "Pilgrim's" house.

PROGRESS REPORTS. These can take the form of written narratives of your children's learning over a quarter, a half year, or a year; the periodicity of these reports will depend on your state laws or regulations. Consider that if you write at least one sentence a day, or at least five sentences at the end of each week, about each child, by the end of the year you will have many pages of detailed information about what your children actually did, rather than just a letter or number for a year's worth of work.

PERFORMANCE ASSESSMENTS. This term refers to the evaluation of the culmination of a body of work. These are becoming more in vogue with some current education reforms. For example, a child could successfully build a working volcano to demonstrate mastery of certain science principles, or actually perform in a play or concert to demonstrate ability and understanding. Many real-life activities demonstrate thought, responsibility, planning, and subject mastery. For example, a child might, for the ultimate purpose of setting up an aquarium, determine how much money he has, budget it properly, and choose the right fish and equipment. Though it may sound like a homeschooling story, this particular example is taken from literature by the Wisconsin Department of Education about how it plans to evaluate students as part of its education reforms.

Assessments can also take the form of interviews with other types of educators (child psychologists, school counselors, etc.); written reports from people other than relatives and parents who work with your child; and videotapes, audiotapes, and newspaper clippings of activities your children do that prove they can use the skills and knowledge they have learned.

Many homeschoolers have been admitted to college or found work worth doing without college degrees. Researchers who study grown homeschoolers find them to be doing well individually and economically, and the list of selective colleges that admit homeschooled students continues to grow.

In general, homeschoolers apply to college just like everyone else, except they need to prepare their own transcripts or summarize what they have been doing to provide evidence that they can handle college-level courses and ensure they have covered the subject matter that each college requires for entrance as first-year students. There are also several books, websites, and newsgroups that focus on college admissions for homeschoolers (see Appendices A and D).

Teenage homeschoolers can sometimes participate in dual-enrollment programs offered by their local high schools; this enables qualified teens to take community college courses instead of high school courses. However, if the school is not cooperative you can simply go directly to your local community college and see if your child can enroll in or audit classes. Our daughter, Lauren, when she was sixteen, took biology and psychology classes at two area community colleges; the biology class, by the way, was offered just to high school–age homeschoolers. Lauren was able to prove that she can handle college-level work in more tangible ways than many of her peers who have only high school diplomas. Now that Lauren is 34, and as I note in my Foreword, she went from community college to a four-year college, and earned a master's degree in social work without ever needing to present a high school diploma.

Further, home-based education programs run by private schools, such as the Clonlara School and others (see Private Schools and Curriculum Providers in Appendices B and C), will provide high school degrees and transcripts for colleges. There are other types of homeschooling programs for teenagers as well. They are oriented toward internship and apprenticeship opportunities rather than conventional schoolwork (see Learning Materials, Appendix E).

Besides questioning the conventional wisdom that all children must go to school, many homeschoolers also question if college is the best place for all teenagers to go in order to become successful adults. Many famous people who were homeschooled or who never graduated from or attended college have made important contributions to society: Susan B. Anthony, Pearl S. Buck, Andrew Carnegie, Thomas Edison, Winston Churchill, Charles Dickens, Michael Faraday, Benjamin Franklin, Jane Goodall, Alex Haley, Patrick Henry, Eric Hoffer, Claude Monet, General George Patton, Bertram Russell, Harry S. Truman, Woodrow Wilson, Gloria Steinem, Mark Twain, and the Wright Brothers, among others. Attending school, and college in particular, is not the only way for people to become valuable members of society and contributors to our culture. For more current listings do an online search for "successful people without college degrees."

In this chapter I've tried to show how homeschooling can be inherently different from traditional schooling. Once you start investigating resources (see Appendices), talking with your children about learning, and meeting other homeschoolers, you will find for yourself how one subject naturally leads to another and you will discover that you have, indeed, created your own "curriculum." The most important thing to do now is to do it! Enjoy your time with your children and the rest will follow. ■

12

SCHOOL RESPONSE

THE VALUE OF COOPERATION

How should the schools respond to parents who want to teach their children at home? Even in terms of their most immediate bread-and-butter interests—improving their public image, maintaining their budgets and salaries, keeping their jobs, and so on—the schools would be wise to try to help rather than hinder.

As we have seen, many school systems still oppose homeschoolers by every possible means, some even trying to take their children away from them. They seem to fear that if they let one family teach their children at home, every family will want to, and they will be out of business. Given their present troubles and bad publicity, this worry is natural enough. But it is not realistic. Even with full school cooperation and support, it is unlikely that, in a generation, more than 10 percent of the families of school-age children would be teaching them at home. Most school-age children would still be in some school. There are simply not that many people who like or trust their children that much, or would want to have them around that much of the time, or would take that much time and effort to answer their questions and otherwise help them find out what they want to know.

It is not primarily compulsory attendance laws that keep most children in school so much as the fact that almost no one wants them anywhere else. Until recently, the state of Mississippi had no such laws. They are just now beginning to introduce them; so far they only cover children of ages seven to eight or so. Yet from all we know, about as many children go to school in Mississippi as anywhere else—probably more than in many of our major cities, where as much as half of the high school population is often truant.

Some school people say, "If we let people teach their children at home, the rich will all take their children out of school, and we will have only poor children to teach." One might ask, "Well, what's so bad about that? You will then at last be able to give these poor children your undivided attention." But the fact is, at least so far, that very few of the people who are teaching their children at home are rich. Homeschoolers, as far as I can tell from their letters, have average incomes or less. Perhaps a majority of them have gone to college, though many have not. Many of them have chosen, for different reasons, to live fairly simply in small towns or in the country. One reason why many of them are interested in homeschooling is that they can't afford private schools, even if there were any around that they liked. For a long time to come homeschooling will have little appeal to the rich, who will probably continue to hire other people to look after their children.

In short, there is no reason for school people to see homeschooling as any kind of serious threat to themselves. Such threats do most certainly exist. The rapidly declining birth rate is one. No one can predict the future, and perhaps in the next decade large numbers of people of child-bearing age will suddenly decide to have many more children. But from all we know about young people today in their teens or early twenties, it seems likely that even more of them than now will decide not to marry, or if they marry, not to have children, or if they have any, to have only one or two. They are terribly worried about their own economic futures, about the rapidly rising costs of rearing and educating children, and about the general uncertainty of the world. The best bet seems to be that our rapidly dropping birth rate will continue to drop for some time, so that within a generation the population of school-age children might well fall to half or less of what it is now.

T HE POPULATION OF SCHOOL-AGE CHILDREN is still declining nationally and locally, despite the enrollment bubble caused by the "baby boomlet" toward the end of the last century. For instance, the *Boston Globe* recently reported that the population of school-age children living in Boston in 1970 was 127,405; in 2020 it was 75,394.[64] Some of this decline is the result of white flight from the city's neighborhoods and schools, but it is also due to the declining birth rate. ■

BEYOND THIS, PARENTS, white and nonwhite, are increasingly determined, if they possibly can, to get their children into private schools. In large cities, more and more parochial school students are non-Catholic, nonwhite children. A mother in Chicago writes that her son is the only white child in such a school. Fundamentalist church schools are springing up in all parts of the country. Private school attendance, after declining for many years, has increased rapidly in recent years. There is no reason to believe this trend will stop.

P RIVATE SCHOOL ATTENDANCE was in a slow decline since the 1990s, but the pandemic has given them a boost. Due their ability to remain open for students to attend in person during the pandemic, many private and religious schools saw enrollment increases. However, the cost of private schools will continue to rise. CNBC notes, "Overall, the average cost of tuition at private schools across all grades is $26,866 a year, with roughly a quarter of all families receiving financial aid, according to the National Association of Independent Schools."[65] ■

ALONG WITH THIS there is the danger—from the public schools' point of view, at least—of voucher plans. Under these programs the various governments, instead of giving education money to schools, give it directly to parents in the form of credits, which they can then use to send their children to whatever public or private school they liked best. Thus many more parents can afford to send their children to private schools or start schools of their own.

VOUCHER PLANS ARE MORE READILY available today than when John wrote about them in 1981, and they continue to be fought by the schools. On June 27, 2002, the U.S. Supreme Court ruled that education vouchers are constitutional. But vouchers as a mechanism for school choice are overtaken in many instances by the charter school movement, which didn't exist at the time John wrote.

On one hand, I think that John would have approved of charter schools in concept, but not in practice because, all too often, government funding turns charter schools into merely slight variations on the theme of state-approved compulsory schooling. John suggested that parents start their own schools where possible, and he often talked about the Danish school system as a model of how this could work on a larger scale. The Danes not only allow small parent-run schools and have done so for years, but they also pay for them with public funds once certain criteria are met. Small, run by and for local families in conjunction with a few like-minded teachers, empowered by flexible curricula and public support, the many "little schools" of Denmark are much more difficult to create in America. The charter school movement, which is supposed to make it easier for the creation of alternatives to public schools, is not growing quickly. For instance, Massachusetts allowed the creation of charter schools in 1995, but only about 78 charter schools have been funded since then.

I've heard of a few charter schools that have been started and operated by parents in some states, but not many. Indeed, in their do-it-yourself fashion, homeschoolers aren't waiting for the state to give them funds and permission to create the schools they want; they're going ahead and doing it anyway. In an article titled "Home-schooled Away from Home,"[66] the *Washington Post* reported on this trend where "parents work together in learning cooperatives, sometimes in each other's homes and increasingly in empty wings of churches and community centers." This may be a new trend for people who follow a school-at-home approach, but as you've read here, John was writing about these clubs and cooperatives, and unschoolers have been creating and using them, for decades. Any fears school officials may have about homeschoolers siphoning off their funding in order to start their own schools are simply overstated: home-schoolers are determined to create what they need regardless of government funding. Schools would be wiser to seek accommodation with homeschoolers rather than continue to drive away these educators, especially now that there are so many free or for-profit options for learning outside of school.

Public schools will gain much-needed allies among the growing number of motivated parents seeking to homeschool if they would work with them rather than against them. As John notes, fighting homeschoolers should not be a big issue for public schools when there are so many more pressing dangers for them. ■

T HE PUBLIC SCHOOLS HAVE REASON enough to worry about all these problems. But they have no good reason to worry about homeschooling. By opposing it they stand to gain little and to lose much of what is left of their good reputation and the confidence and trust of the public.

An example. A woman, a skilled performing classical musician, teacher, and conductor, moved to a small town in northern Minnesota. Her youngest daughter was herself training for a career as a professional violinist and had played with professionals in small concerts. Since the school itself had no advanced music programs, and since the girl was two or three years ahead of her class, the mother decided to take her out of school and teach her, in music and school subjects, at home. The school called the mother's home education program inadequate and took her to court. She lost there, but that decision was overturned by a higher court.

This story from a small Minnesota town was printed in papers all over the country. Two *GWS* readers sent me long news stories about it, one from a paper in Louisville, Kentucky, and the other from a paper in southern New Jersey. Both stories were wholly sympathetic to the mother and the family.

In Providence, Rhode Island, Peter and Brigitta Van Daam, intelligent and well-educated, wanted to take their daughter out of public school. They tried in repeated letters and visits to school officials to find out what kind of forms they needed to fill out and what procedures to follow to do this. The school people (perhaps in ignorance) repeatedly told them, *contrary to fact*, that there were no such forms or procedures. When at length the family, weary of this runaround, began teaching their child at home, the schools took legal action against them, and eventually had the entire family arrested and taken to jail. The Van Daams had worked hard to take their case to the public and the media. When the police came for them, all three major TV networks had cameras there. Soon after, on at least one nationwide TV show, millions of Americans could see these obviously intelligent, concerned, and capable parents, with their obviously intelligent small children, being taken to jail.

Such acts only make the schools look arrogant, greedy, cruel, and stupid. No need to cite other examples, of which there are many. In tough times like these the schools simply cannot stand any more of this kind of publicity. Public opinion on education is making a U-turn. Since they were founded, the public schools have enjoyed almost limitless public trust and confidence. People might criticize them on details, but in principle almost everyone agreed that the public schools were a great thing. The idea of an effective government monopoly in education was accepted almost without question. Now, suddenly, more and more citizens no longer believe that the government should have such a monopoly, and many are beginning to ask whether the government should be in the school business at all.

Some claim that it is still only a minority who are turning against the schools, and then mostly for reasons that lie outside the schools themselves. To some extent this may be true. Today's antischool sentiment is clearly part of a larger reaction against all giant, remote, uncontrollable institutions—big corporations, big unions, big hospitals, above all big government itself. Part of it is the response of people to a shrinking economy, to worries about inflation, their homes, their jobs, gas for the car, and oil for the furnace. But how much the schools may be responsible for this sudden turning against them makes little difference. The change of opinion is here and growing. In such a time the schools can't afford to do things that will make them still more enemies. Spending time and the public's money to make trouble for parents who want to teach their own children will surely do this.

But this is only the negative side of the picture. The real point I want to make here is that the schools have a great many things of real value to gain by cooperating fully with homeschooling families. Let me (in no particular order of importance) discuss some of them here.

RESEARCH

The schools have always needed places where people could do research in teaching. Here I don't mean research as the word is usually understood, with experimental groups, control groups, statistics, and so on. I mean the kind of research I myself did in most of my years as a classroom teacher, in which I was continually trying out and improving new ways of teaching my students. This kind of research, done by teachers in their own classrooms, based on *experience* rather than experiments, is the only kind that will significantly improve teaching.

But it is almost impossible for schools, or teachers in schools, to do such research. One reason is that when schools or teachers use "tried-and-true" methods that everyone is used to—that is, rote learning, drills, and the like—and these methods don't work, as they usually don't, the public is willing to let the schools blame the students. But when a school or teacher uses a method that people consider new and it doesn't work, the public blames *them*. So the rule is, to avoid trouble, stick to the old methods, *even* if they don't work.

Furthermore, whenever the schools do persuade the public to allow and the government to pay for some fairly fundamental research, they are always under heavy pressure to show quick results, that is, higher test scores. The federally funded Follow Through programs were very rarely given even as much as three years to learn how to teach in a new way and to show that it worked; more often they had to produce their results in a year or two. So a really serious project, like finding out what would happen if children could decide for themselves when they wanted to read, with no teaching unless and until they asked for it, has no chance of being tested fairly or at all. A boy I know, by no means unique among children given such freedom and choice, did not learn to read at all until after he was eight, taught himself, and three years later, when tested by a school, scored at the twelfth-grade level in reading. In one of these short-term research projects, this boy would have simply gone down in the statistics as a nonreader, "proof" that the experiment of letting children decide when they would read did not work.

For all these reasons, it seems very likely that the one place where we can hope and expect to see some really fundamental and long-term research on learning, on the kinds and amounts of teaching that most help learning and on the usefulness of different methods and materials, is in the homes of people teaching their own children. They can afford to be patient, to wait a long time for results; they are in complete control of their work and can change their methods as they wish; they can observe closely; they are free from all the routine distractions of large schools; and they are interested only in results rather than excuses. From these people and their work, all serious schools and teachers, many of them now severely limited and handicapped by the conditions under which they have to work, stand to learn a great deal.

First, let it be clear what they will *not* learn. They will not learn that this or that is the *best* way to teach reading, or addition, or multiplication, and so on; or that certain books are the *best* books for children; or that such and such is the *best* curriculum for this or that grade; or that you should always teach this particular subject in this particular order. Homeschoolers will not teach the schools what they so yearn to know, the *one best way* to do anything. What they will teach is that there *is* no one best way, and that it is a waste of time and energy to look for it; that children (like adults) learn in a great many different ways; that each child learns best in the ways that most interest, excite, and satisfy her or him; and that the business of school should be to offer to learners the widest possible range of choices, both in what to learn and ways to learn it. If a number of parents report, as they regularly do in *GWS*, that their children love reading books about astronomy or architecture or anthropology or aircraft or atoms or rockets or space travel or microbes, or working with colored pencils or computers or puzzles or violins or typewriters or gardens or tape recorders or whatever, then that is a sign that these books and materials should be in the schools, not so that all children will have to use them, but so that any child who wants *can* use them.

Beyond this, homeschoolers may be able to teach the schools some very important general principles of teaching and learning. Right now, there are so few homeschoolers that the things they learn from their experience, about which I have written in *GWS* and in this book, can be and are dismissed by conventional educators as rare examples proving nothing. But as the numbers of homeschoolers increase, it will be harder for even their bitterest enemies to ignore or deny their findings. When we can show, as in time we surely will, tens of thousands of children who, having learned to read only when they wanted to, and with only as much instruction as they asked for, are a few years later reading two or three or more years beyond most children of their age in schools, it cannot fail to have a great impact on the schools themselves. The people in schools who want to move in these directions will be much encouraged, while the rest will find it harder and harder to oppose them.

FEEDBACK

People doing a task can only do it better when they can find out how well they are doing it. Experiments have shown this time and time again. If we are estimating the weight of objects, and if we never learn whether our guesses are too low or too high, we never get any better. But if we learn whether each guess was too low or too high, and by how much, we quickly improve. If you shoot at a target but can't see where your shots hit, you have no way to improve them.

One of the reasons why schools and teachers usually find it so hard to do their work better is that they get so little good feedback from their students—candid information about how well they are teaching. A good friend of mine, while a brilliant, successful, and on the whole very happy student at a leading university, once told me that he and his friends never argued or disagreed with their professors, either in class discussions or in writing. He said, "The only way to be sure of an A on a paper or in a course is to say what you think the professor thinks, putting it of course in your own words so he won't think you are just imitating him." Since then, many other college students, in conversations, in letters, or in books about how to succeed at college, have said more or less the same thing. Professors who see themselves as telling truths to the ignorant may not care that students act this way. But others care a great deal. They chose to teach so that they might have lively talks with students about matters they all cared about, and are disappointed and hurt to find themselves dealing more and more with students who care only about getting a good (or at least passing) grade. They grow sick to death of hearing, "What do we have to do to get a good mark in this course? Are we going to be held responsible for this? Is this going to be on the exam?" Such questions drive many of them out of teaching altogether.

Teaching fifth grade, I finally learned that my hardest and most important task was to help my students become enough unafraid of me, and each other, to stop bluffing, faking, and playing testing games with me. Only when they were enough at ease in the class to be truly themselves could they begin to reveal their true interests and strengths, as well as their fears and weaknesses. Only then could I think about how to build on the strengths and overcome or avoid the weaknesses. All this took time and patience. Some of them would not for a long time tell me that they did not understand how to do a problem, or something I had told them or written on the board. A few never told me; their masks never came off.

If only to learn to do our work as teachers, we need students who are not afraid of us, and so not afraid to tell us what they think, or what they know and don't know. There may be a few such students in our schools right now, but not enough—we need many more. And we will have more as more and more children who are for the most part learning outside of school come to school for special classes and activities that they are interested in.

AUTHORITY AND LEADERSHIP

Because they don't understand natural authority, the schools are in an authority crisis. Their coercive authority breaks down more and more, but it is the only kind they know. They find it hard to imagine what it might be like to deal with children who were not in the least afraid of them and whom they had no reason to make afraid. Words alone won't change this. The schools will only learn about natural authority from those children for whom they *have* natural authority, that is, the children who come to school because they want to, to use it as a resource for purposes of their own. From them will come much of the kind of leadership that the schools so badly need.

While teaching fifth grade, I thought often about educational leadership. For a long time, I had no idea what it was. Slowly I began to see that the atmosphere and spirit of my classes were largely determined by the students themselves, above all by two or three who, whatever might be their schoolwork or behavior, were in fact the real leaders. Of the five fifth-grade classes I taught, all of which I liked, the last was much the best—the most interesting and active, the most fun for me, the most valuable for the children. But by all usual standards it should have been one of the worst; only three of the children were really good students, and more than half the class had serious academic and/or emotional problems. What made that class the best was the two children who (without knowing or trying) led it.

One, a Black boy, was by far the most brilliant student I have ever taught, and not just school-smart but life-smart, smart in everything. The other, a girl, just as much a leader, was a very poor student, but exceptionally imaginative and artistic, and also smart in the real world. What made these children such a joy to be with, and such a powerful influence on the other children, was not just their obvious alertness, imagination, curiosity, good humor, high spirits, and interest in many things, but their energy, vitality, self-respect, courage, and, above all, their true independence. They did not need to be bossed, told what to do. Nor were they interested in playing with me, or against me, the old school game of "You Can't Make Me Do It." No doubt they were helped by the fact that I, unlike so many adults, obviously enjoyed and valued those qualities in them that they most valued in themselves. But I did not create these qualities, they brought them to the class. What, without these children, might have been a miserable year turned out to be the most interesting and exciting year I ever spent in a schoolroom.

A few such children can make an enormous difference to a class or even an entire school. Far more than any principal or teacher, they set the tone of the place. If, on the other hand, the children with the most energy, imagination, and courage are constantly defying the school, and if the only ones who are "good" are obviously the ones who are too scared to be bad, most of the children will admire and envy the outlaws even if they don't dare imitate them. No one can maintain law and order, or authority, or discipline in such a place.

In my fifth-grade class the most admired children were not the outlaws. Not that the two leaders were docile teacher's pets, far from it. If they didn't like something I was doing, or wanted to do something else, or thought I was being unfair, they would tell me. But this had nothing to do with a struggle over who was boss. Our relationship was about something else altogether. They were in many ways interested in the world, and I knew more about the world than they did, so they were glad to find out and use much of what I knew. Meanwhile, we enjoyed each other's company. To be sure, the class had its cutups and You-Can't-Make-Me's. When they were really funny, as they sometimes were, the other kids might laugh at them, as I did myself. But they were not admired for being cutups. Their antics were often a distraction and a nuisance to kids who had better things to do. What was important and admired was being as alive, alert, active, curious, and committed as those leaders. The class discipline that grows out of that kind of feeling is as different as night from day from the discipline in a class where the children say to each other, "If you do that, I'll tell the teacher and you'll get in trouble." Not only is it a great deal more pleasant, it is also a great deal more permanent.

The schools desperately need, if only as an example to the others, more of that kind of children, children whose dealings with them are not governed by fear. Such children will bring to the school not only a different attitude about the world (interesting and exciting), themselves (independent and competent), and the school (useful), but also interests that go far beyond last night's TV shows. Some of these interests, the other children will pick up. My Black fifth-grader *taught* the other children in that class far more than I did; admiring him, they talked with him as much as they could (which I allowed), and from that talk they learned a great deal. In the same way, homeschooled children who come to school as part-time volunteers will bring with them many ideas, skills, activities, resources, for other children to share. Even if these children make up only a very small percentage of the student body, they will make the school a very different, and much nicer and more interesting place.

ALL THREE OF OUR HOMESCHOOLED girls, now adults, have been in and out of public and private schools, both as full-time and part-time students. I don't want to sound too much like a bragging father, but my girls have received compliments from their schoolteachers and from other adults for bringing energy and leadership to their play, their classes, and their work with other children. I know many other homeschooling parents who can boast the same—so much for fears that homeschooling stunts social abilities! More often than not, school is considered an all-or-nothing-at-all proposition by its administrators, but, as our experiences and many homeschoolers' experiences indicate, the smorgasbord approach to schooling works quite well. Homeschoolers often use outdoor activities, parks, and recreation spaces to socialize, learn, and play largely because the outdoors is one of the few places people can gather without having to purchase or rent the space. In fact, there are "forest schools" around the world that use the outdoors as their classroom. Outdoor education, like homeschooling, was started by parents seeking alternatives to school for their children, as the Growing Child Forest School in Asheville, NC, notes in its brief history of forest schools:

> The world's first known forest school was created by Ella Flautau in Denmark in 1952. The idea formed when her and neighbors' children began gathering daily in a nearby forest, an unofficial form of daycare which elicited great interest among other parents in the community. The parents formed a group and created an initiative to establish "walking kindergartens" out of the Waldorf-Steiner approach to education—child-led and play-based—with adults as facilitators not teachers. Forest schools, or Naturbørnehavens, started popping up throughout Denmark in the 1950s as the country struggled with a lack of indoor space for young childhood education centers. Regular outdoor learning for older children is referred to with the term *udeskole*.[67]

Forests are not a requirement for outdoor education. Dr. Maysaa Bazna founded a school, Pono, a decade ago in the middle of Manhattan. She writes:

> Our first group of children, as young as two and three years old, repeatedly responded, "Walk in the woods!" whenever we asked what they liked best or what they wanted to do. We found the most wild parts of the biggest NYC parks and the children spent many hours there, freely exploring the wilderness—touching, feeling,

smelling, and engaging their vivid imaginations while taking in the surrounding endless beauty of nature.

On indoor days, the children still often chose to spend their time outdoors in the park across the street. They loved jumping in rain puddles, running in the open field, throwing fall leaves around, painting their feet on the grass, or planting daffodils. We partnered with public parks, community gardens, and urban farms because our children loved digging in the soil, watering, weeding, harvesting, and getting messy in nature.[68]

Another variation on using the outdoors for learning is the Flying Squads program, which links using public spaces in cities to youth empowerment:

Each day starts in a public space (typically a library) documenting and reflecting on previous time together in a communal journal. The group then sets out into the world to explore common interests as a collective, experimenting on how to build community and deciding how to voice group concerns on the social justice issue of being youth in a city built for adults.[69]

Though they pay lip service to the social needs of children, policy makers could help this happen in other ways besides waiting for schools to "get back to normal." Educators and politicians could shift their thinking from maintaining the status quo of schooling to enabling other ways for children to be together. School facilities can be prioritized for use by those with special needs and children who depend on school for their meals and safety; classrooms will be less full since many students can be at home or engaged in other activities, so teachers can have more time with each student in school.

Remote learning suffers not just due to content issues but also due to connectivity issues. Millions of American families don't have internet access or personal computers powerful enough for online schooling. This should encourage teachers and schools to use outdoor learning and social activities for children, instead of tying students at home to computer screens or their desks in school. A few public and private schools have done so, but their example has not caught on. There is support for doing so from the National COVID-19 Outdoor Learning Center, created by the nonprofit Green Schoolyards America,[70] but it appears the school system isn't agile enough to do this pivot for children.

Schoolteachers can "map" many of the activities done by the children outside of school to their school goals, just as schools give academic credit for life experiences or as unschoolers document learning after it occurs. Does it matter if a third-grader learned to add fractions from a school-assigned text or from their use of a measuring cup while helping to cook?

In *Unschooled*, Kerry McDonald writes about a variety of recent opportunities for teenagers to learn in unschooled ways, such as apprenticeship programs and learning centers that meet their needs. *Worldschooling* is a term that encompasses learning through travel for families and individuals, which was much easier to do before COVID-19 and likely to grow in the future. Interestingly, there are now two unschooling programs that are supported and operated in public high schools. McDonald writes about Unschool San Juan in California and the Powderhouse School in Massachusetts, which use unschooling principles (such as no grades, learner-directed study, etc.) for individualized learning that also meets school standards.

Fortunately, parents are doing this on their own and not waiting for schools to figure out how to work outside the computer and the classroom. The outdoor school movement was started by parents, as was the homeschooling movement, because their children were not getting what they needed from school. Play, exploration, and socialization are the primary ways children learn; when will schools embrace this? ■

MONEY, PUBLICITY, CLIENTS

ONE REASON THE SCHOOLS worry about people teaching their children at home has to do with money. Most school districts receive financial aid from the state—so many dollars per pupil per day. This aid often makes up an important part of the school's income. So when a family talks about teaching their children at home, the schools think, "If they do, we will lose X hundred dollars a year, which we can't afford, so we'd better not let them." But clearly, if the schools cooperated with the parents, and the children came to school part-time for activities they liked, the school would be able to mark them present, and so would not lose their share of state aid.

In fact, there is no legal reason why a school district, having decided to cooperate with a homeschooling family, could not enroll their children and list them as attending the school, even if they seldom *came* to school. Nothing in any state education laws I have seen says that "attendance" can only mean physical presence in the school building or would prevent any school district from doing what, for a while at least, the Philadelphia schools did in their Parkway Project or the Toronto schools in their Metro Project. In these programs the students spent their days, not in school buildings, but in various institutions of the city itself. No one ever claimed, or could have sustained a claim, that in sending students around the city instead of shutting them up in school buildings these school systems were violating state attendance laws. Other public school systems have very wisely sent children out of the schools to work as apprentices in various local businesses, giving them school credit for the experience. No one ever claimed that this was a violation of the law.

Since the law gives school districts the right to define attendance in any way they and their constituents choose, there is no reason why a school district could not claim that children learning at home, with the school's support and supervision, were "attending" the school.

Indeed, the school might claim that it was not only legally but morally justified in collecting state aid for such students, since in some ways they might be getting more individualized attention than the children in the school building. So there is no reason why schools have to see homeschooling as an immediate financial threat.

Cooperating with homeschooling families is not only a way to avoid bad publicity, but a way to get good publicity, which most school systems would very much like to have. During an appearance on a local TV talk show, I happened to mention briefly that the schools in Barnstable, Massachusetts, were cooperating fully with a homeschooling family, whose children, whenever they wanted, could and did go to the school to take part in activities they liked. This very brief mention brought and is still bringing the school district a number of inquiring letters and phone calls, some even from outside the state, and all very favorable in tone. School folks, like everyone else, like to feel and have others feel that they are at the forefront of progress, blazing new trails, leading the way. Cooperating with homeschooling families is an easy and an authentic way for schools to put themselves in that position. Then why not do it? Why look bad when it is so easy to look good?

JOHN'S QUESTION CONTINUES TO RESONATE with me as I watch public schools shoot themselves in the foot time and again as they attempt to limit homeschooling. For years, local school districts in Massachusetts could count homeschooled students in their average daily attendance (ADA) formulas and receive funding for them. Massachusetts homeschoolers, by and large, had nothing to complain about as schools that took the funding often let homeschoolers take courses or use school resources without much difficulty. But in 1996 the Massachusetts State Department of Education decided to push away homeschoolers; it passed a regulation that forbids counting homeschooled students in a school's ADA formula. Whatever funds the school would have received for these students now go to the general state fund. Though this move has hardened the "all-or-nothing-at-all" mentality among many Massachusetts's school administrators, nonetheless a few superintendents continue to cooperate openly with homeschoolers and to show how easy it can be to look good and support learning for all the children in their districts. ∎

Because of the decline of the birth rate, no matter what else they do, schools are going to continue to lose more and more of their clients. To stay in business, they must find new ones. Many seem to think they can solve this problem by making compulsory education begin earlier and go on longer, if possible, forever. Educators in many parts of the country are trying to make kindergarten compulsory; some teachers' unions have even proposed that compulsory schooling should begin as early as age two or three. At the same time, educators talk a great deal about a rather sinister idea called Mandatory Continuing Education, which, if they can push it through, will mean that more and more people, having gone to school for years in order to get a job, will then have to keep going to school in order to keep the job. A prominent educator, a gifted promoter of education (and himself), used to say proudly that he considered himself a "womb-to-tomb" schooler. What he had in mind was, of course, that *other people* would have to spend their whole lives going to school. Not him; he would be running those schools.

This is the wrong approach. It might have sold in the days when everyone but a handful of cranks was behind the schools, or when people were sure that every extra year spent in school automatically meant so many extra dollars on your paycheck. But it won't sell now, in today's growing antischool climate, and our declining economy, where college and even graduate degrees are worth less and less every year. If the schools are to survive and thrive, as a few understand quite well, they must become places that people go to *only because they like to*, because they think of school as a place where you can find out about and do interesting things.

Exceedingly few people now feel that way. Even when most people still supported the schools in principle, hundreds of parents, many of whom had even been good students, were telling or writing me that most of their worst anxiety dreams were still school dreams, or that every time they went into their children's school, for whatever reason, they could feel their insides tighten up and their hands begin to sweat. Many kinds of places—concert halls, baseball parks, theaters, parks, beaches, to name a few—make most people feel good as soon as they step into them. They think that something pleasant, interesting, exciting, is about to happen. For their very survival, the schools *need* people who feel that way about them, for in the long run such people are the ones the schools will have to depend on for their support, they are their only true friends.

Some school districts understand this very well. Here are some words from "Declining Enrollments," a pamphlet published by the Center for Community Education Development of the Santa Barbara County Schools.

> When schools exist apart from the community, they stand as monuments to the School Board and their ability to get bond issues passed...as reminders to citizens of the unpleasant past of their own educational experiences...as symbols of something to vote against in the future...they stand empty, unused, and economically unfeasible, they create a further segmented and fragmented society. On the other side of the coin is the school which is an integral part of the total resources of the community.

> There is also what has become almost a classic story of making a building so indispensable that the School Board could not consider its closing. The principal of Fairlington Elementary School in Arlington, Virginia, saw her enrollment drop from 440 to 225. She first turned

space over to a play school, then invited the recreation department to use the school for some of its programs, and then reserved space for use by a senior citizens group. A community theatre and several other local organizations soon joined in using the school's facilities. Before long, talk of closing the school ceased, and some began to wonder if perhaps it needed an addition.

TEACHER TRAINING

In time, the homeschooling movement could become exceptionally useful, at least to the more innovative schools of education, as a way of training teachers.

Professors of education have asked me many times over the years how we might improve teacher training. Until recently I have said that as long as we define teacher training as sending people to college to take education courses, nothing could make that process any less harmful than it already is. Young teachers so trained go into the classroom thinking that they know a great deal about children, learning, and teaching, when in fact they know next to nothing—which I would say even if I had taught all their classes. People so taught have nothing in their minds but words. They know no more about children and teaching than people who had lived all their lives in desert or jungle would know about snow-covered mountains just from hearing people talk about them. We cannot, by turning a complicated experience into words, *give* that experience to someone who has not had it. Hearing mountains or children described, even seeing photos or films of mountains or children, is no substitute at all for seeing and climbing actual mountains or working with actual children.

Since student teachers in their training hear and read only words, and have no experience in teaching or otherwise dealing with children to which they can relate and compare these words, they have no sound basis for saying that some ideas seem to make more sense or fit better with experience than others. What they are told about teaching, they tend to swallow whole. Such students, when they first enter classrooms as teachers, come in, so to speak, with a box of gummed labels: "underachiever," "overachiever," "learning disability," "brain damaged," "acting out," "emotionally disturbed," "culturally deprived," and so on. Once in the class, instead of looking at what is before them, and slowly learning to describe and judge this experience in their own way, they look for children or events on whom they can stick one or more of the ready-made labels from their box. Thinking that a child labeled is a child understood, they quickly decide that Juan is an underachiever, and Susie is a typical this, and Tommy a typical that. This would be bad even if the labels themselves were good. Thus, even if the word *underachiever* described something real and important, instead of a mere discrepancy between the results of two different kinds of tests (neither worth much), there would be many different kinds of underachievers and ways of underachieving. But most teachers, satisfied with this kind of instant diagnosis, don't take time, or don't know how, to look further. And so these labels, wrong to start with and hastily slapped on, become a part of the official record of schoolchildren, and largely determine how the schools, and beyond that the world, will see them and deal with them.

None of these faults in teacher training are improved by having teachers, usually in their last year of education school, do some "student teaching" or "practice teaching" in the classrooms of regular teachers in local public schools. What this "teaching" amounts to is mostly watching the regular teacher and helping out with minor chores. Only rarely, usually under the eye of the regular teacher, are the student teachers allowed to teach a "unit" or two of their own. To expect anyone to learn to teach by such methods is like expecting children to learn to drive a car by sitting in their parents' laps and holding the wheel while they steer it.

When student teachers worked with me in my fifth-grade class, from time to time I used to turn the class over to them. When I did I would always leave the room, first telling the students that while I wasn't there Miss So-and-so was the boss and they had to do exactly what she said. But they knew, and she knew, that I was the real boss; I gave out any serious punishments that had to be given out, and beyond that, the grades which were the true and ultimate reward and punishment. Their fate as fifth-graders lay in my hands, not Miss So-and-so's. I, and not the student teacher, was still holding the wheel.

In any case, whether or not the regular "cooperating" teachers are in the room during this practice teaching, they will always demand a report on it and will know if it went badly. Since student teachers need good reports from their cooperating teachers, they will not, as many have told me, run the risk of using in their practice teaching any methods that these teachers might not like. They will be thinking not about what will most help the students, but what will get the best report from the regular teacher. Beyond this, they get so few chances to teach, and these so brief, that they don't have time to make a serious trial of whatever teaching methods they want to use, far less find out how to improve them.

Student practice teaching is mostly a sham and a fraud. It gives the students a too brief look at the inside of a real schoolroom, and enables schools of education to say to future employers of their graduates that these graduates have had some "field experience." But that's all it does.

A more helpful way to train people for the work of teaching in classrooms would be to have them *begin* by teaching real classes in real schools, all the while giving them places and plenty of time to talk about their work with other new teachers in the same position, sometimes (but not always) in the company of a sympathetic and more experienced teacher. Along with these discussions, the new teachers could read and discuss a number of books about teaching, child psychology, and so on, looking for ideas that might help them make sense of their experience, and so teach better. They would be encouraged to read these books critically, not passively. Perhaps, out of their experience, their discussions, and their reading, they might write some manuals or books of their own. We might then have many more textbooks about classroom teaching "methods" written by people who had actually and recently worked in classrooms.

But even if we could make these changes in the ways in which we hire and train teachers, teaching classes in compulsory schools would not tell them very much about learning. My own work as a teacher began exactly in the way described above. I started teaching without any formal training whatever. I read no books about education until after I had taught for a number of years. I had plenty of time and occasions to talk with other young teachers like myself about our mutual problems, and many of these talks, with my friend and colleague Bill Hull, were the seed of my first book. Yet in all my years in the classroom what I learned was not so much how children learn as how they defend themselves against learning, not so much how they explore and make sense of the world as how they work out slippery strategies for dodging the dangers of school, the pain and shame of not knowing, being wrong, failing.

What I really learned about *learning*, in its best and deepest sense, I learned partly from my own adult experiences in learning languages, music, and sports, but mostly from watching and playing with babies and preschool children in their parents' homes. Only as I began to understand how human beings learned when they learned *best* did I begin to understand what was wrong with the classroom and my own and others' teaching. Seeing human learning at its most powerful, that is, the learning of infants, above all their amazing and always unique discovery and conquest of language, gave me a yardstick against which I could measure all other teaching and learning.

There is no better way to understand human learning than by closely watching babies and infants during those years in which they are learning (among many other things) to stand, walk, and talk, and no better place to do this than in the home, not as a teacher or coldly detached scientist but as *an attentive, concerned, and loving member of the family*. Such an experience, living like an older sister or brother in families with young children, would be invaluable to people who want to be teachers or helpers of learning of any kind. It is the only kind of training for teaching, other than teaching itself, which has any chance of being any use at all.

Looking into the future, I can see a day when at least a certain number of student teachers would have such an experience as part of their training. Of course, there would be problems to work out. Families would have to be paid, not just for the expense and trouble of housing and feeding students but in fair return for the important service they were doing them. Such an experience should not be compulsory; only those students who felt they could learn something important by living in another family with small children should be allowed to do it. Schools of education would have to give generous academic credits for such training. Nor should they demand from students too much in the way of papers and reports, since the whole point is to have the student in the family *not* as a reporter but as a family member. You can't play with little children and take notes at the same time. Any education professors who need piles of paper to prove that their students are learning anything would be better off left out of such a program. I would never have learned half as much from my own experience of living in families with children if I had been required to write papers about them. When I wrote, as I often did, it was only because, I realized later, I had seen something so interesting that I wanted to be sure to remember it, and perhaps to tell others about it.

Student and family would have to agree about how much the student, living as a family member, would be subject to the family's routines and disciplines. Many families would not want students in their homes doing things that they would not allow their own children to do. Families and students would also have to agree on how much of the family housework the students were expected to do, and how much free time they would have and when. There might well be other problems. But any education department that wanted to put such a program into effect could surely find a way to do so.

It will of course be essential to find the right kind of families. Students will not learn much about the learning of infants and children except in families that like, trust, and respect their children and enjoy watching their learning and helping it if and when they can. Here is where the homeschooling movement might be particularly useful to schools. People who are teaching children at home, or who would like to, or even think they might like to, are almost certain to be people who treat their children with loving courtesy and allow and encourage them to explore the world in their own way.

This training might very well be valuable, not just to teachers but to future psychologists, psychiatrists, therapists, social workers, and others whose work might someday bring them into contact with children. Some young people might want to do it for a while just to get themselves more ready for having their own children. We hear much about the need for young people to take courses in "parenting." Six months living in a family with young children would be a great deal more valuable than any such course.

ALTHOUGH I DO KNOW OF SITUATIONS where young adults lived with homeschooling families in exchange for help with tutoring and day care, and where anthropology and education researchers lived with homeschooling families, I know of no teachers-to-be who were encouraged by schools of education to spend time learning about young children in this way. Nevertheless, the internet and the growing number of homeschooling resources at the local and state levels can be a great help to students interested in how children learn "in the field." ■

CONCLUSION

HAVING SAID THIS much about why I think schools would be wise to give their full support to homeschooling families, I have to make two things clear. First, I do not claim that supporting homeschooling is going to be a quick solution to the schools' problems. For these there are no quick solutions. It took the schools many years to get into their present bad position, and even after they come to understand how and why they got into it, it will take them many years to get out. Secondly, I am not proposing homeschooling *so that* the schools will change their ways and/or solve their problems. I would like to see both these things happen, and I believe that homeschooling may in time help them to happen. But that is not why I am for homeschooling. It is an important and worthwhile idea in its own right.

To repeat once again the idea with which I began this book, it is a most serious mistake to think that learning is an activity separate from the rest of life, that people do best when they are not doing anything else and best of all in places where nothing else is done. It is an equally serious mistake to think that teaching, the assisting of learning and the sharing of knowledge and skill, is something that can be done only by a few specialists. When we lock learning and teaching in the school box, as we do, we do not get more effective teaching and learning in society, but much less.

What makes people smart, curious, alert, observant, competent, confident, resourceful, persistent—in the broadest and best sense, intelligent—is not having access to more and more *learning* places, resources, and specialists, but being able in their lives to do a wide variety of interesting things that matter, things that challenge their ingenuity, skill, and judgment, and that make an obvious difference in their lives and the lives of people around them. It is foolish to think that through "education" we can have a society in which, no matter how low may be the quality of work, the quality of learning and intelligence will remain high. People with dull and meaningless jobs are hardly likely to lead active, interesting, productive lives away from those jobs. They are much more likely to collapse in front of the TV set and take refuge from their own dreary daily life in a life of fantasy, by imagining for a while that they are one of those rich, beautiful, sexy, powerful, laughing, fast-moving, successful people on the screen.

I have used the word *homeschooling* to describe the process by which children grow and learn in the world without going, or going very much, to schools, because this word is familiar and quickly understood. But in one very important sense it is misleading. What is most important and valuable about the home as a base for children's growth into the world is not that it is a better school than the schools but *that it isn't a school at all*. It is not an artificial place, set up to make "learning" happen and in which nothing except "learning" ever happens. It is a natural, organic, central, fundamental human institution, one might easily and rightly say the foundation of all other institutions. We can imagine and indeed we have had human societies without schools, without factories, without libraries, museums, hospitals, roads, legislatures, courts, or any of the institutions which seem so indispensable and permanent a part of modern life. We might someday even choose, or be obliged, to live once again without some or all of these. But we cannot even imagine a society without homes, even if these should be no more than tents, or mud huts, or holes in the ground. What I am trying to say, in short, is that our chief educational problem is not to find a way to make homes *more* like schools. If anything, it is to make schools *less* like schools.

Whatever we may call the activity I have tried to describe in this book, it will go on more quickly, easily, painlessly, and productively if the schools will cooperate with it rather than trying to resist it. In these last chapters I have tried to say why I think they would be not simply generous but wise to do so, as some are already doing. (For a list of schools that are helping and supporting homeschooling families, see Appendix C.)

When John Merrow interviewed me for National Public Radio, I told him why I thought schools would be wise to support homeschooling. He said, "Aren't you being a bit naïve?" Well, I certainly would be if I thought that large numbers of school districts were going to do this in the next year or so. I don't at first expect many of them to take this path. But the path is there for those who are willing to take it. The list of supporting school districts is still very small. But, like the homeschooling movement itself, it is growing and will continue to grow, and for the same reason—because it makes sense, and because it works.

I N 1999 I WAS INTERVIEWED by John Merrow for National Public Radio as part of a panel discussing "The New Homeschoolers." We were "new" due to the number of support systems, recognition, and success stories that emerged since Merrow interviewed John in 1981. In 2021, COVID-19 has created a much larger number of new homeschoolers, supported by the growth of online courses and social media. John Holt died in 1985, too soon to see homeschooling flourish, but I think he felt homeschooling would grow no matter what the schools and politicians did to stop it.

While the state has made it a goal to ensure all its children are educated to become "good citizens," the state is constitutionally prohibited from dictating any particular way of educating children, thus allowing alternatives to state schools. However, education has been changing the definition of citizenship with very little debate.

Being a citizen seems to mean merely being an "employed consumer" today. It's not uncommon for education policy makers to refer to children as "resources" to be developed, rather than as individuals to be nurtured. It is hard to imagine how students are expected to become citizens who make and shape society when so much of their time is spent being shaped to fit the demands of schooling. We need other shared experiences and projects to create a national identity instead of our unequal distribution of opportunity based on schooling.

Despite homeschooling's considerable growth and impact since John founded *Growing Without Schooling* magazine in 1977, most school officials appear determined to fight it or ignore it. But they are not in step with public opinion, changing technologies, changing family and work schedules, nor the long body of research that challenges how we teach and learn in schools. Fortunately, you don't have to wait for schools to change to help your children learn: You can teach your own. ■

APPENDIX A

SELECTED BIBLIOGRAPHY

EDUCATION AND SOCIETY

AbdelRahim, Layla. *Wild Children—Domesticated Dreams: Civilization and the Birth of Education*. Fernwood Publishing, 2013.

Appleton, Matthew. *A Free-Range Childhood: Self-Regulation at Summerhill School*. Foundation for Educational Renewal, 2001.

Arons, Stephen. *Compelling Belief: The Culture of American Schooling*. University of Massachusetts Press, 1986.

Avrich, Paul. *The Modern School Movement*. AK Press, 2005.

Axline, Virginia. *Dibs—In Search of Self*. Ballantine, 1990.

Betts, Roland. *Acting Out*. Little, Brown, 1978.

Bowles, Samuel, and Herbert Gintis. *Schooling in Capitalist America: Educational Reform and the Contradictions of Economic Life*. Basic Books, 1977.

Brown, Jerry. *Dialogues*. Berkeley Hills, 1998.

Caplan, Bryan. *The Case Against Education: Why the Education System Is a Waste of Time and Money*. Princeton University Press, 2018.

Cardozo, Philip. *The Nature of the Judicial Process*. Yale University Press, 1921.

Cayley, David. *Ivan Illich: In Conversation*. House of Anansi, 1992.

_____. *Ivan Illich: An Intellectual Journey.* Pennsylvania State University Press, 2021.

_____. *The Rivers North of the Future: The Testament of Ivan Illich.* House of Anansi, 2005.

Dennison, George. *The Lives of Children: The Story of the First Street School.* Heinemann/Boynton/Cook, 1999.

Dickerson, Adam. *John Holt: The Philosophy of Unschooling.* Springer, 2019.

Ferm, Elizabeth Byrne. *Freedom in Education.* Modern School, 1925.

Elias, Stephen, and Susan Levinkind. *Legal Research: How to Find and Understand the Law.* Nolo Press, 2001.

Farenga, Patrick, and Carlo Ricci, eds. *The Legacy of John Holt: A Man Who Genuinely Understood, Trusted, and Respected Children.* HoltGWS, 2013.

Fader, Daniel. *The Naked Children.* Heinemann/Boynton/Cook, 1996.

Freire, Paulo. *Pedagogy of the Oppressed.* Penguin, 1970.

Gatto, John Taylor. *A Different Kind of Teacher.* Berkeley Hills Books, 2000.

_____. *Dumbing Us Down: The Hidden Curriculum of Compulsory Schooling.* New Society Press, 2002.

_____. *The Exhausted School.* Oxford Village Press, 1993.

_____. *The Underground History of American Education: A Schoolteacher's Intimate Investigation into the Problem of Modern Schooling.* Oxford Village Press, 2001.

Goodman, Paul. *Compulsory Miseducation.* Horizon Press, 1964.

_____. *Growing Up Absurd: Problems of Youth in the Organized Society.* Random House, 1960.

_____. *Nature Heals: The Psychological Essays of Paul Goodman.* Free Life Editions, 1977

Goyal, Nikhil. *Schools on Trial: How Freedom and Creativity Can Fix Our Educational Malpractice.* Doubleday, 2016.

Greenberg, Daniel. *Free at Last: Sudbury Valley School.* Sudbury Valley School Press, 1987.

Hern, Matt, ed. *Deschooling Our Lives.* New Society Publishers, 1996.

_____. *Everywhere All the Time: A New Deschooling Reader.* AK Press, 2008.

_____. *Field Day: Getting Society Out of School.* New Star Books, 2003.

_____. *Watch Yourself: Why Safer Isn't Always Better.* New Star Books, 2007.

Herndon, James. *How to Survive in Your Native Land.* Simon and Schuster, 1971.

_____. *The Way It Spozed to Be*. Heinemann/Boynton/Cook, 1997.

Hirsch, E. D. *What Your First Grader Needs to Know*. Bantam, 2014.

Holt, John. *Escape from Childhood*. Holt Associates, 2013.

_____. *Freedom and Beyond*. Heinemann/Boynton/Cook, 1972.

_____. *How Children Fail*. Perseus, 1995.

_____. *How Children Learn*. Perseus, 1995.

_____. *Instead of Education*. Sentient, 2004.

_____. *Learning All the Time*. Perseus, 1990.

_____. *A Life Worth Living: Selected Letters of John Holt*. Ohio State Univ. Press, 1990.

_____. *Never Too Late*. Perseus, 1991.

_____. *Teach Your Own: The John Holt Book of Homeschooling*. Perseus, 2003.

_____. *The Underachieving School*. Sentient, 2005.

_____. *What Do I Do Monday?* Heinemann/Boynton/Cook, 1995.

Illich, Ivan. *Deschooling Society*. Boyars, 1999.

_____. *In the Mirror of the Past: Lectures and Addresses 1978–1990*. Boyars, 1992.

_____. *Shadow Work*. Boyars, 1981.

_____. *Tools for Conviviality*. Boyars, 2001.

Lipson, Eric. *Everyday Law for Young Citizens*. Lorenz Educational Press, 2000.

Marsh, John. *Class Dismissed: Why We Cannot Teach or Learn Out Way Out of Inequality*. Monthly Review Press, 2011.

Meighan, Roland. *John Holt*. Bloomsbury, 2014.

Mercogliano, Chris. *Making It Up As We Go Along: The Story of the Albany Free School*. Heinemann/Boynton/Cook, 1998.

_____. *In Defense of Childhood: Protecting Kids' Inner Wildness*. Beacon Press, 2008.

Miller, Ron. *Free Schools, Free People: Education and Democracy After the 1960s*. SUNY Press, 2002.

Neill, A. S. *Freedom—Not License!* Hart Publishing, 1966.

_____. *Summerhill: A Radical Approach to Child-Rearing*. Hart Publishing, 1960.

Novak, Mark W. *Living and Learning in the Free School*. McGill–Queen's Press, 1975.

Postman, Neil. *The Disappearance of Childhood*. Delacorte, 1982.

Prakash, Madhu S., and Gustavo Esteva. *Escaping Education: Living as Learning within Grassroots Cultures*. Peter Lang, 2008.

Purdy, Bryn. *A. S. Neill: Bringing Happiness to Some Few Children.* Educational Heretics Press, 1997.

Reimer, Everett. *School Is Dead: Alternatives in Education.* Penguin, 1971.

Rembar, Charles. *The End of Obscenity.* HarperTrade, 1986.

Richards, Akilah S. *Raising Free People: Unschooling as Liberation and Healing Work.* PM Press, 2020.

Rietmulder, Jim. *When Kids Rule the School: The Power and Promise of Democratic Education.* New Society, 2019.

Rust, Carl. *Get Out of the Way and Let Kids Learn!: How We Can Transform Schools and Reintroduce Natural Learning.* KDP, 2019.

Salisbury, Harrison. *Travels Around America.* Walker, 1976.

Sheffer, Susannah, ed. *A Life Worth Living: Selected Letters of John Holt.* Ohio State University Press, 1990.

Shute, Chris. *Compulsory Schooling Disease: How Children Absorb Fascist Values.* Educational Heretics Press, 1993.

_____. *Edmond Holmes and the Tragedy of Education.* Educational Heretics Press, 1998.

Silberman, Charles. *Crisis in the Classroom.* Random House, 1970.

Sizer, Theodore and Sizer, Nancy Faust. *The Students Are Watching: Schools and the Moral Contract.* Beacon Press, 2000.

Smith, Frank. *Essays into Literacy.* Heinemann, 1983.

_____. *Insult to Intelligence.* Arbor House, 1986.

_____. *Joining the Literacy Club: Further Essays into Education.* Heinemann, 1988.

_____. *Reading without Nonsense.* Teacher's College Press, 1997.

Spring, Joel. *Education and the Rise of the Corporate State.* Beacon Press, 1972.

HOMESCHOOLED TEENAGERS AND COLLEGE ADMISSIONS

Arnall, Judy. *Unschooling to University: Relationships Matter Most in a World Crammed with Content.* Professional Parenting, 2018.

Boles, Blake. *The Art of Self-Directed Learning: 23 Tips for Giving Yourself an Unconventional Education.* Tells Peak Press, 2014.

_____. *Better Than College: How to Build a Successful Life without a Four-Year Degree.* Tells Peak Press, 2012.

_____. *College without High School: A Teenager's Guide to Skipping High School and Going to College*. New Society Publishers, 2009.

_____. *Why Are You Still Sending Your Kids to School? The Case for Helping Them Leave, Chart Their Own Paths, and Prepare for Adulthood at Their Own Pace*. Tells Peak Press, 2020.

Cohen, Cafi. *And What About College? How Homeschooling Leads to Admissions to the Best Colleges and Universities*. Holt Associates, 2000.

_____. *Homeschoolers' College Admissions Handbook: Preparing 12- to 18-year-olds for Success in the College of Their Choice*. Prima, 2000.

_____. *Homeschooling the Teen Years*. Prima, 2000.

Danford, Kenneth. *Learning Is Natural, School Is Optional: The North Star Approach to Offering Teens a Head Start on Life*. Golden Door Press, 2019.

Hern, Matt, ed. *Stay Solid! A Radical Handbook for Youth*. AK Press, 2013.

Heuer, Loretta. *The Homeschoolers Guide to Portfolios and Transcripts*. Arco, 2000.

Kamenetz, Anya. *DIY U: Edupunks, Edupreneurs, and the Coming Transformation of Higher Education*. Chelsea Green, 2010.

Llewellyn, Grace. *Real Lives: Eleven Teenagers Who Don't Go to School*. Lowry House, 1993.

_____. *The Teenage Liberation Handbook: How to Quit School and Get a Real Life and Education*. Lowry House, 1998.

Sheffer, Susannah. *A Sense of Self: Listening to Homeschooled Adolescent Girls*. Heinemann/Boynton/Cook, 1995

Soling, Cevin. *The Student Resistance Handbook*. Spectacle Films, 2014.

Stephens, Dale. *Hacking Your Education. Ditch the Lectures, Save Tens of Thousands, and Learn More Than Your Peers Ever Will*. Penguin, 2013.

Wood, Danielle. *The Uncollege Alternative: Your Guide to Incredible Careers and Amazing Adventures Outside College*. ReganBooks, 2000.

HOMESCHOOLING

Albert, David. *And the Skylark Sings with Me: Adventures in Homeschooling and Community-Based Education*. New Society Press/Holt Associates, 1999.

_____. *Homeschooling and the Voyage of Self-Discovery*. Common Courage Press, 2003.

Aldrich, Clark. *Unschooling Rules: 55 Ways to Unlearn What We Know about Schools and Rediscover Education*. Greenleaf Book Group, 2011.

Allee, Judith, and Melissa Morgan. *Educational Travel on a Shoestring.* Harold Shaw, 2002.

_____. *Homeschooling on a Shoe String.* Harold Shaw, 1999.

Bogart, Julie. *The Brave Learner: Finding Everyday Magic in Homeschool, Learning, and Life.* TarcherPerigee, 2019.

Colfax, David, and Micki Colfax. *Hard Times in Paradise: An American Family's Struggle to Carve Out a Homestead in California's Redwood Mountains.* Warner, 1992.

_____. *Homeschooling for Excellence.* Warner, 1988.

Dobson, Linda. *The Art of Education: Reclaiming Your Family, Community, and Self.* Holt Associates, 1997.

_____. *Homeschooler's Success Stories: 15 Adults and 12 Young People Share the Impact That Homeschooling Has Made on Their Lives.* Prima, 2000.

_____. *The Homeschooling Book of Answers.* Prima, 2002.

Dodd, Sandra. *Sandra Dodd's Big Book of Unschooling.* Forever Curious Press, 2019.

Duffy, Cathy. *The Christian Home Educator's Curriculum Manual.* Grove Publishing, 2000.

Eldridge, Lehla, and Anthony Eldridge-Rogers. *Jump Fall Fly.* Jump Fall Fly Press, 2017.

Farenga, Patrick, and Carlo Ricci, eds. *Growing Without Schooling: A Record of a Grassroots Movement.* Volumes 1–4. Holt Associates, 2021.

Fitzenreiter, Valerie. *The Unprocessed Child: Living without School.* Unbounded Publications, 2003.

Fortune-Wood, Jan. *Bound to Be Free: Home Education as a Positive Alternative to Paying the Hidden Costs of "Free" Education.* Educational Heretics Press, 2001.

_____. *Doing It Their Way: Home-Based Education and Autonomous Learning.* Educational Heretics Press, 2000.

Gold, LauraMaery, and Joan M. Zielinski. *Homeschool Your Child For Free: More Than 1,200 Smart, Effective, and Practical Resources for Home Education on the Internet and Beyond.* Prima, 2000.

Hammon, Joel. *The Teacher Liberation Handbook: How to Leave School and Create a Place Where You and Young People Can Thrive.* Grelton Group, 2016.

Hayes, Lenore. *Homeschooling the Child with ADD (or Other Special Needs).* Prima, 2002.

Hood, Mary. *The Relaxed Home School.* Ambleside Educational Press, 1994.

Griffith, Mary. *The Unschooling Handbook: How to Use the Whole World as Your Child's Classroom.* Prima, 1998.

____. *The Homeschooling Handbook.* Prima, 1999.

Guterson, David. *Family Matters: Why Homeschooling Makes Sense.* Harcourt Brace Jovanovich, 1992.

Hewitt, Ben. *Home Grown: Adventures in Parenting off the Beaten Path, Unschooling, and Reconnecting with the Natural World.* Roost Books, 2014.

Hunt, Jan, ed. *The Unschooling Unmanual: Nurturing Children's Natural Love of Learning.* The Natural Child Project, 2016.

____. *The Natural Child: Parenting from the Heart.* New Society Publishers, 2001.

Joudry, Patricia. *And the Children Played.* Tundra Books, 1975.

Kaseman, Larry, and Susan Kaseman. *Taking Charge Through Homeschooling.* Koshkonong Press, 1990.

Kesson, Kathleen. *Unschooling in Paradise.* Inner World Publications, 2018.

Laricchia, Pam. *The Unschooling Journey: A Field Guide.* Living Joyfully Enterprises, 2018.

Leistico, Agnes. *I Learn Better by Teaching Myself / Still Teaching Ourselves.* Holt Associates, 1997.

Llewellyn, Grace, ed. *Freedom Challenge: African American Homeschoolers.* Lowry House, 1996.

Llewellyn, Grace, and Amy Silver. *Guerilla Learning: How to Give Your Kids a Real Education with or without School.* John Wiley & Sons, 2001.

McDonald, Kerry. *Unschooled: Raising Curious, Well-Educated Children Outside the Conventional Classroom.* Chicago Review Press, 2019.

McDonald, Milva. *Slow Homeschooling: Essays about Mindful Homeschooling.* KDP, 2017.

McKee, Alison. *Homeschooling Our Children, Unschooling Ourselves.* Bittersweet House, 2002.

Montgomery, Pat. *The School That's Inside You.* Clonlara Press, 2017.

Moore, Raymond, and Dorothy Moore. *Better Late Than Early.* Readers Digest Press, 1989.

____. *School Can Wait.* Brigham Young University Press, 1989.

____. *The Successful Homeschool Family Handbook: A Creative and Stress-Free Approach to Homeschooling.* Thomas Nelson, 1994.

Orr, Tamra. *A Parent's Guide to Homeschooling.* Parent's Guide Press, 2002.

Polanco, Julie. *God Schooling: How God Intended Children to Learn.* Morgan James Faith, 2018.

Pride, Mary. *The Big Book of Home Learning.* Alpha Omega, 2000.

Prince, Daniel. *Choose Life: The Tools, Tricks, and Hacks of Long-Term Family Travelers, Worldschoolers, and Digital Nomads.* Kindle Direct Publishing, 2017.

Rainbolt, Rachel. *Sage Homeschooling: Wild and Free.* Kindle Direct Publishing, 2017.

Ransom, Marsha. *The Complete Idiot's Guide to Homeschooling.* Alpha Books, 2001.

Ray, Brian. *Worldwide Guide to Homeschooling.* Broadman & Holman, 2002.

Reed, Donn. *The Home School Source Book.* Brook Farm Books, 2001.

Ricci, Carlo. *The Willed Curriculum, Unschooling, and Self-Direction: What Do Love, Trust, Respect, Care, and Compassion Have to Do with Learning?* Ricci Publishing, 2012.

Riley, Gina. *Unschooling: Exploring Learning Beyond the Classroom.* Palgrave Macmillan, 2020.

Rowland, Ellen. *Everything I Thought I Knew: An Exploration of Life and Learning.* Kindle Direct Publishing, 2017.

Sheffer, Susannah. *Writing Because We Love To: Homeschoolers at Work.* Heinemann/Boynton/Cook, 1992.

Shute, Chris. *Joy Baker: Trailblazer for Home-Based Education and Personalized Learning.* Educational Heretics Press, 2008.

Wade, Ted. *The Homeschool Manual.* Gazelle, 2000.

Wallace, Nancy. *Better Than School.* Larson, 1983.

____. *Child's Work: Taking Children's Choices Seriously.* Holt Associates, 1991.

Weldon, Laura Grace. *Free Range Learning: How Homeschooling Changes Everything.* Hohm Press, 2010.

Westover, Tara. *Educated: A Memoir.* Random House, 2018.

Wise, Jessie, and Susan Wise Bauer. *The Well-Trained Mind: A Guide to Classical Education at Home.* Norton, 1999.

Worldbook. *Typical Course of Study, K–12.* https://www.worldbook.com /typical-course-of-study.aspx.

HUMAN PSYCHOLOGY AND DEVELOPMENT

Armstrong, Thomas. *The Human Odyssey: Navigating the Twelve Stages of Life*. Ixia Press, 2019.

_____. *If Einstein Ran the Schools: Revitalizing U.S. Education*. Praeger, 2019.

_____. *In Their Own Way: Discovering and Encouraging Your Child's Personal Learning Style*. Tarcher, 1988.

_____. *The Myth of the ADD Child: 50 Ways to Improve Your Child's Behavior and Attention Span without Drugs, Labels, or Coercion*. Houghton Mifflin, 1997.

_____. *Smarts! Everybody's Got Them*. Free Spirit, 2019.

Bateson, Gregory. *Steps to an Ecology of Mind*. University of Chicago Press, 2000.

Breggin, Peter. *Talking Back to Ritalin: What Doctors Aren't Telling You about Stimulants and ADHD*. Perseus, 2001.

Csikszentmihalyi, Mihaly. *Flow: The Psychology of Optimal Experience*. HarperCollins, 1991.

Fortune-Wood, Mike. *Can't Go Won't Go: An Alternative Approach to School Refusal*. Educational Heretics Press, 2007.

Goleman, Daniel. *Working with Emotional Intelligence*. Bantam, 1998.

Gopnik, Alison. *The Gardener and the Carpenter: What the New Science of Child Development Tells Us About the Relationship Between Parents and Children*. Farrar, Straus and Giroux, 2016.

_____. *The Philosophical Baby: What Children's Minds Tell Us About Truth, Love, and the Meaning of Life*. Farrar, Straus and Giroux, 2009.

Goodman, Paul. *Nature Heals: Psychological Essays*. Free Life Editions, 1977.

Greenspan, Stanley. *Challenging Child: Understanding, Raising, and Enjoying the Five "Difficult" Types of Children*. Perseus, 1996.

Healy, Jane. *Failure to Connect: How Computers Affect Our Children's Minds—for Better and Worse*. Simon and Schuster, 1998.

Kohn, Alfie. *Beyond Discipline: From Compliance to Community*. Professional Learning & Community for Educators, 1996.

_____. *No Contest: The Case Against Competition*. Mariner, 1992.

_____. *Punished by Rewards: The Trouble with Gold Stars, Incentive Plans, A's, Praise, and Other Bribes*. Mariner, 1993.

_____. *Schooling Beyond Measure and Other Unorthodox Essays about Education*. Heinemann, 2015.

_____. *The Schools Our Children Deserve*. Mariner, 2000.

_____. *Unconditional Parenting: Moving from Rewards and Punishments to Love and Reason*. Atria Books, 2006.

Langer, Ellen. *Mindfulness*. Addison-Wesley, 1989.

_____. *The Power of Mindful Learning*. Addison-Wesley, 1997.

Liedloff, Jean. *The Continuum Concept: Allowing Human Nature to Work Successfully*. Addison-Wesley, 1985.

Mercogliano, Chris. *Teaching the Restless: One School's Remarkable No-Ritalin Approach to Helping Children Learn and Succeed*. Beacon Press, 2004.

Sacks, Peter. *Standardized Minds: The High Price of America's Testing Culture and What We Can Do to Change It*. Perseus, 1999.

Schrag, Peter and Divoky, Diane. *The Myth of the Hyperactive Child*. Pantheon, 1975.

Shinn, Millicent W. *The Biography of a Baby*. 1900, Addison Wesley, 1985

Shute, Chris. *Alice Miller: The Unkind Society, Parenting, and Schooling*. Educational Heretics Press, 1994.

Skenazy, Lenore. *Free-Range Kids: How to Raise Safe, Self-Reliant Children—Without Going Nuts with Worry*. Jossey-Bass, 2009.

Stallibrass, Alison. *The Self-Respecting Child: Development through Spontaneous Play*. Addison-Wesley, 1989.

Tizard, Barbara, and Martin Hughes. *Young Children Learning*. Harvard University Press, 1984.

Winnicott, D. W. *Winnicott on the Child*. Perseus, 2002.

LEARNING COOPERATIVES AND COMMUNITIES

Ellis, William, et al. *A Guidebook for Creating Learning Communities*. Coalition for Self Learning, 2002.

Houk, Katherine. *Creating a Cooperative Learning Center: An Idea-Book for Homeschooling Families*. Longview, 2000.

Miller, Ron, ed. *Creating Learning Communities: Models, Resources, and New Ways of Thinking about Teaching and Learning*. Foundation for Educational Renewal, 2001.

Pearse, Innes, and Crocker, Lucy. *The Peckham Experiment: A Study of the Living Structure of Society*. George Allen and Unwin, 1947.

Stallibrass, Alison. *Being Me and Also Us: Lessons from the Peckham Experiment*. Scottish Academic Press, 1989.

PERIODICALS

Compleat Mother. https://compleatmother.com.

Education Revolution Magazine. www.educationrevolution.org/store /magazine/.

Empathic Parenting: Journal of the Canadian Society for the Prevention of Cruelty to Children. www.torontopubliclibrary.ca/detail.jsp?Entt=RDM239 2169&R=2392169.

Growing Without Schooling. www.johnholtgws.com.

Home School Researcher Journal. See National Home Education Research Institute under National Organizations.

Homeschooling Today. https://homeschoolingtoday.com.

Life Learning Magazine: Personalized, Non-Coercive, Active, Interest-Led Learning from Life. http://www.lifelearningmagazine.com.

Practical Homeschooling. https://www.practicalhomeschooling.com.

The Teaching Home. www.teachinghome.com.

Tipping Points Magazine. www.self-directed.org/tipping-points.

RESEARCH

WEBSITES AND JOURNALS ABOUT HOMESCHOOLING RESEARCH

International Center for Home Education Research. icher.org.

Journal of Unschooling and Alternative Learning. https://jual.nipissingu.ca/.

National Home Education Research Institute. https://www.nheri.org.

Other Education: The Journal of Educational Alternatives. https://www .othereducation.org/index.php/OE.

SELECTED RESEARCH BOOKS AND ARTICLES

Dwyer, James, and Peters, Shawn. *Homeschooling: The History and Philosophy of a Controversial Practice.* University of Chicago Press, 2019.

Gray, Peter. *Evidence That Self-Directed Education Works.* Tipping Points Press, 2020.

_____. *Children's natural ways of learning still work—even for the three rs.* In D.C. Geary & D.V. Berch (eds.). *Evolutionary Perspectives on Child Development and Education* (pp.63—93). Springer, 2016.

_____. *Free to Learn: Why Unleashing the Instinct to Play Will Make Our Children Happier, More Self-Reliant, and Better Students for Life*. Basic Books, 2013.

_____. *The Harm of Coercive Schooling*. Tipping Points Press, 2020.

_____. *How Children Acquire "Academic" Skills Without Formal Instruction*. Tipping Points Press, 2020.

_____. *Mother Nature's Pedagogy: Biological Foundations for Children's Self-Directed Education*. Tipping Points Press, 2020.

_____. *Self-Directed Education—Unschooling and Democratic Schooling*. Oxford Research Encyclopedia of Education, 2017.

Gray, Peter, and David Chanoff. "Democratic Schooling: What Happens to Young People Who Have Charge of Their Own Education?" *American Journal of Education* 94, no. 2 (1986).

Gray, Peter, and Jay Feldman. "Playing in the Zone of Proximal Development: Qualities of Self-Directed Age Mixing Between Adolescents and Young Children at a Democratic School." *American Journal of Education* 110, no. 2 (2004).

Gray, Peter, and Gina Riley. (2013). "The Challenges and Benefits of Unschooling, According to 232 Families Who Have Chosen That Route." *Journal of Unschooling and Alternative Learning* 7, no. 14 (2013).

_____. "Grown Unschoolers' Evaluations of Their Unschooling Experiences: Report I on a Survey of 75 Unschooled Adults." *Other Education: The Journal of Educational Alternatives* 4, no. 2 (2015).

Kunzman, Robert. *Write These Laws on Your Children: Inside the World of Conservative Christian Homeschooling*. Beacon Press, 2009.

Mayberry, Maralee, J. Gary Knowles, Brian Ray, and Stacey Marlow. *Home Schooling: Parents as Educators*. Corwin Press, 1995.

Meighan, Roland. *Comparing Learning Systems: The Good, the Bad, the Ugly and the Counter-productive and Why Many Home-Based Educating Families Have Found a Learning System Which Is Fit for a Democracy*. Educational Heretics Press, 2005.

_____. *Learning Unlimited: The Home-Based Education Case Files*. Educational Heretics Press, 2001.

_____. *The Next Learning System and Why Homeschoolers Are Trailblazers*. Educational Heretics Press, 1997.

Murphy, Joseph. *Homeschooling in America: Capturing and Assessing the Movement*. Corwin, 2012.

Pattison, Harriet. *Rethinking Learning to Read*. Educational Heretics Press, 2016.

Riley, Gina. "Differences in Competence, Autonomy, and Relatedness between Home Educated and Traditionally Educated Young Adults." *International Social Science Review* 90, no. 2 (2015).

———. "Exploring Unschoolers' Experiences in Learning to Read: How Reading Happens Within the Self-Directed Learning Environment." *Journal of Unschooling and Alternative Learning* 12, no. 24 (2018).

———. "The Role of Self-Determination Theory and Cognitive Evaluation Theory in Home Education." *Cogent Education* 3, no. 1 (2016).

———. "Unschooling in Hong Kong: A Case Study. *Journal of Unschooling and Alternative Learning* 10, no. 20 (2016).

———. "Worldschooling: Homeschooling Away from Home." *International Journal of Education* 9, no. 1 (2017).

Riley, Gina, and Peter Gray. "Grown Unschoolers' Experiences with Higher Education and Employment: Report II on a Survey of 75 Unschooled Adults." *Other Education: The Journal of Educational Alternatives* 4, no. 2 (2015).

Stephens, Mitchell. *Kingdom of Children: Culture and Controversy in the Homeschooling Movement*. Princeton University Press, 2001.

Thomas, Alan. "Autonomous and Informal Education Under Threat: Summerhill, UK, Sudbury Schools in The Netherlands and Home Education." *Other Education: The Journal of Educational Alternatives* 2, no. 1 (2013).

———. *Educating Children at Home*. Continuum, 1999.

Thomas, Alan, and Harriet Pattison. *How Children Learn at Home*. Continuum, 2007.

Van Galen, Jane, and Mary Anne Pitman. *Home Schooling: Political, Historical, and Pedagogical Perspectives*. Ablex, 1991.

APPENDIX B

CORRESPONDENCE SCHOOLS OR CURRICULUM SUPPLIERS

Abeka; 1-877-223-5226. Home Video School/Book Publications. https://www.abeka.com.

Accelerated Christian Education. https://schooloftomorrow.com.

Alpha Omega Publications, 804 N. 2nd Avenue E, Rock Rapids, IA 51246; 1-800-622-3070. https://www.aop.com.

American School, 2200 East 170th Street, Lansing, IL 60438; 708-418-2800. High school only. https://www.americanschoolofcorr.com.

American Association of Christian Schools, 6170 Shallowford Road, Suite 103, Chattanooga, TN 37421; 423-629-4280. https://www.aacs.org.

Autonome. Self-directed education offerings using an online platform. https://a.utono.me.

Brigham Young U-Dept of Independent Study, 770 E. University Parkway, Provo, UT 84602; 1-800-914-8931. https://is.byu.edu.

Calvert Education, 804 N. 2nd Avenue East, Rock Rapids, Iowa 51246-1759, 1-877-878-8045.

https://www.calverteducation.com/.

CLASS Homeschools, 502 West Euclid Avenue, Suite 68, Arlington Heights, IL 60004; 1-800-348-0899. https://www.homeschools.org.

Clonlara Distance Learning Program, 1289 Jewett Street, Ann Arbor, MI 48104; 734-769-4511. https://clonlara.org.

Galileo, 2230 Fillmore Street, San Francisco, CA 94115. An online school for self-directed learners aged 8–18. https://galileoxp.com.

Hewitt Learning, PO Box 28010, Spokane, WA 99228; 360-835-8708. https://hewittlearning.org.

The Hub. All-ages online programming and support. https://thehub.community.

International Institute, 4433 Broadway, Gary, IN 46409. https://iilcnwi.org.

Khan Academy. Free online courses in many subject areas. https://www.khanacademy.org.

Kolbe Academy, 1600 F Street, Napa, CA 94559; 707-255-6499. homeinfo@kolbe.org. https://kolbe.org.

Language Kids. Language programs for children. https://languagekids.com.

Laurel Springs School, 1615 West Chester Pike, West Chester, PA 19382. https://laurelsprings.com.

The Moore Foundation, PO Box 534, Dufur, OR 97021; 541-467-2444. https://www.moorefoundation.com.

NatureGlo's eScience Unschool. https://natureglosescience.com.

Oak Meadow School, PO Box 615, Putney, VT 05346; 802-251-7250. https://www.oakmeadow.com.

Our Lady of Victory School, 421 S. Lochsa Street, Post Falls, ID 83854; 208-773-7265. https://www.olvs.org.

Outschool. Live online classes and camps. https://outschool.com.

Rod & Staff Publishers, PO Box 3, Highway 172, Crockett, KY 41413-0003; 606-522-4348. https://www.anabaptists.org/ras.

School Specialty, 80 Northwest Boulevard, Nashua, NH 03063; 1-800-225-5750. https://eps.schoolspecialty.com.

Seton School Home Study, 1350 Progress Drive, Front Royal, VA 22630; 540-636-9990. https://www.setonhome.org.

APPENDIX C

HELPFUL PRIVATE SCHOOLS AND LEARNING CENTERS

Abbington Hill School, 602 Higgins Avenue, #146, Brielle, NJ 08730. http://www.school-your-way.com.

The Attic Learning Community, 24023 51st Avenue SE, Woodinville, WA 98072. info@the-attic.org. http://www.the-attic.org.

ALC Mosaic, 6100 Monroe Road, Charlotte, NC 28212. https://www.alcmosaic.org.

Bloom Academy, Las Vegas, NV; bloomacademylv@gmail.com. https://www.bloomacademylv.com.

Bay Shore School; bayshoreedu@gmail.com. https://bayshoreeducational.com.

Bungalow Lane ALC, Fresno, CA. https://www.bungalowlanealc.com.

Clonlara Distance Learning Program, 1289 Jewett Street, Ann Arbor, MI 48104; 734-769-4511. https://clonlara.org.

Cottonwood ALC, 322 Fuller Avenue, Helena, MT 59601; info@cottonwoodalc.org. https://www.cottonwoodalc.org.

Dayspring Christian Academy, 120 College Avenue, Mountville, PA 17554; 717-285-2000. https://www.dayspringchristian.com.

Eleanor Roosevelt Community Learning Center, 31191 Road 180, Visalia, CA 93292; 559-592-9160. https://erclc.org.

Family Academy, PO Box 157, Arlington, WA 98223. https://familyacademy .org.

Free To Learn ALC, 628 Royer Street, Roseville, CA 95678; hello@Free toLearnCommunity.com. http://freetolearncommunity.com.

Grassroots Free School, 2458 Grassroots Way, Tallahassee, FL 32301; 850-656-3629. https://www.grassrootsschool.org.

Headwaters School, Red Star, AR; raynbo.entropy@gmail.com. Homeschooler-run community school. https://www.facebook.com/pg/HeadwatersJuneBug Jam.

Heartwood School, 3983 Church Street, Clarkston, GA 30021; info@heart woodalc.org. https://www.heartwoodalc.org.

Learn Beyond the Book, Santa Clarita, CA; LearnBeyondTheBook@gmail .com. Homeschool/hybrid school classes & resources. https://learnbeyondthe book.com.

Lilac Agile Learning Community, Clovis, CA; lilacalcinfo@gmail.com. https://lilacalcinfo.wixsite.com/lilacagilelearningco.

Market Square Education, 13120 NE 177th Place A104, Woodinville, WA 98072; jcihak@marketsquare.education. https://marketsquare.education.

Puget Sound Community School, 660 S. Dearborn Street, Seattle, WA 98134; 206-324-4350. https://pscs.org.

Rivers & Roads ALC, 11301 N. Meridian Avenue, Oklahoma City, OK 73120; riversandroadsok@gmail.com. https://sites.google.com/view/riversand roadsok.

Rock Tree Sky, Ojai, CA. https://www.rocktreesky.org.

Sidney Ledson Institute, 220 Duncan Mill Road, Suite 7, North York, Ontario, Canada, M3B 3J5; 416-447-5355. https://www.sidneyledsoninstitute.net.

u.school, Springfield, MO. https://u.school.

West River Academy. https://www.westriveracademy.com.

APPENDIX D

HOMESCHOOLING ORGANIZATIONS

US NATIONAL GROUPS

Homeschool Legal Defense Association, PO Box 3000, Purcellville, VA 20134; 540-338-5600. https://hslda.org.

National Homeschool Association, 9249 S. Broadway, #200-368, Highlands Ranch, CO 80129. https://www.nationalhomeschoolassociation.com.

STATE OR LOCAL GROUPS (ALPHABETICALLY BY STATE)

Lists are out of date the minute you complete them because lists don't move but people do. Further there are so many state and local homeschooling support groups that a web search, or browsing through another book about homeschooling, will inevitably turn up new listings. Therefore, don't use this list as your sole resource, use it as a networking tool. One contact will lead to another until you locate the information or people you trust.

Statewide groups are likely to have information about state laws or regulations, and they may have conferences and packets of information for new homeschoolers. Other groups are local support groups that are likely to have meetings and activities. Both state and local groups may have newsletters. Try getting in touch with a state group even if it's far away from where you live since many state groups can refer you to families, or smaller support groups, in your immediate area.

ALABAMA

Alabama Homeschooling. https://www.facebook.com/alabamahome schooling.

Alabama Unschoolers. https://www.facebook.com/groups/1506567350 56065.

Homeschool Alabama. https://www.facebook.com/HomeschoolAlabama.

Valleydale Christian Academy, 2408 Valleydale Road, Birmingham, AL 35244; 205-987-6286. Acts as cover school. https://valleydale.net.

ALASKA

Alaska Homeschool Community. https://www.facebook.com/Alaska HomeschoolCommunity

Alaska Private and Home Educators Association, 189 E. Nelson Avenue, #179, Wasilla, AK 99654. https://aphea.org.

Alaskan Unschool Supporters. https://www.facebook.com/groups/216812 171677661.

Anchorage Life Learners. https://www.facebook.com/groups/Anchorage LifeLearners.

ARIZONA

Arizona Families for Home Education, PO Box 2035, Chandler, AZ 85244-2035. homeschool@afhe.org. https://www.afhe.org.

Desert Dreamers Unschooling Group, Goodyear, AZ. https://www.face book.com/groups/189618822099493.

Free To Be Unschooling Conference, Phoenix, AZ. http://www.freetobe conference.com.

Phoenix Unschoolers. https://www.facebook.com/groups/1805606786 85890.

Sonoran Desert Homeschoolers, Tucson, AZ. www.tucsonhomeschoolers .com.

ARKANSAS

Arkansas Unschoolers. https://www.facebook.com/groups/cafe.life1.

Cabot Area Home Education; cabotareahomeeducation@gmail.com. https://www.homeschool-life.com/279/signup.

The Education Alliance, 414 South Pulaski Street, Suite 9, Little Rock, AR 72201. info@arkansashomeschool.org. https://arkansashomeschool.org.

Social Homeschoolers Network, Northwest AK. https://www.nwasocial homeschoolers.com.

CALIFORNIA

Alcove Learning Cooperative, 321 1/2 East 1st Street #206, Los Angeles, CA 90012. alcove.learning@gmail.com. https://sites.google.com/view/alcove learning.

Bay Area Unschooling Connections. https://www.facebook.com/groups /bayareaunschoolingconnections.

Big Oak Homeschoolers, Sacramento, CA; bigoakhomeschoolers@gmail .com. http://bigoakhomeschoolers.com.

California Homeschool Network, 2166 W. Broadway #266, Anaheim, CA 92804. mail@californiahomeschool.net. https://www.californiahomeschool .net.

Diablo Valley Unschooling Co-op, Pleasant Hill, CA. https://www.meetup .com/The-Contra-Costa-Unschooling-Group.

East Bay Self-Directed Education, Oakland, CA. https://www.facebook .com/groups/408464636774540.

Full Circle Schooling, Fremont, CA; hello@fullcircleschooling.org. https:// www.fullcircleschooling.org.

Homeschooling LA, Los Angeles, CA. https://www.facebook.com/groups /1159840177409093.

HUGS | SF (Homeschoolers+Unschoolers Group Support), San Francisco, CA. https://www.facebook.com/groups/1931740383552142.

Homeschool Association of California; 1-888-HSC-4440. https://www.hsc.org.

Humboldt Homeschoolers, Humboldt County, CA. https://www.facebook .com/groups/humboldthomeschoolers.

Kids Out In Daylight (!) Homeschoolers, Alameda, CA. https://www .meetup.com/EB-Young-Homeschoolers.

Lassen Life Learners, Susanville, CA. https://www.facebook.com/groups /lassenlifelearners.

LEAP Homeschool Conference, San Diego, CA. https://www.learningjour neysforum.com/leap-2020.

Los Angeles Unschoolers. https://www.facebook.com/LAUnschoolers.

Monterey Self-Directed Educators, Monterey, CA. https://www.facebook .com/groups/934772353330533.

Natural Learners, Wildomar, CA. https://www.meetup.com/Natural Learners.

Peninsula Self-Directed Education, Woodside, CA. https://www.facebook .com/groups/PeninsulaSDE.

Sacramento Area Self-Directed Education. https://www.facebook.com /groups/159430147981519.

Sacramento Spark. https://sacramentospark.com.

SF Bay Area Homeschool Network. https://www.facebook.com/groups /1537398423139116.

San Diego Homeschooling Co-op. https://www.meetup.com/San-Diego -Homeschooling-Meetup-Group.

San Diego Learning Revolution. https://www.facebook.com/groups/SD LearningRevolution.

San Francisco Homeschooling & Unschooling Group. https://www.face book.com/groups/166286810672946.

Sonoma County Homeschoolers Nonprofit. http://schnonprofit.org.

Sonoma County Unschoolers, Santa Rosa, CA. https://www.facebook.com /groups/1607628806200803.

South Bay Homeschoolers Community, Torrance, CA. https://www.face book.com/groups/southbayhomeschoolerscommunity.

South Bay Unschoolers, Los Angeles, CA. https://www.facebook.com /SouthBayUnschoolers.

South Street Centre, 15685 Forest Hill Drive, Boulder Creek, CA 95006. https://southstreetcentre.wordpress.com.

Sticky Buns—East Bay Unschoolers & Homeschoolers, Orinda, CA. https:// www.meetup.com/StickyBuns.

Unschooling Homies of Solano County, Vacaville, CA. https://www.face book.com/groups/169055117095516.

Unschooling LA, Los Angeles, CA. https://www.facebook.com/groups /234120860601975.

Ventura County Unschoolers, Thousand Oaks, CA. https://www.facebook.com/groups/vcunschoolers.

COLORADO

BLDG 61: Boulder Library Makerspace; 1001 Arapahoe Avenue, Boulder, CO 80302. https://boulderlibrary.org/bldg61.

Colorado Community of Wholelife Unschooling. https://www.facebook.com/groups/103800093055344.

Denver Area Unschoolers. https://www.facebook.com/groups/274677689556807.

Denver-Boulder Unschoolers. https://www.facebook.com/groups/249960438390148.

Denver Unschoolers. https://denverunschoolers.weebly.com.

Green Mountain Area Homeschoolers, Lakewood, CO. https://thehappinesshere.com/green-mountain-area-homeschoolers.

Northern Colorado Homeschool Association. https://www.ncha.info.

CONNECTICUT

Beacon Self-Directed Learning, 123 Whalley Avenue, New Haven, CT 06511; 203-747-8735. http://www.beaconlearning.org.

Quiet Corner Homeschoolers (Northeastern CT). https://www.facebook.com/groups/268476756562076.

TEACH CT—The Education Association of Christian Homeschoolers in Connecticut. https://www.teachct.org.

Unschoolers' Unlimited, Guilford, CT; 203-458-7402. http://unschoolersunlimited.blogspot.com.

Wild Child Bliss—Unschool Community, Mossup, CT. https://www.facebook.com/WildChildBliss.

DELAWARE

Delaware Homeschoolers. https://www.facebook.com/Dehomeschooling.

Delaware Secular Homeschoolers. https://www.facebook.com/groups/DelawareSecularHomeschoolers.

Homeschool Action Network of Delaware. https://handde.org.

Homeschool Delaware. https://www.facebook.com/groups/118853418201199.

Tri-State Homeschool Network. https://www.tristatehomeschoolnetwork.org.

Walnut Grove Coop (homeschoolers and unschoolers), 91 Salem Church Road Newark, DE 19711. http://walnutgrovecoop.com.

FLORIDA

Branches Unschoolers of Pinellas County, Dunedin, FL. https://www.facebook.com/groups/608286892604774.

Florida Parent Educators Association; 877-275-3732. https://fpea.com.

Florida Unschoolers; director@floridaunschoolers.net. https://sites.google.com/site/floridaunschoolers.

Florida Unschooling Adventures. https://www.facebook.com/groups/389706827885465.

Gainesville Unschooling Community, Gainesville, FL. https://www.facebook.com/groups/466357783377830.

Miami Homeschoolers. https://www.facebook.com/MiamiHomeschoolers.

Not Exactly Florida Unschoolers. https://www.facebook.com/groups/271960499991802.

Real Life Agile Learning Center, Tampa, FL; reallifeinc.org@gmail.com. https://reallifeincorg.wixsite.com/reallifealc.

River City Unschoolers, Jacksonville, FL. https://www.facebook.com/groups/Rivercityunschoolers.

SOAR (Society of Autodidactic Radicals), Brevard Space Coast, FL. https://www.facebook.com/groups/665185260279253.

Spark Agile Learning Center, 1805 30th Avenue W, Bradenton, FL 34205. sparkagilelearningcenter@gmail.com. https://www.sparkalc.org.

Unschoolers of Brevard, Brevard Co., FL. https://www.facebook.com/groups/UnschoolersBrevard.

GEORGIA

AAEN—Atlanta Alternative Education Network, 10495 Woodstock Road, Roswell, GA; 404-636-6348. https://www.facebook.com/AAENgroup.

Anna Julia Cooper Learning & Liberation Center, 790 Welch Street SW, Atlanta, GA 30310; 678-210-6155. http://www.learningandliberation.org.

Atlanta SDE + Social Justice Group. https://www.heartwoodalc.org.

Atlas Agile Learning Center, 101 Parkview Drive, Winterville, GA 30683. AtlasALC@gmail.com. https://www.atlasalc.org.

Augusta–Aiken Unschooling. https://www.facebook.com/groups/565565 666881390.

Georgia Homeschool Network. https://www.facebook.com/groups/115573 126412.

Georgia Unschoolers. https://www.facebook.com/groups/GeorgiaUnschoolers.

Middle Georgia Unschoolers, Thomaston, GA. https://www.facebook.com /groups/1015311358527062.

Oasis Agile Learning Center, 4561 Church Street, Acworth, GA 30101; 678-813-1336. https://www.oasisalc.com.

Union County Homeschoolers/Unschoolers. https://www.facebook.com /groups/2271941756384343.

HAWAII

Big Island Unschoolers. https://www.facebook.com/bigislandunschoolers.

Christian Homeschoolers of Hawaii; 808 664-9608; info@christianhomes choolersofhawaii.org. http://christianhomeschoolersofhawaii.org/w.

Hawaii Homeschool Association; hha-info@hawaiihomeschoolassociation .org. https://www.hawaiihomeschoolassociation.org.

Kauai Unschoolers. https://www.facebook.com/groups/380584349171093.

Liberating Hawaii's Youth. https://www.facebook.com/groups/50825329 5918162.

IDAHO

Homeschool Idaho; info@homeschoolidaho.org. https://homeschoolidaho .org.

Southwestern Idaho Unschoolers. https://www.facebook.com/groups /219237298097848.

Twin Falls Homeschoolers & Unschoolers, Twin Falls, ID. https://www.face book.com/groups/TFHaU.

ILLINOIS

Chicagoland Unschoolers. https://www.facebook.com/groups/3147769760 49945.

Illinois Christian Home Educators, PO Box 617, Antioch, IL 60002-0617; 847-603-1259. https://iche.org.

Illinois Homeschool/Unschooling Support. https://www.facebook.com /groups/1123189554365080.

Illinois Unschoolers. https://www.facebook.com/groups/IllinoisUnschoolers.

Lake County, Illinois Unschoolers and Life Learners. https://www.face book.com/groups/264703697484110.

NIAH (Northern Illinois Alternative Homeschoolers). https://www.face book.com/groups/NIAHhomeschoolers.

Northside Unschoolers of Chicago. http://www.northsideunschoolers.org.

INDIANA

Fort Wayne Unschoolers. https://www.facebook.com/groups/14166360 5992663.

Indiana Association of Home Educators, PO Box 217, Stilesville, IN 46180; 317-467-6244; info@iahe.net. https://iahe.net.

Indianapolis' Freeschoolers/Lifeschoolers. https://www.facebook.com/groups /unschooledIndy.

Northwest Indiana Unschoolers. https://www.facebook.com/groups/1865 437240348063.

Steuben County Homeschoolers. https://www.faccbook.com/groups/Steuben CountyHomeschoolers.

IOWA

Homeschool Iowa, Box 158, Dexter, IA 50070; niche@homeschooliowa.org . https://homeschooliowa.org.

Iowa Unschoolers. https://www.facebook.com/groups/130034355310.

Radical Unschool Iowa. https://www.facebook.com/groups/5857180048 44229.

KANSAS

Christian Home Educators Confederation of Kansas, PO Box 1332, Topeka, KS 66601. http://kansashomeschool.org.

Kansas Home Educators, PO Box 3968, Wichita, Kansas 67201; editor@ KShomeeducators.com. https://www.teachingparents.org.

Kansas Unschoolers. https://www.facebook.com/Kansas-Unschoolers -156985535069414.

Wichita Unschoolers. https://www.facebook.com/groups/1707373564 10053.

KENTUCKY

Bluegrass Homeschool Learning Cooperative, Inc., PO Box 23901, Lexington, KY 40523. https://www.my-bhlc.org.

Christian Home Educators of Kentucky, PO Box 397, Bloomfield, KY 40008. http://www.chek.org.

Louisville SDE. https://www.facebook.com/groups/1005545809608124.

Louisville Unschooling, Self-Directed, and Relaxed Homeschooling. https://www.facebook.com/groups/155348361670016.

POP Louisville. https://poplouisville.com.

Unschool Central Kentucky, https://www.facebook.com/groups/unschool centralkentucky.

LOUISIANA

Dat School, 2231 Arts Street, New Orleans, LA 70117. Agile Learning Center-model homeschool community. http://www.datschoolnola.org.

Lafayette Homeschool Collective for Self-Directed Learning, Lafayette, LA; 337-247-8316. https://www.lafayettehomeschool.org.

Louisiana Unschoolers. https://www.facebook.com/groups/LAUnschoolers.

NOLA Homeschoolers. https://www.nolahomeschoolers.com.

Westbank Homeschool Organization. http://www.who2000inc.org.

MAINE

Homeschoolers of Maine, PO Box 159, Camden, ME 04843; 207-763-2880. https://www.homeschoolersofmaine.org.

Maine Homeschoolers & Unschoolers. https://www.facebook.com/maine homeschool.

Maine Unschooling Network. https://www.facebook.com/groups/131272 143567112.

MARYLAND

Eastern Shore Unschoolers, Salisbury, MD. https://www.facebook.com /groups/1454156428022147.

Maryland Homeschool Association; mdhsa.info@gmail.com. https://mdhsa.com.

Maryland Unschoolers. https://www.facebook.com/groups/Maryland Unschoolers.

MASSACHUSETTS

AHEM—Advocates for Home Education in Massachusetts. www.Ahem.info.

Bay State Learning Center, 45 Bullard Street, Dedham, MA 02026. https://www.baystatelearning.org.

Camberville Unschoolers, Somerville, MA. https://www.facebook.com/groups/cambervilleunschoolingfamiles.

Cape Cod Unschoolers. https://www.facebook.com/groups/148671938532043.

Hilltown Families: Community-Based Education Network, PO Box 332, Williamsburg, MA 01096. https://hilltownfamilies.org.

LearnMV, 16 Knight Lane, Edgartown, MA 02539. https://www.learnmv.org.

LightHouse Holyoke, 208 Race Street, Holyoke, MA 01040. https://www.lighthouseholyoke.org.

Northeast Unschooling Conference, Wakefield, MA; neucinfo@gmail.com. https://www.facebook.com/groups/NEUnschooling.

Macomber Center, 1 Badger Road, Framingham, MA 01702. https://macombercenter.org

Massachusetts Home Learning Association. https://www.mhla.org.

Massachusetts Homeschool Organization of Parent Educators (MassHope). https://masshope.org.

North Suburban Homelearners. https://www.facebook.com/groups/1967867903514004.

North Star: Self-Directed Learning for Teens, 45 Amherst Road, Sunderland, MA 01375. http://www.northstarteens.org.

Nuts About Learning. Group for Northeastern MA/Southeastern NH unschoolers. https://www.facebook.com/groups/202309239950482.

Parts and Crafts: The Center for Semi-Conducted Learning, 577 Somerville Avenue, Somerville, MA 02143. https://www.partsandcrafts.info.

Southcoast Homeschoolers & Unschoolers. https://www.facebook.com /groups/1807199842850335.

South Shore Unschoolers. https://www.facebook.com/groups/16729340 49657626.

Talking Radical Unschooling in MA. https://www.facebook.com/groups /904692352945921.

MICHIGAN

Blue Bridge School, 1711 Walker Avenue NW, Grand Rapids, MI 49504; 616-710-1347; hello@bluebridgeschool.com. https://bluebridgeschool.com.

FLASH: Families Learning and Schooling at Home, Calhoun County, MI; 269-589-5166; info@miflash.org. https://miflash.org.

Harambee Homeschool Cooperative (African-centered), Detroit, MI; hhsc .detroit@gmail.com. https://www.facebook.com/HHSCDetroit.

Homeschooling in Detroit. https://homeschoolingindetroit.com.

Michigan Christian Homeschool Network, 4407 W. St. Joseph Street, Lansing, MI 48917. https://michn.org.

Michigan Homeschoolers & Unschoolers Unite. https://www.facebook .com/groups/564371506944301.

Michigan Unschoolers. https://www.facebook.com/groups/Michigan Unschoolers.

Lupine Learning Community, 1517 Bayliss Street, Midland, MI 48640; 989-423-0363. https://lupinelearningcommunity.org.

Unschooling Michigan. https://www.facebook.com/groups/1646281802 276694.

West Michigan Unschoolers. https://www.facebook.com/groups/638675 346744704.

MINNESOTA

Home Education Resource Organization, Minneapolis, MN; herohome school@gmail.com. https://herohomeschool.org.

Homegrown Kids, Minneapolis, MN. Secular group of unschoolers and relaxed homeschoolers. https://www.facebook.com/groups/858672794248882.

Little Urban Explorers, Minneapolis, MN. https://www.facebook.com /groups/810214712343517.

Minnesota Homeschoolers Alliance; mha@homeschoolers.org. https://homeschoolers.org.

Twin Cities Unschoolers, Minneapolis and St. Paul, MN. https://www.facebook.com/groups/400623420612573.

MISSISSIPPI

Homeschoolers of Central Mississippi. https://www.facebook.com/groups/HS.Central.MS.

Mississippi Home Educators Association; 662-494-1999. https://www.mhea.net.

PEAK Homeschool Network. https://www.facebook.com/PEAKHomeschoolNetwork.

MISSOURI

Families for Home Education, PO Box 3096, Independence, MO 64055. 1983fhemo@gmail.com. https://fhe-mo.org.

L.E.A.R.N. Home Education Network, Kansas City, MO (includes families in Kansas). www.kclearn.org.

St. Louis Homeschool Network. https://stlouishomeschoolnetwork.org.

Unschoolers of Kansas City. https://www.facebook.com/groups/275615852579450.

Unschooling in Missouri. https://www.facebook.com/groups/263198304979309.

Unschoolers of Missouri. https://www.facebook.com/groups/unschoolers.

Zen Mamas–Homeschooling and Unschool Group of Kansas City. https://www.facebook.com/groups/160657074049283.

MONTANA

Billings Area Homeschoolers. https://www.facebook.com/groups/338713966214446.

Bitterroot Homeschooling. https://bitterroothomeschooling.com.

Bozeman Area Homeschoolers. https://www.facebook.com/groups/370189256395959.

Flathead Home Educators Association. http://fheaonline.org.

Helena Homeschool Network. https://www.facebook.com/groups/158421437503409.

Homeschooling in Montana. https://www.homeschoolinginmontana.com.

Missoula Homeschool. https://missoulahomeschool.com.

Montana Coalition of Home Educators, PO Box 43, Gallatin Gateway, MT, 59730. https://www.mtche.org.

Rosebud County Home Educators Association, Forsyth, MT. https://www.facebook.com/groups/1521575284775921.

We, Montana! https://wemontana.org.

Yellowstone Coalition of Homeschoolers; ychemt@gmail.com. http://www.yche.org/index.html.

NEBRASKA

Nebraska Homeschool. https://www.facebook.com/nebraska.homeschool.

Nebraska Secular Home Educators. https://www.facebook.com/NebraskaSecularHomeEducators.

Omaha Unschoolers. https://www.facebook.com/groups/1491271290960660.

Wild Learning, Lincoln, NE; wildlearninglincoln@gmail.com. https://www.wildlearninglincoln.com.

NEVADA

Home Schools United-Vegas Valley; homeschooluvv@yahoo.com. http://homeschool8.tripod.com.

Las Vegas Life Learners. https://www.facebook.com/groups/lasvegaslifelearners.

Nevada Middle/High Homeschool Support. https://www.facebook.com/groups/NNHSHighSchoolSupport.

Reno Homeschoolers/Unschoolers: Adventure, discover, build, explode! https://www.facebook.com/groups/471500579569340.

NEW HAMPSHIRE

BigFish Learning Community, 61 Locust Street, Dover, NH 03820. https://www.bigfishnh.org.

Latitude Learning Resources, PO Box 16542, Hooksett, NH 03106. https://www.latitudelearning.org.

New Hampshire Homeschooling Coalition, PO Box 2224, Concord, NH 03302. https://nhhomeschooling.org.

Seacoast Unschooling. https://www.facebook.com/groups/8996835400
98549.

UnschoolingNH. https://www.facebook.com/groups/UnschoolingNH.

NEW JERSEY

Amber Colibri Center, 902 N. 5th Street, Newark, NJ 07107; ambercoli
bricenter@gmail.com. http://ambercolibricenter.org.

New Jersey Homeschool Association; https://www.facebook.com/NJhome
school. https://jerseyhomeschool.net.

Princeton Learning Cooperative, 16 All Saints Road, Princeton, NJ 08540.
Liberated Learners center. https://princetonlearningcooperative.org.

Raritan Learning Cooperative, 168 Main Street, Flemington, NJ 08822.
Liberated Learners center. https://raritanlearningcooperative.org.

Self-Directed Education in Central Jersey. https://www.facebook.com
/groups/sdecentraljersey.

NEW MEXICO

The Homeschool Classroom, 1500 5th Street, Suite 3, Santa Fe, NM
87505; thehomeschoolclassroomsantafe@gmail.com. https://thehomeschool
classroomsantafe.com.

NM Unschooling. https://www.facebook.com/groups/422574748265892.

NEW YORK

Agile Learning Center NYC, 115 E. 106 Street, Floor 2, New York, NY 10029.
https://nycagile.org.

Brooklyn Apple Academy, 545 5th Avenue, Brooklyn, NY 11215; brookly
nappleacademy@gmail.com. https://www.brooklynappleacademy.org.

Cottonwood Cooperative NYC, 203 Driggs Avenue, Brooklyn, NY 11222.
https://www.cottonwoodnyc.org.

Deep Root Center for Self-Directed Learning, 48 Riverside Drive, Canton,
NY 13617. https://www.deeprootcenter.org.

Dida Academy, Brooklyn, NY; 718-395-7401. Serving ages 1–18. https://
didaacademy.org.

Flying Squad—Brooklyn; brooklyn@flyingsquads.org. http://www.flying
squads.org.

Home Learners Association of Central New York. https://www.hlacny.com.

Ithaca NY Area Homeschoolers. https://www.facebook.com/groups/4354 97099879666.

New York City Home Educators Alliance, 511 Avenue of the Americas #332, New York, NY 10011; nychea.info@gmail.com. https://www.nychea.org.

RUNNY – Radical Unschoolers in New York. https://www.facebook.com /groups/runny.

Unschoolers of Western NY. https://www.facebook.com/groups/713731 902141360.

NORTH CAROLINA

Asheville Unschoolers & Homeschoolers. https://www.facebook.com /groups/AshevilleHomeschoolUnschool.

Gastonia Freedom School (agile learning center), 208 N. Pryor Street, Gastonia, NC 28052; gastoniafreedomschool@gmail.com. https://gastoniafreedom .org.

Greensboro Area Unschoolers. https://www.facebook.com/groups/1226 23695090990.

Homeschool Park Days, Jacksonville, NC. https://www.facebook.com /groups/530554070618015.

NC Unschooling – Triangle Area. https://www.facebook.com/groups /684654211597415.

North Carolinians for Home Education, 4441 Six Forks Road, Suite 106, Box 144, Raleigh, NC 27609; 1-844-NCHE-EDU; nche@nche.com. https://www.nche .com.

Pathfinder Community School, 2400 Broad Street, Suite 5, Durham, NC 27704. https://pathfindercommunityschool.com.

Unschoolers of Central Wake, Cary, NC. https://www.facebook.com /groups/CaryUnschoolers.

Unschoolers of Eastern NC. https://www.facebook.com/groups/Un schoolersOfEasternNC.

Unschoolers of North Carolina. https://www.facebook.com/groups/2391 35689856468.

Wildwood Agile Learning Community, Boone, NC; wildwoodagilelear ning@gmail.com. https://www.wildwoodalc.org.

Wilmington Cooperative School, 2166 Dexter Street, Wilmington, NC 28403. Homeschool coop using ALC tools. https://welearnfreely.com.

ZigZag Liberation Station & ALC, 22 Thompson Road, Asheville, NC 28806; 828-378-6993. https://www.zigzagalc.org.

NORTH DAKOTA

Bismarck/Mandan Area Home Educators. https://www.bmahe.com/2437.

Fargo-Moorhead Homeschooling Network. https://www.facebook.com /groups/488824394478273.

North Dakota Homeschool Association, PO Box 1066, Devils Lake, ND 58301; 701-662-6347; office@ndhsa.org. https://www.homeschool-life.com/nd /ndhsa.

OHIO

Akron-Cleveland-Canton Area Radical/Whole Life Unschooling. https:// www.facebook.com/groups/149878705115040.

Alliance Area Home Educators; allianceareahomeeducators@gmail.com . https://www.facebook.com/AllianceAreaHomeEducators.

Annual Unschoolers' Waterpark Gathering, Kalahari Waterpark Resort, Sandusky, OH. https://www.unschoolerswaterparkgathering.com.

Bloom Learning Community, 44 Front Street, Berea OH 44017. https:// www.growatbloom.com.

Chagrin Valley School, 14040 Auburn Road, Newbury Township, OH 44065; chagrinvalleyschool@gmail.com. https://chagrinvalleyschool.org.

Christian Home Educators of Ohio. https://www.cheohome.org.

Cincinnati-Dayton Unschoolers and Relaxed Homeschoolers. https://www .facebook.com/groups/232931826776913.

Columbus Area Self-Directed Teens. https://www.facebook.com/groups /964223543620420.

Columbus Unschoolers' CoOp. https://www.facebook.com/columbus unschoolers.

Dayton/ SW Ohio Unschoolers. https://www.facebook.com/groups/Dayton Unschoolers.

Northeast Ohio Unschooling Community, Cleveland, OH. https://www .facebook.com/groups/135252350149199.

Ohio Homeschooling Parents. https://ohiohomeschoolingparents.com.

Spark Homeschool Co-op, Cincinnati, OH; sparkhomeschoolcoop@gmail .com. https://sparkhomeschool.org.

Unschool Community Connection, Lorain Co., OH. https://www.facebook
.com/groups/1558870177665568.

Unschoolers of Fairfield County. https://www.facebook.com/groups/1883
469925115710.

Unschooling Ohio. https://www.facebook.com/unschoolingohio.

OKLAHOMA

Homeschool Oklahoma. https://www.homeschooloklahoma.org.

Radical Unschoolers of Oklahoma. https://www.facebook.com/groups
/radicalunschoolersok.

Tulsa Unschooling Co-op. https://www.facebook.com/groups/30856285
2491072.

OREGON

Alder Commons, 4212 NE Prescott Street, Portland, OR 97218; hello@alder
commons.org. https://aldercommons.org.

Cascadia Learning Cooperative, 95 S. Bertelsen Road, Eugene, OR 97402;
info@cascadialearning.com. https://www.cascadialearning.com.

Flying Squad—Portland; portland@flyingsquads.org. http://www.flying
squads.org.

The Hive: Self-Directed Learning for Teens, Springfield, OR; hiveteens@
gmail.com. http://www.thehiveforteens.org.

Imagine Cooperative, Corvallis, OR; 1234lookingup@gmail.com. https://
www.facebook.com/imaginecooperative.

Marrow, 7025 N. Lombard Street, Unit 100, Portland, OR 97203; info@
marrowpdx.org. https://www.marrowpdx.org.

Notschool Eugene/Springfield. https://www.facebook.com/groups/341581
619909531.

Oregon Home Education Network, PO Box 80155, Portland, OR 97219;
503-893-2744; info@ohen.org. http://www.ohen.org.

Oregon Unschoolers. https://www.facebook.com/groups/OregonUnschoolers.

Portland Self-Directed Education. Advocacy group and book club. https://
portlandsde.com.

Portland Unschoolers. https://www.facebook.com/groups/portlandun
schoolers.

Rogue Valley Unschoolers, near Ashland, OR. https://www.facebook.com /groups/RogueValleyUnschoolers.

Unschooling in Curry County, Oregon. https://www.facebook.com /groups/1855849641137126.

Village Home Education Resource Center; info@villagehome.org. http:// www.villagehome.org.

PENNSYLVANIA

Bucks Learning Cooperative, 315 W. Maple Avenue, Langhorne, PA 19047. http://buckslearningcooperative.org.

Lancaster Secular Homeschoolers. https://www.facebook.com/groups /474715539304295.

Natural Creativity Center, Germantown, Philadelphia, PA. https://natural creativity.org.

Open Connections, 1616 Delchester Road, Newtown Square, PA 19073. http://www.openconnections.org.

Pennsylvania Homeschoolers Accreditation Agency. https://www.phaa.org.

Pennsylvania Home Educators Association. https://phea.net.

Pennsylvania Unschooling Info. https://www.facebook.com/groups/paun schoolers.

People Always Learning Something (PALS), 905 Mifflin Avenue, Pittsburgh, PA. https://www.facebook.com/pg/PalsPittsburgh.

Philly ALC, 756 S. 11th Street, Philadelphia, PA. https://www.phillyalc.org.

Talking Stick Learning Center, 1 Awbury Road, Philadelphia, PA 19138. https://talkingsticklearningcenter.org.

Unschoolers in Pennsylvania. https://www.facebook.com/groups/922899 647829068.

RHODE ISLAND

Providence Unschoolers. https://www.facebook.com/groups/1038628722 880404.

RIGHT: Rhode Island Homeschooling. https://www.rihomeschool.com.

Rhode Island Unschoolers. https://www.facebook.com/groups/RIun schoolers.

SOUTH CAROLINA

South Carolina Association of Independent Home Schools; scaihs@scaihs .org. https://schomeschooling.com.

South Carolina Homeschool Connection. https://www.homeschoolingsc .org.

South Carolina Unschoolers. https://www.facebook.com/groups/909874 212732534.

SOUTH DAKOTA

Our Way of Learning, Sioux Falls, SD. http://www.owlsiouxfalls.org.

Natural Learning Network of South Dakota. https://www.facebook.com /NaturalLearningNetwork.

SMASH—Sioux Metro Area Social Homeschoolers. https://www.facebook .com/groups/1306966619323884.

South Dakota Unschoolers. https://www.facebook.com/groups/388884 478157359.

TENNESSEE

East Tennessee Unschoolers, Knoxville, TN. https://www.facebook.com /groups/636798906330428.

Eclectic Homeschoolers of Middle Tennessee. https://www.facebook.com /groups/EHSMT.

Make-A-Space Unschool Coop, Nashville, TN; marie.mckinney@gmail .com. https://www.facebook.com/groups/2641875295878494.

Tennessee Home Education Association. https://www.tnhea.org.

Village Coop, Murfreesboro, TN; villagecooptn@gmail.com. Coop of homeschooling families. https://www.villagecooptn.com.

TEXAS

ATX Homeschool. https://atxhomeschool.com.

Austin Area Homeschoolers. https://www.facebook.com/groups/austin areahomeschoolers.

Austin Unschoolers. https://www.facebook.com/groups/1394841424103117.

EPIC Life Learning Community, 1641 W. Hebron Parkway, Carrollton, Texas 75010; info@epiclifelearningcommunity.com. http://www.epiclifelearning community.com.

Families Learning Freely, Houston, TX. Meet-up group for unschooling-compatible families. https://www.facebook.com/groups/familieslearningfreely.

Holistic Global Education Community, Houston, TX. https://www.holisticglobaled.org.

Houston Unschooling Kids. https://www.facebook.com/groups/realschoollittles.

Inspired Learning Academy, Fairview, TX. http://www.inspiredlearningacademy.org.

Katy/West Houston Unschoolers. https://www.facebook.com/groups/katyunschoolers.

Odyssey: A Self-Directed Learning Community, New Braunfels, TX. http://www.odysseylearning.org.

Open Skies Learning Community, Midland, TX. https://www.openskieslearning.com.

Self-Directed Path Conference & Workshop. https://self-directedpath.org.

Texas Homeschool Coalition. https://thsc.org.

Texas Unschoolers. https://www.texasunschoolers.com.

Unschool Austin. https://www.facebook.com/groups/UnschoolAustin.

Unschooling Center San Antonio. https://www.facebook.com/groups/170514750231158.

Unschooling San Antonio. https://www.facebook.com/groups/UnschoolingSanAntonio.

UTAH

Salt Lake Unschoolers. https://www.facebook.com/groups/SaltLakeUnschoolers.

Utah County Unschoolers. https://www.facebook.com/groups/1416729405286537.

Utah Home Education Association. http://www.uhea.org.

Utah Unschoolers. https://www.facebook.com/groups/1444203939129441.

Wasatch Home Educators Network. https://whenonline.org.

VERMONT

Learning Through Living VT Unschool Conference; LTLconferencevt@hotmail.com. http://www.facebook.com/LTLVT.

Open Path Homeschooling Resources, 180 Bartlett Road, Plainfield, VT 05667. http://www.openpathhomeschooling.com.

Vermont Home Education Network, PO Box 72, Woodbury, VT 05681. https://vhen.org.

Vermont Homeschoolers & Unschoolers Unite. https://www.facebook.com /groups/305422002936927.

VIRGINIA

BR FUN (Blue Ridge Family Unschoolers Network), Blue Ridge, VA. https:// www.facebook.com/BRFunUnschoolers.

Embark Center for Self-Directed Education, 103 Loudoun Street SW, Leesburg, VA 20175; 540-277-3172. Liberated Learners center. https://embark center.org.

Funschooling, Winchester, VA. Group for homeschooling families to plan events, coops, classes, or recreation dates. https://www.facebook.com /groups/1696209297279128.

Home Educators Association of Virginia, 2100 W. Laburnum Avenue, Suite 108-A, Richmond, VA 23227; 804-278-9200. https://heav.org.

The Organization of Virginia Homeschoolers. https://vahomeschoolers.org.

Raw Learning, Lexington, VA. Self-directed homeschool coop. https:// www.rawlearning.org.

Southern Virginia Unschoolers, Norfolk, VA. https://www.facebook.com /groups/southernvirginiaunschoolers.

Virginia Unschoolers. https://www.facebook.com/groups/136139983241768.

WASHINGTON

Family Learning Organization (assessment and testing services), 37 E. Cozza Drive, Spokane, WA 99208; homeschool@familylearning.org. www .familylearning.org.

Flying Squad—Seattle; seattle@flyingsquads.org. http://www.flyingsquads .org.

Homeschoolers & Unschoolers of Washington State. https://www.face book.com/groups/869889723078527.

Learning Outside The Box, Tacoma, WA. https://www.facebook.com /groups/learningoutsidethebox.

Life Is Good Unschooling Conference, Vancouver, WA; lifeisgoodconference@comcast.net. http://lifeisgoodconference.com.

Mid-Columbia Self-Directed Education Collaborative, Tri-Cities, WA; mcsdecollab@gmail.com. https://www.facebook.com/mcsdecollab.

Seattle Unschoolers. https://www.facebook.com/groups/196093957110003.

Snohomish County Unschoolers. https://www.facebook.com/groups/466935506718257.

Tacoma Unschoolers. https://www.facebook.com/groups/615223771906687.

Unschool Spokane. https://www.facebook.com/groups/UnschoolSpokane.

Washington Homeschool Organization, PO Box 66960, Seattle, WA 98166-0960; WHOContact@washhomeschool.org. https://washhomeschool.org.

WEST VIRGINIA

Better with Thyme, Shepherdstown, WV. https://betterwiththyme.farm.

WV Home Educators Association, PO Box 4241, Clarksburg, WV 26302; 800-736-9843. https://wvhea.org.

WV Homeschool Haven. https://www.facebook.com/groups/177600318942178.

WISCONSIN

Wisconsin Homeschooling Parents Association, PO Box 2502, Madison, WI 53701; wpa@homeschooling-wpa.org. https://www.homeschooling-wpa.org.

Wisconsin Unschoolers. https://www.facebook.com/groups/wisconsinunschoolers.

WYOMING

Cheyenne, Wyoming Homeschoolers and Unschoolers. https://www.facebook.com/groups/325887874283095.

Common Ground Homeschoolers of Laramie. https://www.facebook.com/groups/commongroundlaramie.

Homeschoolers of Wyoming. Christian homeschooling organization. https://homeschoolersofwy.org.

Wyoming Homeschool Network. https://www.facebook.com/groups/770242963006926.

Wyoming Homeschool Support. https://www.facebook.com/groups/161115450748938.

HOMESCHOOL GROUPS OUTSIDE OF THE UNITED STATES

ARGENTINA

Homeschooling Argentina. https://www.facebook.com/homeschoolingAr.

Unschooling Argentina. https://www.facebook.com/groups/4450879159 25331.

AUSTRALIA

Arcadia ALC, Crn Villa Road & Park Street, Yeronga, QLD 4104. https://www.arcadiaalc.com.

Brisbane Unschooling and Natural Learning Homeschooling Community. https://www.facebook.com/Brisbane-Unschooling-and-Natural-Learning -Homeschooling-Community-BUS-BNL-201070770245722.

Central Coast Home Educators. https://www.facebook.com/groups /cchomeed.

Home Education Network, 13 Waterford Drive, Strathfieldsaye VIC 3551. https://home-ed.vic.edu.au.

Home Education Network of Canberra and the Southern Tablelands. https://www.hencast.org.au.

Homeschooling in the Yarra Ranges. https://www.facebook.com/groups /YarraRangesHomeschooling.

Homeschooling Perth. https://www.facebook.com/groups/homeschooling perth.

Home Education Association Inc., PO Box 245, Petersham, NSW 2049; 1300-72-99-91. https://www.hea.edu.au.

Melbourne Unschoolers. https://www.facebook.com/groups/melbourne unschoolers.

NT Homeschool Network. https://www.facebook.com/NTHomeschool Network.

Sunshine Coast Homeschool Community. https://www.facebook.com /groups/Sunshinecoasthomeschool.

Teen Homeschooling & Unschooling Australia. https://www.facebook .com/homeschooleraustralia.

Unschool Australia. https://www.facebook.com/groups/193822784049280.

Unschooling Info Australia. https://www.facebook.com/groups/unschooling infoaustralia.

Unschooling Queensland. https://www.facebook.com/groups/57398644 9389172.

Victorian Homeschoolers and Unschoolers. https://www.facebook.com /groups/214510892049120.

BELGIUM

ALC Talent-in, Ghent; alcghent@gmail.com. https://www.facebook.com /ALC.Talent.in.

Unschooling België. https://www.facebook.com/Unschooling-Belgi%C3% AB-108399217178334.

BRAZIL

ALC São Paulo; agilelearningcentersp@gmail.com. https://www.facebook .com/alcsaopaulo.

Unschooling Brasil. https://www.facebook.com/groups/unschoolingbrasil.

BULGARIA

Center for Democratic Learning, Sofia; dem.edu.bg@gmail.com. https:// odo.bg/centur-za-demokratichno-uchene.

CANADA

Barrie Area Unschoolers. https://www.facebook.com/groups/24342439 9473886.

Burlington-Hamilton Unschoolers. https://www.facebook.com/groups /309562122564272.

Calgary Homeschooling & Unschooling. https://www.facebook.com /groups/CalgaryHomeschooling.

Canadian Home-Based Learning Resource Page. https://homebased learning.ca.

Canadian Home Education Resources. https://www.canadianhomeedu cation.com.

Cedar Hill Open Learning, Panorama Ridge, Surrey, BC. https://www .cedarhillopenlearning.com.

Edmonton and Northern AB Homeschooling & Unschooling. https://www .facebook.com/groups/Edmontonandnorthernalbertahomeschoolers.

Edmonton Natural Learners & Unschoolers. https://www.facebook.com /groups/206799972800243.

Fort McMurray Funschool Friday. https://www.self-directed.org/resource /fort-mcmurray-funschool-Friday.

Fort McMurray Homeschoolers. https://www.facebook.com/groups/5204 35911322425.

Greater Vancouver Home Learners. https://www.facebook.com/groups /12061571570.

Home Educators of New Brunswick, 507 Route 616, Keswick Ridge, NB E6L 1S4. https://henb.ca.

Homeschoolers & Unschoolers of London, Ontario. https://www.facebook .com/groups/londonontariocanadahomeschoolers.

KW Unschooling Club. Natural learners of the Kitchener/Waterloo/Cam bridge, Ontario area. https://www.facebook.com/groups/253685614832685.

Mont-Libre, 8440 St. Laurent Boulevard, Montreal, QC H2P 2M5. Agile learning center for young people ages 8 to 18. http://montlibre.org.

Nova Scotia Unschoolers. https://www.facebook.com/groups/1857871082 25516.

Ontario Federation of Teaching Parents. https://ontariohomeschool.org.

Ontario Radical Unschoolers. https://www.facebook.com/groups/374673 806327880.

Ontario Unschoolers. https://www.facebook.com/groups/449068978484008.

Ontario Unschooling Families. https://www.facebook.com/groups/326997 164778186.

Unschooling Calgary & Area. https://www.facebook.com/groups/142563 472472443.

Unschooling Canada Association, 12018 Lake Erie Road SE, Calgary, AB T2J 2L8. http://unschoolingcanada.ca.

Unschooling Manitoba. https://www.facebook.com/groups/239724372759270.

Unschooling Montreal. https://www.facebook.com/groups/1702899706623717.

Unschooling Ottawa. https://www.facebook.com/groups/388018001250238.

Unschooling Toronto. https://www.facebook.com/groups/653106004735833.

VicHomeLearn. Place for Victoria-area home learners to post meet-ups, get -togethers, and park days. https://www.facebook.com/groups/518089604961617.

Wellington County Unschoolers. https://www.facebook.com/groups/1275 58534448045.

Westman Homeschool Connection. https://www.facebook.com/groups
/westmanhomeschoolers.

Winnipeg Homeschoolers. https://www.facebook.com/groups/36119940
7275065.

Yukon Home Education Society. https://www.yhes.ca.

CHILE

Educar En Libertad Unschooling Chile. https://www.facebook.com
/pedagogiaanarquista.

Peumal ALC, Santiago, Chile; varignia@gmail.com. Agile learning center
start-up. https://www.peumal.org.

CZECH REPUBLIC

Komunitní Školy Holubníku, Nebílovy 37, Nebílovy 332 04; holubnik
prusiny@gmail.com. Self-directed learning program co-created by children
ages 5–12. http://holubnikprusiny.cz/skola.

Prague Worldschooling. https://www.facebook.com/pragueworldschooling.

Svobodná Škola Ronja, Jindřichovice pod Smrkem; (+420) 605-345-467.
Summerhill-inspired learning center for unschoolers ages 6-15+. https://www
.facebook.com/svobodnaskolaronja.

DENMARK

Frilæring: Foreningen for Danske Hjemmeundervisere. https://frilæring.dk.

Unschooling Bornholm. https://www.facebook.com/unschoolingbornholm.

Unschooling in Denmark. https://www.facebook.com/groups/20856024
78338986.

ECUADOR

Unschooling red Ecuador. https://www.facebook.com/692813030908191
/posts/d41d8cd9/1259752770880878/.

EGYPT

Mesahat Learning Community, Cairo; sde.egypt@gmail.com. https://mesa
hat.agilelearningcenters.org.

ENGLAND

Education Otherwise, 61 Bridge Street, Kington, HR5 3DJ. https://www.educationotherwise.org.

The Garden, 222 Mina Road, Bristol BS2 9YP. Consent-based, inclusive and nurturing woodland space for young people. https://www.thegarden bristol.org.

The Greenhouse Education Project, Bitton, South Gloucestershire. Agile learning center. http://www.ourgreenhouse.org.

Home Education Advisory Service, PO Box 98, Welwyn Garden City, Hertfordshire AL8 6AN. https://www.heas.org.uk.

Home Education in London. https://www.facebook.com/groups/209101 845926025.

Home Education UK. www.home-education.org.uk.

The Otherwise Club, South Kilburn, London. Community center for families choosing to learn together without school. http://www.theotherwiseclub .org.uk.

Taking Children Seriously, https://www.takingchildrenseriously.com.

UK Radical Unschooling Network. https://www.facebook.com/groups /134546556668155.

Unschooling London. https://www.facebook.com/Unschooling-London -224452584238382.

FRANCE

La Fabrique Démocratique, 27 Rue Yves Kermen, Boulogne-Billancourt 92100. https://www.fabriquedemocratique.org.

La Maison Inspirée, 1996 route Nationale, La Chapelle-d'Armentières 59930. http://www.lamaisoninspiree.org.

L'écolieu Terr'Azïl, Ferme de Lessé, Le Mas d'Azil 09290. https://www .terrazil.org.

L'écovillage de Pourgues, Pourgues, Le Fossat, Occitanie 09130. https:// www.villagedepourgues.coop.

Les Enfants D'Abord. https://www.lesenfantsdabord.org.

Unschooling en France. https://www.facebook.com/groups/unschoofrance.

GERMANY

Die Lernwerkstatt (Learning Workshop), Karl-Kunger-Str. 55, Berlin 12435. https://www.die-lernwerkstatt.org.

Freilernen in der Praxis. https://www.facebook.com/groups/FreilerneninderPraxis.

GREECE

Nature Play ALC, North Evia. https://www.facebook.com/natureplayalc.

Unschooling Greece. https://www.facebook.com/pg/unschoolgr.

HONG KONG

Hong Kong Homeschool Meetup Group. https://www.meetup.com/hongkong-homeschool.

INDIA

Calcutta Unschoolers. https://www.facebook.com/calcuttaunschoolers.

The Learning Community at Quest, 4/375 Chari Avenue, Palavakkam, Chennai, Tamil Nadu 600041. http://questcommunity.in.

Sadhana Forest; india@sadhanaforest.org. Self-directed eco community in Tamil Nadu. http://www.sadhanaforest.org.

Swa-Adhyayan, B 804 Venkatesh Bilva, Pune, Maharashtra 411041; chetanerande@gmail.com. https://www.self-directed.org/resource/swa-adhyayan.

Swashikshan—Indian Association of Homeschoolers; mail@homeschoolers.in. http://swashikshan.org.

IRELAND

Home Education Network Ireland. https://www.henireland.org.

Irish Unschoolers. https://www.facebook.com/groups/371767552900664.

ITALY

Flow ALC, Via Vigo 60, Vigo, Vicenza 36050; info@flowalc.org. Self-directed learning community for ages 6–14. https://www.facebook.com/FlowALC.

Homeschooling & Unschooling in Italia. https://www.controscuola.it.

Unschooling eco-village, Calabria. https://www.workaway.info/en/host/468867971922.

LUXEMBOURG

Association Luxembourgeoise pour la liberté d'Instruction. https://alliasbl.lu.

Homeschooling in Luxembourg. https://www.facebook.com/groups/248275408672476.

LuDUS, 6A, rue de la Forêt, Gosseldange 7432. https://www.ludus.lu.

MEXICO

ALC Querétaro. Agile learning center. https://www.facebook.com/ALCQueretaro.

CAAD (Comunidad de Aprendizaje Autodirigido), Jurica La Campana, 76230 Querétaro. https://aprendizajealternativo.org.

Educambiando ALC, Rancho Viejo, Tlalnelhuayocan Xalapa, Veracruz. https://www.educambiando.org.

Homeschooling, Unschooling y otros en Xalapa. https://www.facebook.com/groups/713134555510505.

Iyari ALC, Aldama 31 45645 Tlajomulco de Zúñiga. https://www.facebook.com/IyariALC.

La Tribu, San Luis Potosí. https://www.facebook.com/La-Tribu-100727061442323.

Mochicahui, Singuilucan, Hidalgo; mochicahuilibre@gmail.com. https://www.facebook.com/mochicahuilibre.

Unschooling México. https://www.facebook.com/pg/unschoolingmexico.

THE NETHERLANDS

UnschoolingNL. https://www.facebook.com/groups/unschoolingnl.

Radical Unschooling Nederland. https://www.facebook.com/groups/301091520067909.

NEW ZEALAND

Auckland Unschoolers/Natural Learners. https://www.facebook.com/groups/westaklunschool.

Hawke's Bay Unschoolers; hbunschoolers@gmail.com. https://www.facebook.com/pg/HBUnschoolers.

Home Education in New Zealand. https://www.facebook.com/groups/174211400495.

Home Schooling NZ, PO Box 4107, Kamo 0141. https://homeschoolingnz.org.

National Council of Home Educators New Zealand. https://www.nchenz.org.nz.

Unschooling Christchurch. https://www.facebook.com/groups/unschooling christchurch.

Unschooling NZ Networking. https://www.facebook.com/groups/2990 82366772694.

PHILIPPINES

Abot Tala, Unit 2A Tres Palmas Commercial Arcade, Pedro Cayetano Boulevard, Taguig. Liberated Learners center near Manila. https://abottala.com.

PORTUGAL

Homeschool Portugal. https://www.facebook.com/groups/1895716753998877.

ROMANIA

Unschooling Bucuresti. https://www.facebook.com/unschoolingBucuresti.

School of Joy, Drumul Sfântul Ioan 107C, Cluj-Napoca 400000. Agile learning center. https://schoolofjoy.eu.

RUSSIA

Время и место/Time and Place, 25 Mironovskaya St, Moscow. https://www.v-m.club.

SAUDI ARABIA

Home Educators of Riyadh. https://www.facebook.com/groups/Riyadh HomeschoolGroup.

SINGAPORE

Homeschooling/Unschooling in Singapore. https://www.facebook.com/Homeschooling-Unschooling-2e-in-Singapore-1657093424587979.

SOUTH AFRICA

Animalia Learning Center for Homeschoolers and Unschoolers, 14A Clement Stott Road, Assagay, Hillcrest, Kwazulu-Natal. http://www.animalia learningcenter.co.za.

Freerange Education, New Plaston Road, White River; freerange.edu@gmail
.com. Open agile learning space. https://www.facebook.com/FreerangeEdu.

Growing Minds. Unschooling info. https://www.growingminds.co.za.

Re-Imagined Learning Community, 61 Bellevue Street, Troyeville, Johannesburg, 2139; reimaginedlearningcommunity@gmail.com. https://vannas911
.wixsite.com/reimaginedlearning.

Riverstone Village, North Riding, Randburg, Johannesburg 2169. Democratic self-directed learning community. http://www.riverstonevillage.co.za.

South Africa Homeschoolers. https://www.sahomeschoolers.org.

Unschooling in South Africa. https://www.facebook.com/UnschoolingIn
SouthAfrica.

SPAIN

Home and Unschoolers in Spain. https://www.facebook.com/groups/2510
43088437422.

Homeschooling en Madrid. http://homeschoolingenmadrid.blogspot.com.

Ojo de Agua–Ambiente Educativo, Partida Racó del Pastor s/n, Orba 03790.
https://ojodeagua.es.

Worldschool Hub Andalucia. https://www.worldschoolhubandalucia.com.

SWEDEN

Unschooling/Oskolning Sverige. https://www.facebook.com/groups/2365
74749814115.

THAILAND

Unschooling Thailand. https://www.facebook.com/groups/707371882670581.

TURKEY

Türkiye'de Okulsuz Eğitim (Unschooling in Turkey). https://www.face
book.com/groups/435555633232766.

UKRAINE

Unschooling in Ukraine. https://www.facebook.com/UnschoolingUkraine.

UNITED ARAB EMIRATES

Al Ain Homeschoolers. https://www.facebook.com/groups/alainhome schoolers.

VIETNAM

Unschooling in Vietnam. https://www.facebook.com/groups/11666451 00089015.

Unschool Vietnam; unschool.vn@gmail.com. http://unschool.vn.

WALES

Coed Cariad Learning Community, Blaen Y Wern, Llangyndeyrn, Carmarthenshire, SA17 5ES. http://www.coedcariad.org.

SPECIAL INTEREST HOMESCHOOLING GROUPS

See "Special Needs" for related listings.

Eclectic Learning Network. Secular, BIPOC-centered unschooling/self-directed learning network. https://www.eclecticlearningnetwork.com.

Educating Our Own Now. Homeschool village community guided by Melanated elders with identifiable voices. https://www.facebook.com/pg/EOONow.

Gifted Unschooling Los Angeles. https://www.facebook.com/groups /giftedunschoolingLA.

Homeschooling Gamers in Perth. https://www.facebook.com/groups/1703 365106545618.

Homeschooling / Unschooling Diversity. Healing space centering those of us that have been "Othered" due to racial, ethnic, (dis)ability, gender, class, age and/or sexual identity. https://www.facebook.com/groups/1021614897 880913/1061280237247712.

Jewish Home Education Network. https://www.facebook.com/Jewish HomeEducation.

Latter-Day Saint Home Educators. https://ldshe.org.

LGBTQ Homeschool Families. https://www.facebook.com/groups/LGBTQ Homeschoolfamilies.

LGBTQ Unschoolers. https://www.facebook.com/lgtbqunschoolers.

Miami Homeschool Rainbow Alliance. Homeschool club that brings together LGBTQAI+ and ally students to support each other. https://www.face book.com/miamihomeschoolrainbowalliance.

Muslim Homeschool Network. http://www.muslimhomeschoolnetwork.com.

My Reflection Matters Village. Secular, co-learning community for primarily BIPOC families. http://www.myreflectionmatters.org.

National LDS Homeschool Association. http://www.lds-nha.org.

Radical Unschooling en Español. https://www.facebook.com/groups/7080 95229264708.

Single and Solo Parents Homeschooling. https://www.facebook.com/single parentshomeschooling.

Single Moms Homeschooling. https://www.facebook.com/groups/918174 031636179.

Single Parent Homeschooling Support. https://www.facebook.com/groups /364710486973514.

Unschooling Every Family: Embracing Neurodivergent and Disabled Learners. https://www.facebook.com/groups/UnschoolingSpecialNeeds.

Worldschooling Single Parents. https://www.facebook.com/groups/5200 95594692477.

OTHER ORGANIZATIONS

These educational, child-raising, or self-reliance organizations and blogs are good sources of help and allies for homeschooling.

Agile Learning Centers. https://agilelearningcenters.org.

The Alliance for Self-Directed Education; info@self-directed.org. https://www.self-directed.org.

Alternative Education Resource Organization, 417 Roslyn Road, Roslyn Heights, NY 11577; 516-621-2195. http://www.educationrevolution.org.

Association of Waldorf Schools of North America, 515 Kimbark, Suite 106, Longmont, CO 80501; 720-204-5505. https://www.waldorfeducation.org.

The Aware Parenting Institute, PO Box 206, Goleta, CA 93116; 805-968-1868; info@awareparenting.com. http://www.awareparenting.com.

Consent Parenting. Abuse-prevention parenting resources, by an unschool ing mom. https://www.consentparenting.com.

Divergent Labs. Neuro-divergence network. http://www.divergentlabs.org.

ERIC (Educational Resources Information Center). https://eric.ed.gov.

Family Policy Compliance Office, US Department of Education, 400 Maryland Avenue SW, Washington DC 20202-4605; 1-800-872-5327. Access to school records. https://www2.ed.gov.

Freechild Institute for Youth & Social Change. 360-489-9680; https://freechild.org.

Freeschoolin' Community. https://www.facebook.com/groups/602104683217231.

Flying Squads Network. Network of outdoor self-directed youth community groups. https://www.flyingsquads.org.

Great Ideas in Education/Holistic Education Press, PO Box 328, Brandon, VT 05733; 1-800-639-4122. www.great-ideas.org.

Grown Unschoolers. Profiles of grown unschoolers, in their own words. https://grownunschoolers.com.

The Higher Process. Artist and single parent blogs about the process of life living in authenticity & unschooling through divorce and trauma. https://magpie64.wordpress.com.

I'm Unschooled. Yes, I Can Write. Blog by a grown unschooler exploring the intersections between self-directed lifelong learning, youth rights, respectful parenting, and social justice. http://yes-i-can-write.blogspot.com/.

International Society for Self-Directed Learning. https://www.sdlglobal.com/.

John Holt: Growing Without Schooling. https://www.johnholtgws.com.

La Leche League International, 110 Horizon Drive, Suite 210, Raleigh, NC 27615, USA; 1-800-LA LECHE. https://www.llli.org.

Let Grow, 228 Park Avenue S. #77212, New York, NY 10003; info@letgrow.org. Advocates for free play and trusting kids. https://letgrow.org.

Liberated Learners. Network of self-directed learning centers for teens. https://liberatedlearners.net.

Liedloff Continuum Network, PO Box 1634, Sausalito, CA 94966; 415 332-1570. www.continuum-concept.org.

Montessori World Educational Institute, 1735 Chester Lane, Cambria, CA 93428; 805-927-3240; montessoriworld@charter.net. https://montessoriworld.org.

National Association for the Legal Support of Alt. Schools, 18520 N.W. 67th Avenue, #188, Miami, FL 33015; 1-800-456-7784. http://www.nalsas.org.

National Center for Fair and Open Testing (FairTest), 196 Spring Street, Arlington, MA 02476; 617-477-9792. https://www.fairtest.org.

National Youth Rights Association, PO Box 5865, Takoma Park, MD 20913; 202-827-5280. https://www.youthrights.org.

NomadTogether. Community of digital nomad families. https://nomad together.com.

The Natural Child Project. https://www.naturalchild.org.

Peaceful Parenting/Unschooling Support. https://www.facebook.com /groups/501568239855574.

Peer Unschooling Network; https://discord.gg/xgdXd45. https://peer unschooling.net.

Recess Revolution. Nonprofit about the importance of self-directed free play. http://www.recessrevolution.org.

School Survival. Support site for kids who hate school. http://www.school -survival.net.

School Without Frontiers. An open movement which supports democratic, nomadic, and agile education by removing partitions in all spheres of learning. https://schoolwithoutfrontiers.org.

Unschooling in Peace. https://www.facebook.com/groups/8761105424 98517.

Unschooling to University (blog). https://unschoolingtouniversity.com.

Unschool Rules (blog). https://unschoolrules.com.

APPENDIX E

LEARNING MATERIALS

This list is just a sampling to help jump-start your thinking about what is available to use at home with your children.

FILMS, AUDIO

Approaching the Elephant. Dir. Amanda Wilder. The Film Sales Company, 2014. Year one at the Teddy McArdle Free School in Little Falls, New Jersey, where all classes are voluntary and rules are determined by vote.

Being and Becoming. Dir. Clara Bellar. Pourquoi Pas Productions, 2014. Invites us to question our learning paradigms and options.

Boles, Blake. *Off-Trail Learning Podcast*. Interviews with self-directed learners, innovative educators, and young people blazing their own paths through life. https://soundcloud.com/blakebo/sets/off-trail-learning-podcast.

Class Dismissed: A Film About Learning Outside of the Classroom. Dir. Jeremy Stuart, 2015. Documentary about a family's journey from conventional school to unschooling.

Davis, Taylor, and James Davis. *One Free Family Podcast*. Husband–wife podcast about gentle parenting, family life, and self-directed education. https://www.youtube.com/channel/UC-E0oGQ2LjJ09Z5Yh1FgrMg.

EDiT—Education in Transformation. Open media platform that amplifies the self-directed education movement through video storytelling. https://educationintransformation.com.

Elvis, Sue. *Stories of an Unschooling Family.* A podcast about radical unschooling. https://storiesofanunschoolingfamily.podbean.com.

Laricchia, Pam. *Exploring Unschooling Podcast.* Interviews, information, and inspiration about unschooling. https://livingjoyfully.ca/podcast-2.

Mintz, Jerry. *Education Revolution Podcast*, Alternative Education Resource Organization. Discussions about different facets of learner-centered education. https://soundcloud.com/aeropodcast.

Rainbolt, Rachel. *Sage Family Podcast.* Sharing meaningful conversations with inspiring and insightful friends around gentle parenting, unschooling, and simple living. https://rachelrainbolt.com/category/podcast.

Richards, Akilah S. *Fare of the Free Child*, Raising Free People Network. Podcast about community centering, Black people, Indigenous people, and People of Color in liberatory living and learning practices. https://raisingfreepeople.com/podcast.

Schooling the World: The White Man's Last Burden. Dir. Carol Black. Lost People Films, 2010. Challenging, sometimes funny, ultimately deeply disturbing look at the effects of modern education on the world's last sustainable indigenous cultures.

Schools of Trust. Dir. Christoph Schuhmann. Tologo Verlag, 2014. A German film about self-directed education.

Self-Taught: Life Stories From Self-Directed Learners. Dir. Jeremy Stuart, 2019. Explores the lives of several adults who chose to follow a self-directed path of learning.

The War on Kids. Dir. Cevin Soling, 2009. Documentary that exposes the many ways the public school system robs students of all freedoms, largely due to irrational fears.

Unschooled. Dir. Rachel Beth Anderson and Timothy Grucza, 2020. Documentary about the Natural Creativity Center in north Philadelphia's Germantown district. https://unschooledthemovement.com/about/.

Use Your Outside Voice! Unschooling Podcast. Living authentically with children and rejecting the school model of relationship. https://podcasts.apple.com/us/podcast/use-your-outside-voice-unschool/id1485566037.

ARTS AND CRAFTS

KidsArt News, PO Box 274, Mt Shasta, CA 96067; service@kidsart.com. Series of art teaching booklets. Children's art supplies catalog. https://kidsart .com.

NASCO Arts & Crafts, 901 Janesville Avenue, PO Box 901, Fort Atkinson, WI 53538-0901; 920-563-2446. Free catalog. https://www.enasco.com/c /Art-Supplies-Crafts.

Sculpture House, 3804 Crossroads Parkway, Fort Pierce, FL; 772-210-6124. Sculpting tools for clay, stone, ceramics, and wood. https://www.sculpture house.com.

BOOKS, GAMES, AND LEARNING MATERIALS

American Printing House for the Blind, 1839 Frankfort Avenue, Louisville KY 40206; 502-895-2405. Cranmer Abacus, books, and materials. https://www .aph.org,

Booklist, American Library Association, 225 N Michigan Avenue, Suite 1300, Chicago, IL 60601; 1-800-545-2433. http://www.ala.org/aboutala/offices /publishing/booklist,

Center for Innovation in Education, PO Box 2070, Saratoga, CA 95070-0070; 1-800-395-6088. Math, reading. www.ccntcr.edu.

Constructive Playthings, 13201 Arrington Road, Grandview, MO 64030. Educational supplies and tools. https://constructiveplaythings.com.

Cricket, 1751 Pinnacle Drive, Suite 600, McLean, VA 22102; 703-885-3400. Children's magazines and online learning products. https://cricketmedia.com.

Family Pastimes, 796 Brook Valley Road RR4, Perth, Ontario K7H 3C6; 613-267-4819. Cooperative board games. https://familypastimes.com.

Follett Educational Service, 3 Westbrook Corporate Center, Suite 200, Westchester, IL 60154. Used textbooks. https://www.follett.com.

Front Row Experience. Materials about movement education, perceptual-motor development, coordination activities for pre-school through sixth-grade age group. http://www.frontrowexperience.com.

FUN Books, Dept. W, PO Box 1394, Pasadena, MD 21123-1394; FUN@FUN -Books.com. www.Fun-Books.com. Original back issues of GWS magazine are for sale here.

A Gentle Wind, Box 3103, Albany, NY 12203; 1-888-FUN-SONG. Downloadable stories and songs. www.gentlewind.com.

Gifted Education Press, 10201 Yuma Court, Manassas, VA 20109; 703-369-5017. Free newsletter. www.giftededpress.com.

The Great Courses. Audio courses for lifelong learners. https://www.thegreatcourses.com.

Hearthsong, 7021 Wolftown-Hood Rd, Madison, VA 22727; 1-800-533-4397. Toy/craft catalog for families. https://www.hearthsong.com.

The Homeschool Resource Roadmap. Free, summative information about more than 4,800 homeschool-oriented resources. https://www.homeschoolroadmap.org.

The Horn Book, Inc.; 617-278-0225. Magazine for children's book recommendations. https://www.hbook.com.

I Can Read Books, HarperCollins Children's Books; 888-965-8737. https://www.icanread.com.

Key Curriculum. Miquon math workbooks and software. https://keycurriculum.com.

Flannery, Jim. *LEAVE SCHOOL: What Teachers Can't Tell You.* App available on Apple and Android.

McGuffey's Readers, Mott Media, 1130 Fenway Circle, Fenton, MI 48430-2641; 810-714-4280. https://www.mottmedia.com/mcguffey-s-readers-2.

Michael Olaf Montessori Publishers, PO Box 1162, Arcata, CA 95518; michaelolafcompany@gmail.com. Tools, playthings, math manipulatives. http://michaelolaf.com/store.

Montessori Services, 11 West 9th Street, Santa Rosa, CA 95401; 877-975-3003. Free supply catalog. https://www.montessoriservices.com.

National Storytelling Network, Woodneath Library, 8900 N.E. Flintlock Road, Kansas City, MO 64157; 1-800-525-4514. https://storynet.org

One Day University. 300+ online lectures from the best professors. https://www.onedayu.com.

Parents' Choice Foundation, 210 West Padonia Road. Suite 303, Timonium, MD 21093. 410-308-3858. Review of children's media and toys. http://www.parentschoice.org.

Project-Based Homeschooling. Offers guidance on how to mentor self-directed learners. http://project-based-homeschooling.com.

Recorded Books, Inc., 270 Skipjack Road, Prince Frederick, MD 20678. Novels, classics, history, science, on tape. https://www.recordedbooks.com.

Saxon Publishers. Mathematics and phonics programs. https://www.hmhco.com/programs/saxon-math.

Scholastic Book Clubs; 1-800-724-6527. Inexpensive paperbacks. https://clubs.scholastic.com.

School Yourself. Free interactive math lessons. https://schoolyourself.org.

Udemy. Online courses. https://www.udemy.com.

CODING AND ROBOTICS

CodaKid. https://codakid.com.

Codecademy. https://www.codecademy.com.

CodeCombat. https://codecombat.com.

CoderZ. https://gocoderz.com.

Home Science Tools. Robotics kits. https://www.homesciencetools.com/physics-engineering/robotics.

Makeblock Ultimate 2.0. Robot kit. http://learn.makeblock.com/en/ultimate2.

MIT App Inventor. https://appinventor.mit.edu.

Ozobot EVO. https://shop.ozobot.com/products/evo.

RoboCamp. https://www.robocamp.eu/en/lessons.

Scratch. https://scratch.mit.edu.

Tello EDU. https://www.ryzerobotics.com/tello-edu.

Tynker. https://www.tynker.com.

FOREIGN LANGUAGES

Babbel. https://www.babbel.com.

Bolchazy-Carducci Publishers; 847-526-4344. Audio and texts for learning Latin. https://www.bolchazy.com.

Duolingo. https://www.duolingo.com.

The Learnables. https://learnables.com.

Lectorum Publications. Spanish children's books and magazines. https://lectorum.com.

Rosetta Stone. https://www.rosettastone.com.

Schoenhofs; 617-547-8855. Source of foreign books. http://www.schoenhofs.com.

Sky Oaks Productions. Total physical response approach to teaching and learning languages. https://www.bookdepository.com/publishers/Sky-Oaks-Productions.

MUSIC

Drumbeat Indian Arts, 4143 N. 16th Street, Phoenix, AZ 85016; 602-266-4823. Native American music and books. https://drumbeatindianarts.com.

Homespun. Audio and video lessons in a variety of roots music styles. https://www.homespun.com.

Lark in the Morning, 830 Gilman Street, Berkeley, CA 94710; 707-964-5569. Musical instruments from all over the world. https://larkinthemorning.com.

Suzuki Association of the Americas, PO Box 17310, Boulder, CO 80308; 303-444-0948. https://suzukiassociation.org.

SCIENCE AND NATURE

Abrams Planetarium, Michigan State University, 755 Science Road, East Lansing, MI 48824; 517-355-4672. Sky calendar. https://www.abramsplanetarium.org.

American Science & Surplus; 888-724-7587. https://www.sciplus.com.

Astronomical Society of the Pacific, 390 Ashton Avenue, San Francisco, CA 94112; 415-337-1100. https://astrosociety.org.

Carolina Biological Supply Company, 2700 York Road, Burlington, NC 27215; 800-334-5551. https://www.carolina.com

Celestial Products. http://www.mooncalendar.com.

Exploratorium, Pier 15, San Francisco, CA 94111; 415-528-4444. https://www.exploratorium.edu.

Ranger Rick's Nature Magazine, National Wildlife Federation. https://rangerrick.org.

Sanctuary Magazine, Massachusetts Audubon Society. https://www.massaudubon.org/news-events/publications/sanctuary-magazine.

Skeptical Inquirer. https://skepticalinquirer.org.

TOPS Learning Systems. https://topscience.org.

Ursa Major, 900 South Deer Road, Macomb, IL; 844-676-8772. https://www
.ursamajorstencils.com.

Virtual Anatomy Center; 1-800-638-3030. http://www.anatomical.com.

SOCIAL STUDIES

Amazon Drygoods, 3788 Wilson Street, Osgood, IN 47037; 1-812-852-1780.
Catalog of historical items and books. http://www.amazondrygoods.com.

Cobblestone, 30 Grove Street, Suite C, Peterborough, NH 03458; 800-821-
0115. US history magazine for children.

DIG Into History Magazine. Children's magazine on world history and
archaeology. https://www.davidsongifted.org/search-database/entry/r11546.

Faces. World cultures magazine for children. https://shop.cricketmedia
.com/faces-magazine-for-kids.

League of Women Voters, 1233 20th Street NW, Suite 500, Washington, DC,
20036; 202-429-1965. Pamphlets: government, current events. https://www.lwv
.org.

National Geographic Society. Magazines, including *Nat Geo Kids*, books,
maps. https://www.nationalgeographic.com.

National Women's History Alliance, 730 2nd Street, PO Box 469, Santa Rosa,
CA 95402; 707-636-2888. Materials about women in history; multicultural.
https://nationalwomenshistoryalliance.org.

Replogle Globes, 125 Fencl Lane, Hillside, IL 60162; 708-593-3411. https://
replogleglobes.com.

Americas Program. Action and communication for social change. https://
www.americas.org.

Smithsonian Magazine; 1-800-766-2149. https://www.smithsonianmag.com.

Wide World Books & Maps, 4411 A Wallingford Avenue North, Seattle, WA
98103; 206-634-3453. https://www.facebook.com/WideWorldBooks.

Young Biz USA. News magazine, curriculum, books. https://youngbiz.com.

SPECIAL NEEDS

See "Special Interest Groups for Homeschoolers" for related listings.

Blind Homeschoolers. https://www.facebook.com/groups/Blindhome
schooler.

Deaf Homeschool Australia. https://www.deafhomeschool.com.

National Association for the Deaf, 8630 Fenton Street, Suite 820, Silver Spring, MD 20910; video phone: 301-587-1788. Sign language videos, books. https://www.nad.org.

National Challenged Homeschoolers Associated Network (NATHHAN). https://www.nathhan.com.

National Federation of the Blind, 200 East Wells Street at Jernigan Place, Baltimore, MD 21230; 410-659-9314. https://www.nfb.org.

T.J. Publishers, Inc., PO Box 702701, Dallas, TX 75370; customerservice@tjpublishers.com. Materials and books about American Sign Language and deafness. https://tjpublishers.com.

WRITING

Child's Play Touring Theatre, 4161 N Damen Avenue, Chicago, IL 60618; 773-235-8911. Develops plays out of stories and poems by kids. http://cptt.org/cms.

School Specialty, 80 Northwest Boulevard, Nashua, NH 03063; 1-800-225-5750. *Keyboarding Exchange* (typing book), educational books, workbooks, and materials. https://eps.schoolspecialty.com.

Heinemann Educational Books. Videos, books on writing. https://www.heinemann.com.

Stone Soup. Literary magazine 100 percent written and illustrated by kids. https://stonesoup.com.

Teachers & Writers Collaborative, 540 President Street, 3rd Floor, Brooklyn, NY 11215; 212-691-6590. Resources for teaching writing. https://twc.org.

APPENDIX F

OPPORTUNITIES AND ACTIVITIES

AFS InterNational Exchange Program, 71 West 23rd Street, 6th Floor, New York, NY 10010; (+1) 212-209-0900; info@afs.org. https://afs.org.

A Little Alaska. Adventure stays for Self-Directed Teens in Cordova, Alaska. https://www.alittlealaska.com.

Center for Interim Programs, 195 Nassau Street, Suite 6 (2nd Floor), Princeton, NJ 08542; 609-683-4300. Matchmaker for apprenticeships. https://www.interimprograms.com.

Chesapeake Bay Foundation, 6 Herndon Avenue, Annapolis, MD 21403; chesapeake@cbf.org; 1-888-SAVEBAY. https://www.cbf.org.

Childhood Redefined: Online Unschooling Summit. https://childhoodredefined.com.

Crow Canyon Archaeological Center, 23390 County Road K, Cortez, CO 81321; 970-564-4346. https://www.crowcanyon.org.

East Tennessee Unschooled Summer Camp, PO Box 821, Jonesborough, TN 37659; laurabowman.etusc@gmail.com. https://www.etusc.com.

Encompass Learning. Whole family and teen program with focus on outdoor education and adventure courses. http://encompasslearning.org.

World Learning, 1015 15th Street NW, 7th Floor, Washington, DC 20005 USA; 202 408-5420. Cultural immersion home study programs for 3, 4, or 5 weeks in summer to 161 countries. https://www.worldlearning.org.

Farm Sanctuary. Apprenticeships in caring for sick animals. https://www.farmsanctuary.org.

Generation On. Provides programs, tools, and resources to engage kids and teens in service and volunteering. https://www.generationon.org.

Great Smoky Mountains Institute at Tremont, 9275 Tremont Road, Townsend, TN 37882; 865-448-6709. Naturalist workshops, programs for teenagers. https://gsmit.org.

Grown Unschooler Opportunity Network. https://www.facebook.com/groups/259346827508248.

Hulbert Outdoor Center, 2968 Lake Morey Road, Fairless, VT, 05045. Camps for children and adults. https://alohafoundation.org/hulbert.

Kids for Saving Earth, 37955 Bridge Road, North Branch, MN 55056; 651-277-2222. https://kidsforsavingearth.org.

Maine Youth Activism Gathering. Annual three-day, youth-run celebration of political action, fierce youth brilliance, and do-it-yourself fun. https://maineyag.weebly.com.

Not Back to School Camp, PO Box 2034, Joshua Tree, CA 92252. Grace Llewellyn's camp for unschooled teens, with locations in Oregon and Vermont. https://www.nbtsc.org.

Project World School. Inspiring temporary learning communities for teens and young adults. https://projectworldschool.com.

Roots & Shoots; rootsandshoots@janegoodall.org. Youth advocacy program. https://www.rootsandshoots.org.

SERVAS. Visit or host foreign family. https://servas.org.

TIA Architects, 592 Main Street, Amherst, MA 01002; 413-256-8025. Ecological architecture internships. https://tiaarchitects.com

Tree People, 12601 Mulholland Drive, Beverly Hills, CA 90210; 818-753-4600. Environmental leadership program. https://www.treepeople.org.

NOTES

FOREWORD

1. Dana Goldstein, "Research Shows Students Falling Months Behind during Virus Disruptions," *New York Times*, June 5, 2020, https://www.nytimes .com/2020/06/05/us/coronavirus-education-lost-learning.html; Laura Meckler and Hannah Natanson, "'A Lost Generation': Surge of Research Reveals Students Sliding Backward, Most Vulnerable Worst Affected," *Washington Post*, December 6, 2020, https://www.washingtonpost.com /education/students-falling-behind/2020/12/06/88d7157a-3665-11eb -8d38-6aea1adb3839_story.html.

2. Raymond Moore and Dorothy Moore, *Better Late Than Early* (Readers Digest Press, 1989); Harriet Pattison, *Rethinking Learning to Read* (Educational Heretics Press, 2016); Alan Thomas and Harriet Pattison, *How Children Learn at Home* (Continuum, 2007).

3. Alfie Kohn, "When school's out, education might suffer less than you think," *Boston Globe*, September 3, 2020. https://www.bostonglobe .com/2020/09/03/opinion/when-schools-out-kids-suffer-less-than-you -might-think/.

4. Peter Gray, *How Children Acquire "Academic" Skills Without Formal Instruction* (Tipping Points Press, 2020), pp. 98–100.

5. Jay Mathews, "Half the World Is Bilingual. What's Our Problem?", *Washington Post*, April 25, 2019, https://www.washingtonpost.com/local /education/half-the-world-is-bilingual-whats-our-problem/2019/04/24 /1c2b0cc2-6625-11e9-a1b6-b29b90efa879_story.html.

6. Harper's Index, *Harper's Magazine*, February 2018, https://harpers.org /archive/2018/02/harpers-index-402/.

7. Kirsty Blake Knox, "Michael D Higgins questions the effectiveness of making Irish compulsory at school," The Independent, https://www .independent.ie/irish-news/michael-d-higgins-questions-the-effective ness-of-making-irish-compulsory-at-school-36268423.html

8. Knox, "Michael D Higgins questions the effectiveness of making Irish compulsory at school."

9. Scott Chacon, "MIT Scientists Prove Adults Learn Language to Fluency Nearly as Well as Children," Medium.com, May 3, 2018, https://medium .com/@chacon/mit-scientists-prove-adults-learn-language-to-fluency -nearly-as-well-as-children-1de888d1d45f.

10. Bryan Caplan, "The Numbers Speak: Foreign Language Requirements Are a Waste of Time and Money," EconLog, The Library of Economics and Liberty, August 10, 2012, https://www.econlib.org/archives/2012/08 /the_marginal_pr.html.

11. Pagan Kennedy, "To Be a Genius, Think Like a 94-Year-Old," *New York Times*, April 7, 2017, https://www.nytimes.com/2017/04/07/opinion/sunday /to-be-a-genius-think-like-a-94-year-old.html.

12. John Holt, *Never Too Late* (Da Capo Press, 1991), p. 4.

13. Carol Black, "Science/Fiction: Evidenced-Based Education, Scientific Racism, and How Learning Became a Myth," 2016, http://carolblack.org /science-fiction.

14. Adam Dickerson, *John Holt: The Philosophy of Unschooling* (Springer, 2019).

15. Dickerson, *John Holt*, p. 30.

16. Rama Lakshmi, "These Indian Parents Climbed a Wall to Help Their Kids Cheat on an Exam," *Washington Post*, March 19, 2015, https://www.wash ingtonpost.com/news/worldviews/wp/2015/03/19/these-indian-parents -climbed-a-school-wall-to-help-their-kids-cheat-on-an-exam/.

17. Manavi Kapur, "India's Culture of High-Stakes Testing Needs to Be Dismantled," Quartz India, October 24, 2019, https://qz.com/india/1728666/indias-high-stakes-testing-culture-needs-to-be-dismantled/.

18. Barak Obama, "State of the Union Address, " Januaray 25, 2011, https://obamawhitehouse.archives.gov/the-press-office/2011/01/25/remarks-president-state-union-address.

19. ABC News, "7-year-old donates more than 6,000 masks, gloves and caps from hotels to hospital workers," April 3, 2020, https://abcnews.go.com/US/year-donates-6000-masks-gloves-caps-hotels-hospital/story?id=69948357.

20. Brent Crane, "The High Schooler Who Became a COVID-19 Watchdog," *The New Yorker*, March 30, 2020, https://www.newyorker.com/magazine/2020/03/30/the-high-schooler-who-became-a-covid-19-watchdog.

CHAPTER 1: CHILDREN ARE NOT THE FUTURE—THEY ARE THE PRESENT

21. Bijan Stephen, "Wuhan Students Tried to Boot Remote Learning App from the App Store by Leaving Bad Reviews," *The Verge*, March 9, 2020, https://www.theverge.com/2020/3/9/21171495/wuhan-students-ding talk-hooky-nyc-columbia-princeton-app-store-reviews; Andrew Whalen, "Students Are Targeting Zoom and Classroom with Bad Reviews to End Homework during Coronavirus," *Newsweek*, March 19, 2020, https://www.newsweek.com/google-zoom-classroom-students-schools-closed-coronavirus-china-1493309.

22. Patrick Farenga and Carlo Ricci, eds., *The Legacy of John Holt* (HoltGWS, 2013), p. 118.

23. Elizabeth Bonawitz, Patrick Shafto, Hyowon Gweon, and Noah D. Goodman, "The Double-Edged Sword of Pedagogy: Instruction Limits Spontaneous Exploration and Discovery," *Cognition* 120, no. 3 (2011): 322.

24. Alison Gopnik, *The Gardener and the Carpenter: What the New Science of Child Development Tells Us About the Relationship Between Parents and Children* (Picador, 2017), p. 15.

25. Gopnick, *The Gardener and the Carpenter*, p. 35.

26. Dickerson, *John Holt*, p. 64.

27. John Holt, *Freedom and Beyond* (Heinemann/Boynton/Cook, 1972), p. 91.

28. Holt, *Freedom and Beyond*, p. 92.

29. Naomi Fisher, *Changing Our Minds: How Children Can Take Control of Their Own Learning* (Robinson, 2021), p. 42.

30. Joseph Murray, *Homeschooling in America*, p. 126.

31. Annie Murphy Paul, "Where's the Joy in Learning?", MindShift, KQED, April 19, 2012, https://www.kqed.org/mindshift/20657/wheres-the-joy-in -learning.

CHAPTER 2: HOMESCHOOLING, PARENTING, AND HIGHER EDUCATION

32. Arianna Prothero and Christina A. Samuels, "Home-Schooling Is Way Up with COVID-19. Will It last?" *Education Week*, November 9, 2020, https:// www.edweek.org/policy-politics/home-schooling-is-way-up-with-covid -19-will-it-last/2020/11.

33. Prothero and Samuels, "Home-Schooling Is Way Up with COVID-19."

34. Carol Black, "On the Wilderness of Children," 2016, http://carolblack.org /on-the-wildness-of-children.

35. Peter Gray, *Evidence That Self-Directed Education Works* (Tipping Points Press, 2020), pp. 73–88.

36. John Holt, *Learning All the Time* (Perseus, 1990), p. 140.

37. John Holt, *How Children Learn* (Da Capo Press, 2017), pp. xii–xiii.

38. John Holt, *Teach Your Own* (Perseus, 2003), p. 10.

39. Susannah Sheffer, ed., *A Life Worth Living: Selected Letters of John Holt* (Ohio State University Press, 1990), p. 196.

40. Children's Defense Fund, *The State of America's Children* (Author, 2021), https://www.childrensdefense.org/policy/resources/soac-2020-child -poverty/.

41. Jon Marcus, "More People with Bachelor's Degrees Go Back to School to Learn Skilled Trades," *Washington Post*, November 20, 2020, https://www .washingtonpost.com/local/education/more-people-with-bachelors-deg rees-go-back-to-school-to-learn-skilled-trades/2020/11/20/06404180 -2aa9-11eb-9b14-ad872157ebc9_story.html.

42. Anthony P. Carnevale, "Ignore the Hype. College Is Worth It," *Inside Higher Ed*, February 13, 2020, https://www.insidehighered.com/views

/2020/02/13/why-one-should-ignore-reports-and-commentary-ques
tion-value-college-degree-opinion.

43. Nikelle Murphy, "10 College Degrees That Are a Dime a Dozen Nowa-
days," Showbiz CheatSheet, March 25, 2018, https://www.cheatsheet.com
/money-career/college-degrees-dime-dozen-anymore.html/.

44. Federal Reserve Bank of New York, "The Labor Market for Recent College Graduates," update February12, 2021, https://www.newyorkfed.org
/research/college-labor-market/college-labor-market_underemploy
ment_rates.html.

45. Tigran Sloyan, "2020 Recruiting Trends," *Forbes*, March 30, 2020, https://
www.forbes.com/sites/forbestechcouncil/2020/03/30/2020-recruiting
-trends/?sh=4fc0bea66779.

46. Sheffer, *A Life Worth Living*, p. 266.

CHAPTER 8: LEARNING DIFFICULTIES

47. Jean Liedloff, *The Continuum Concept* (Warner Books, 1977), p. 72.

48. Liedloff, *The Continuum Concept* (pp. 107–108)

49. Ivan Illich, *Shadow Work* (Marion Boyars, 1981), p. 66.

50. Illich, *Shadow Work*, p. 74.

51. Gregory Bateson, *Steps to an Ecology of Mind* (University of Chicago Press,
2000), p. 369.

52. Bateson, *Steps to an Ecology of Mind*, p. 369.

53. L. A. McKeown, "ADHD Drug Overprescribing Raises Concerns Over
Future CV Events," *TCTMD*, Cardiovascular Research Foundation,
August 11, 2020, https://www.tctmd.com/news/adhd-drug-overprescribing
-raises-concerns-over-future-cv-events.

CHAPTER 9: CHILDREN AND WORK

54. Paul Goodman, *Nature Heals* (Free Life Editions, 1977), p. 98.

55. Jennifer Wadia, *Private Colleges – What Makes Them Different from Public
Colleges,* StudentDebtRelief.com, https://www.studentdebtrelief.us/college
-tips/private-colleges-different-from-public-colleges/.
Farran and Emma Kerr, *See The Average College Tuition in 2020–2021*,
U.S. News & World Report, https://www.usnews.com/education/best
-colleges/paying-for-college/articles/paying-for-college-infographic.

CHAPTER 10: HOMESCHOOLING IN AMERICA

56. Charles Rembar, *The End of Obscenity* (Olympic Marketing, 1986).

57. Rebecca Smithers, "Poor A-Levels Leads Family to Sue." *The Guardian*, October 2, 2001, www.guardian.co.uk/Archive.

58. John Holt. *Escape From Childhood: The Needs and Rights of Children* (Holt-GWS, 2013), p. 163.

59. "School Corporal Punishment in the United States," Wikimedia Foundation, last modified May 9, 2021, https://en.wikipedia.org/wiki/School_corporal_punishment_in_the_United_States).

CHAPTER 11: HOW TO GET STARTED

60. Jon Wartes, *The Relationship of Selected Input Variables to Academic Achievement among Washington's Homeschoolers*, Washington Homeschool Research Project, 1988.

61. Neil Postman, *The Disappearance of Childhood* (Vintage, 1994), p. 49.

62. Milva McDonald, *Slow Homeschooling: Essays about Mindful Homeschooling*, KDP, 2017.

CHAPTER 12: SCHOOL RESPONSE

63. John Holt, *What Do I Do Monday?* (Heinemann, 1995), p. 223.

64. Peter, Ciurczak, Antoniya Marinove, and Luc Schuster, "Kids Today: Boston's Declining Child Population and Its Effect on School Enrollment," Boston Indicators, January 22, 2020, https://www.bostonindicators.org/reports/report-website-pages/kids-today.

65. Jessica Dickler, "During Covid more families switch to private school from public education," CNBC, May 7, 2021, https://www.cnbc.com/2021/05/07/during-covid-more-families-switch-to-private-school-from-public-.html

66. Rosalind S. Helderma, "Home-Schooled Away from Home: Parents Form Academies to Support One Another." *Washington Post*, March 26, 2002, p. B01.

67. Growing Wild Forest School, "A Brief History of Forest Schools Around the World," October 9, 2020, https://www.growingwildforestschool.org/post/the-brief-history-heritage-of-forest-schools-around-the-world.

68. Maysaa Bazna. "Why Did Our Kids Design An Outdoor School?" Pono, October 15, 2020, https://pono.nyc/blog/2020/8/11/top-3-factors-to -consider-in-a-virtual-summer-camp-b8djb.

69. Flying Squads, "Our Program," n.d., https://www.flyingsquads.org/our -program/.

70. Green Schoolyards America, "COVID-19 Outdoor Learning," n.d., https:// www.greenschoolyards.org/covid-learn-outside

INDEX

Homeschooling. (*cont.*)
  curricula and materials for. *See*
    Curricula and materials
  defined, 206, 255
  different approaches to, 19,
    193–194, 205–215
  enjoying family time and, 10,
    58–59, 63, 204–205
  family businesses and, 79–80
  famous people and, 225–226
  getting started with, 193–226.
    See also Getting started in
    homeschooling
  legal issues and, 169–192. *See also*
    Legal issues
  philosophies of, 203, 206–215, 219
  school cooperation and, 227–233,
    244–248, 255–256
  socioeconomic status and, 228
  state laws on, 177, 202, 216,
    218–219, 256
Homeschooling groups
  clubs and cooperatives, 71–74,
    194, 212–214, 231
  international, 298–307
  other organizations, 308–310
  regulation and law information
    from, 170, 202
  special interest, 307–308
  by state, 276–297
Homeschooling in America (Murray),
  13–14
Home Study Institute, 200
Horses, 122
Horticulture, on raising food in
  Boston, 78–79
Houk, Katharine, 216–217
Howard, Jerry, 78–79
How Children Fail (Holt), xxvi, 14,
  123–124, 134, 140

How Children Learn (Holt), xxvi, 22,
  119–120, 137–138
How to Love a Child (Korczak), 105
Hughes, Peggy, 73
Hull, Bill, 251
Hurstpierpoint College (England), 175
Hybrid homeschooling, 15–16
Hyperactivity, 136

I

Illich, Ivan, xii, 3, 68, 70, 118–120
Illinois, greenhouse for biological
  research in, 74–75
Illinois State Court, 179
Imagination, 93, 105, 215. *See also* Play
Inarticulateness of children, 69
India, testing in, xxi–xxii
Infants. *See* Babies
Ingraham v. Wright (1977), 187
Instead of Education (Holt), xxix,
  xxxiv, 72
Interests. *See also* Self-directed
  learning
  parents sharing with children,
    61–62, 97
  retention of information and, 56–57
  stimulation of, 61–62
Internships, 225
Inventors, age of, xviii–xix
Iowa v. Sessions (1978), 172
Iowa State Court, 172, 179
Ireland, required language
  instruction in, xvii

J

Jaffer, Susan, 208–209
Jail, family taken to, 232
Jerome, Jud, 57–58
Jobs. *See* Employment; Work and
  children

Public schools. (*cont.*)
  legal action against homeschool
    parents, 232–233
  litigation against schools for poor
    teaching, 173–175
  as managers of child
    development, 200–201
  metrics for success, 3–4, 13–14
  mimicking employment,
    xxix–xxx, xxxiii
  mistakes forbidden in, 157, 180
  Natural Creativity Center
    (Philadelphia), 6–7
  play, lack of, 215
  remote learning through, 1, 3, 7–8,
    15, 242–243
  research conducted in, 233–236
  schedules and, 21, 222
  skills not taught in, 215
  socioeconomic status and, xxi–xxii
  subject categories, limitations of,
    xii–xiii, 10–11, 209
  summer learning losses and,
    xiv–xv
  unschooling programs in, 243
Punished by Rewards (Kohn), 13

R
Racism, 229
Reading
  children resisting teaching of,
    99–100
  late, xii–xiii, 201–202, 235–236
  lawsuit for school failing to teach,
    174
  learning difficulties and, 126–133,
    135
  self-teaching, 117–118
  summer learning losses and, xiv
Real-life experiences, 203

Real-world skills, 64–68
Record keeping, 216–221. *See also*
    Evaluations for homeschoolers
*The Relationship of Selected Input
    Variables to Academic
    Achievement among
    Washington's Homeschoolers*
    (Wartes), 199–200
Religious schools, xxxi, 229
Rembar, Charles, 171
Remedial classes, xv
Remote learning, 1, 3, 7–8, 15, 242–243
Requiem for a Turtle (child's chant),
    90–91
Research
  homeschooling parents vs.
    teacher parents, child
    outcomes and, 199–200
  on learning, 9–10, 13–14, 199
  in public schools, 233–236
  on reading, 201–202
Resource centers, 213–214
Resource librarians, 195
Retention of information, 13–14, 56–57
RetractionWatch.com, xxiii
Rewards, inappropriate, 48–49
Right/left confusion, 133, 137–140
Rights
  of children, 187
  parents' legal right to homeschool,
    172–173, 178–180, 186–187
Riley, Gina, 20
Ritalin, 136
Robotics, 315
Rote learning, xiv, 234
Rulings, reversal of, 171–172

S
Safety issues, 45–48
San Francisco, lawsuit against, 175, 180

Santa Barbara County Schools, "Declining Enrollments" pamphlet, 247–248
Schedules
flexibility of, 59–64, 80, 194–195, 203–205
homeschool rhythm and, 2, 79–80
public schools and, 21, 222
unschooling and, 1, 20–21, 62, 211–212
Schiffmann, Avi, 5
Schmitt, Ken, 154
School-at-home, 1–2, 17, 21, 120, 193–194, 206–207
Schools. *See also* Private schools; Public schools
alternative, 50, 71–74, 151–152, 188, 203
necessity of, xxxiii
for outdoor education, 241–243
parents starting, xxxiv–xxxv, 71–74, 230–231
Science
age of inventors and, xviii–xix
biochemistry lab, child learning in, 158
biological research center, Chicago, 74–75
facilitating learning in, 195–197
learning resources for, 316–317
Screen time, remote learning and, 15
Secrets of a Buccaneer-Scholar (Bach), 26
Seeing-backward hypothesis, 126–133, 136
Self-directed learning
adult support of, 7, 194–195
computer skills and, 116–117
direct instruction vs., xx–xxi, 9–13, 98–104

higher education and employment, 27
as homeschooling approach, 207–215
reading and, 117–118
record keeping and, 216–219
Self-discipline, 11–12
Self-education, 26–27, 106–109
Self-efficacy, 2
Self-teaching, 116–118
Sense of direction, 140–142
Sessions, State of Iowa v. (1978), 172
Seymour David, xvii
Shadow Work (Illich), 68, 118
Shaw, George Bernard, 8
Sheffer, Susannah, 210–211
Skeptics, 206
Skills, real-world, 64–68
Slow homeschooling, 205
Smith-Heavenrich, Sue, 197–198
Smithsonian Institution (Washington DC), 51–52
Social capital, xxi
Socialization, 31, 179, 240–241
Social mobility, xxii
Social studies learning resources, 317
Socioeconomic status, xiv, xxi–xxii, 228. *See also* Poverty
Solar Age, 154
Songs/chants, children making up, 91–92
Specialists, 125–126, 136
Special needs learning resources (reference list), 317–318
Speech and language, 68–70
Sports Illustrated, 153–154
Standardized tests, xxiii, 216, 222–223
Starting homeschool. *See* Getting started in homeschooling